The Andy Griffith Show
B·O·O·K

Swinging in Mayberry

The Andy Griffith Show

B·O·O·K

From Miracle Salve to Kerosene Cucumbers: The Complete Guide to One of Television's Best-Loved Shows

Ken Beck and Jim Clark

St. Martin's Press
New York

To the cast and crew

All photos are courtesy of the Nashville *Tennessean* and the *Nashville Banner,* unless otherwise noted.

THE ANDY GRIFFITH SHOW BOOK. Copyright © 1985 by Ken Beck and Jim Clark. All rights reserved. Printed in the United States of America. No part of this book may be used or reproduced in any manner whatsoever without written permission except in the case of brief quotations embodied in critical articles or reviews. For information, address St. Martin's Press, 175 Fifth Avenue, New York, N.Y. 10010.

Design by Paolo Pepe

Library of Congress Cataloging-in-Publication Data

Beck, Ken.
    The Andy Griffith show book / Ken Beck and Jim Clark. —35th anniversary ed.
        p.   cm.
    ISBN 0-312-11741-8 (pbk.)
    1. Andy Griffith show (Television program)   I. Clark, Jim.
    II. Title.
PN1992.77.A573B4   1995
791.45′72—dc20   94-46271
                                                                              CIP

Revised Edition: April 1995

10   9   8   7   6   5   4   3   2   1

Acknowledgments

Our thanks to the many folks who possess the Mayberry spirit and helped make this book possible: Judy Jenkins, John Seigenthaler, Philippa Brophy and Ruthanne Sutor of the Sterling Lord Agency, Al Knight and Gus Winter, Richard Kelly, Earle Hagen, Paul Henning, Steve Tamerius, Mike Price, Ken Cauthern, Rachel B. Smith, Barbara Wall Spearman, Wendy Beck, Roger Beck, Blake and Nancy Clark, Ann Clark, Tonya Hamel, Robert W. Shockley, Jr., and Tom Hotchkiss.

We also received valuable assistance from Terry Beck, Blake Hendrickson, Tommy Ford, Ken Draughn, Larry Locke, Wendell Melvin, Billy Batson, Robert Clinard, Bob Bell, Frank Empson, Lee Kaplan, Jim Lamberson, Yvonne and Ronnie White, Gene Wyatt, Jack Gunter and Bill Thorup, Dan Loftin, Douglas Downs, Doug Dillard, Hal Smith, Rance Howard, Jack Dodson, Joyce Jameson, William Keene, George Lindsey, Howard Morris, Ken Lynch, Fred Goodwin, Richard Abraham, and Bob Turner (for his excellent rendering of the Mayberry County map).

Our special thanks to Bob Miller and Lisa DiMona of St. Martin's.

We're especially grateful to Paul Harvey, a man as truly All-American and legendary as Mayberry itself, for his wonderful foreword to this anniversary edition. His poignant commentary surely captures the essence of what Mayberry represents to many people.

We also wish to thank several other people for their help with the revisions for the 1995 edition. We're grateful to "Andy Griffith Show" writers Harvey Bullock and Everett Greenbaum for their assistance with the spelling of names in scripts that each wrote. We also thank the staff at the Collier Library of the University of North Alabama for access to their collection of "Andy Griffith Show" scripts donated to the school by George Lindsey.

Likewise, several other folks helped us with all-important trivial verifications and research: Donny Whitehead, Judson F. Sandlin, Dale Robinson, David Fernandes, Neal Brower, Jim Schwenke, Dennis Hasty, Joel Rasmussen, John and Mary Lock, Greg Carson, and Steve Cox.

In addition to our family members listed in the book's original edition, we appreciate support from Jim's wife, Mary, and Ken's daughter and son, Kylie and Cole.

And once again, we express our gratitude to the folks at St. Martin's Press who continue to believe in this book and the appeal of Mayberry—especially our editor, Gordon Van Gelder and his assistant, Matthew Rettenmund.

Contents

Foreword   xi

Preface   xiii

Introduction   xv

History of Mayberry, North Carolina   1

Andy Taylor   6

Barney Fife   14

Cops and Robbers   29

Codes and Cases   36

Opie Taylor   40

Mayberry Menagerie   50

Aunt Bee   53

Clara Edwards Johnson   60

Mayberry Morsels   62

Floyd Lawson   64

Otis Campbell   69

Rafe Hollister   73

Ellie May Walker   74

Thelma Lou   76

Helen Crump   79

Mayberry Media   82

Gomer Pyle   85

Goober Pyle   89

Howard Sprague   94

Emmett Clark   100

Warren Ferguson   102

Ernest T. Bass   104

The Darlings   107

Music From Mayberry   112

Folks Around Town   115

Mayberry, R.F.D.   126

Away From Mayberry   128

Contradictions   132

Odds and Ends   134

Miss Crump's Final Exams   138

Cast Credits   147

Episode Summaries   149

Mayberry Memories   172

Mayberry Town Directory   175

Mt. Pilot Directory   189

Mayberry Yellow Pages   191

Mt. Pilot Yellow Pages   195

The Andy Griffith Show
Rerun Watchers Club   199

Foreword

Mayberry—Where are you?

Since television ran away from home it's been wandering, searching, trying to find its way back—to Mayberry.

These days, whatever I'm watching I'm unfulfilled.

I can close my eyes and smell the crayon in Miss Crump's classroom.

I can smell the bay rum in Floyd's Barbershop.

But when I open my eyes I see mostly mayhem.

And, as Charlene Darling would say, "That makes me cry."

From our weekly visits to Mayberry we learned tolerance for Otis Campbell's weakness and for Aunt Bee's pickles and we learned compassion from Opie's misused slingshot and we were introduced to soft-love at Myers Lake.

The bumbling "Goobers" among us learned that we may still be smarter than anybody when it comes to fixin' cars.

Barney Fife, taking himself so very seriously, was a mirror reflection of most of us.

And Sheriff Andy Taylor understood.

Mayberry, where are you now when we need you so?

Those of us who grew up with patchwork quilts and square-head nails and gourd dippers would be considered poor by today's ways of measurin'. . . .

But how rich we were back home in Mayberry!

Might television ever find its way back to Mayberry?

Is the image of a father and son hand-in-hand going fishing too trite, too provincial for contemporary palatability?

One might think so, except that episodes remain evergreen in reruns after thirty-five years.

After all these years the bullet in Barney's pocket still evokes a smile.

After all these years we recall the tedious front porch deliberations between Andy and Barney over which flavor ice cream.

City folks, intimidated, are seduced by drifters. Buddy Ebsen as a hobo was helped to discover his own conscience—in Mayberry.

Remember the impatient city visitor with "no time to spare" who ended up in the porch swing singing, "Church in the Wildwood." Opie slept on the ironing board that night. "Adventure sleeping," he called it.

Today we laugh at one another; in Mayberry we cared about one another. That was confirmed even in the way the writers wrote around Floyd's incapacity.

An observation which this professional people-watcher considers most impressive is that everybody for whom

Mayberry was home might have been assumed by cynics to be play-actors.

Yet each in real life turned out real good. Aunt Bee remained in character until death did us part.

Whatever it was about that small town "Brigadoon" appears to have become an indelible influence on those who lived there and on us who visited.

Television owes us. And that accruing debt will be amortized at least in part if it keeps Mayberry alive against the day when "behave yourself" and "love your neighbor" come back into style.

—Paul Harvey

What a great place to rest your bones, and mighty fine for skippin' stones

Preface to Revised Edition

When St. Martin's Press asked us if we would like to update this book to commemorate the thirty-fifth anniversary of "The Andy Griffith Show" in 1995, we jumped at the chance. Doing so would give us an opportunity to make some corrections, include a few additional photos, and otherwise add some new snap to the book, which itself is celebrating its tenth year in 1995.

Most of the corrections have to do with spellings of names of characters mentioned in Mayberry. In the last ten years, we've been able to review additional scripts from the show and find correct spellings that were not available to us in 1985. Also, two of the show's key writers, Harvey Bullock and Everett Greenbaum, lent a helping hand with spellings in scripts they wrote.

In this new edition, we've also found space to tuck in a few more photographs, plus St. Martin's has provided additional pages for a special section of photographs, a number of which are in color. We're particularly pleased to include photographs of several Mayberry characters that were not in the first edition.

We have continued with our original objective of not introducing into this book any information about Mayberry that is gathered from places beyond the 249 episodes of "The Andy Griffith Show." Our goal has always been to focus on what happens in those eight seasons of Mayberry and simply leave it at that. That's why you'll not find information here from the pilot episode on "The Danny Thomas Show," "Gomer Pyle, U.S.M.C.," "Mayberry R.F.D.," and the 1986 TV movie, *Return to Mayberry.*

And while you'll notice some obvious changes in this book, one thing never changes much—Mayberry. It's still the friendly little town that always feels like home. That's one of the reasons that millions of fans around the world agree that "The Andy Griffith Show" remains perhaps the best television show ever made.

—Ken Beck and Jim Clark
September 1994

Introduction

With the birth of "The Andy Griffith Show" on October 3, 1960 (9:30 P.M. EST), Mayberry, North Carolina, became our hometown. (Mayberry was introduced to the world earlier on February 15, 1960, on an episode of "The Danny Thomas Show.")

The show ran for eight seasons, with 249 episodes on the CBS television network. "The Andy Griffith Show" was number one in the Nielsen ratings during its final season and it was never out of the Top Ten during its eight-year reign. Having entered its fourth decade in 1990, the show remains one of the finest American television series ever produced. The scripts were superb, and the actors formed an ensemble that was almost too good to be true. Mayberry may never again be equalled.

"The Andy Griffith Show" continues to be an all-American favorite across the country and is currently broadcast in about 100 local markets. Fans of the show number in the millions, and every year more and more TV watchers are discovering the joys of life in Mayberry.

"The Andy Griffith Show" has enjoyed great popularity in syndication because Mayberry and its inhabitants represent more than just a small town in North Carolina—Mayberry is pure Americana. We've tried to capture some of the spirit and flavor of Mayberry in this book and we hope "Andy Griffith Show" fans enjoy it. Still,

there's no substitute for watching Mayberry come to life on television.

This is not so much a study of the production of "The Andy Griffith Show" (already ably documented in Richard Kelly's *The Andy Griffith Show* in 1981). Rather, this book is a chronicle of Andy Taylor's town—a biography of Mayberry, North Carolina—everybody's hometown.

Throughout the years, towns have been vividly brought to life by great writers. Sir Arthur Conan Doyle offered us the London of Sherlock Holmes, and William Faulkner literally mapped out Yoknapatawpha County for his readers. The creative people behind "The Andy Griffith Show" have achieved the same realism. It is one of the few television shows to convey that kind of believability on the air.

Ironically, it was a North Carolinan, Thomas Wolfe, who concluded one of his novels with the statement "You can't go home again." But that was before television and before "The Andy Griffith Show." We can go back to Mayberry. Television allows us to visit the folks there just about any time we feel like it.

The fictional town of Mayberry was partially influenced by the town of Mt. Airy, North Carolina, Andy Griffith's hometown. Much of the show's realism draws from Andy Griffith's use of Mt. Airy as a model for Mayberry. The names of many of Mayberry's townspeople, businesses, and streets, and landmarks can be found in and around Mt. Airy. We have tried to include these same details here. Along with biographies of prominent Mayberrians, we have included information on a variety of topics pertaining to Mayberry. We have made every effort to be as accurate as possible. (Especially with the spelling of some names, we've had to depend on our assistant, Opie, to help us.)

We have also asked Miss Crump to prepare assorted quizzes, which we hope will be both entertaining and challenging for all Mayberry lovers. Lots of luck to you and yours!

Ready to go dancing

The Andy Griffith Show

B·O·O·K

History of Mayberry North Carolina

Goin' fishin'

Upon driving into the town of Mayberry, North Carolina, a visitor would have to be enchanted. There is a sign at the Mayberry city limits that reads, "Welcome to Mayberry, The Friendly Town." Mayberry is located in the northeastern part of the state and it is the county seat of Mayberry County. The elevation of the town is 671 feet, and its population was a little less than 2,000 at the beginning of the 1960s. According to the statistics on a sign at the train depot, the population rose to 5,360 by the mid-1960s.

Mayberry is a beautiful place. Because of the abundance of lovely flower gardens, Mayberry has earned the nickname the "Garden City of the State." The Garden Club sponsors an annual flower show, with competition in gladiola, snapdragon, pansy, and rose divisions.

A notable town landmark is the big old oak tree in the middle of the town. (Andy Taylor recalls, "Many's the time

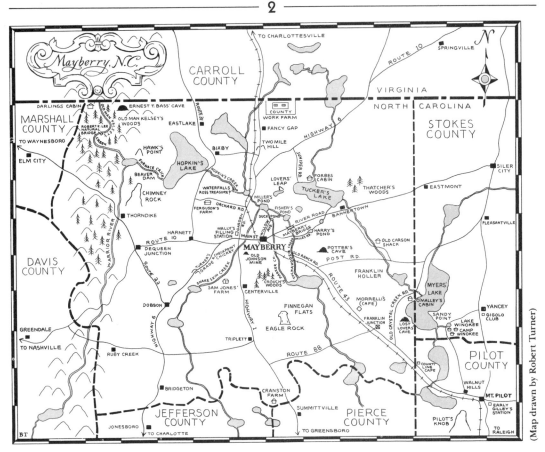

(Map drawn by Robert Turner)

Map of Mayberry County, North Carolina

This map is a rendering of what Mayberry County, North Carolina, *might* look like. Even though Mayberry is a fictional place, "The Andy Griffith Show" provides a lot of information about the county that makes it seem like an actual place.

Every item on our map is mentioned on the show. The locations of the items are based chiefly on the descriptions and directions given by the characters on the show. We have also used the map behind Andy's desk in the courthouse to chart the bodies of water.

Some items on the map are simply mentioned on the show, with no reference to their location. In those cases, we have selected what we feel are their likely (or possible) locations. As a guide we have relied somewhat on the geography of North Carolina (particularly Surry County).

Although you won't find a place quite like Andy Taylor's Mayberry in North Carolina, we hope this map will be an entertaining companion to watching Mayberry come to life on TV.

—K.B. and J.C.

I've clumb up this old oak tree when I was a young 'un.") On the town square there is a cannon (with the initials T.R. scratched on it—the handiwork of Tracy Rupert, not Teddy Roosevelt) whose muzzle was busted after it misfired one Fourth of July. Near the center of town is the David Mendelbright Memorial Horse Water Trough ("Let no horse go thristy here," 1870–1933). And, of course, all the folks in Mayberry can point out the old Remshaw place, a haunted house where Old Man Remshaw is rumored to have killed his hired hand with an ax.

The town's National Guard Armory houses several objects of historical significance, including an RJ300 motorcycle from World War I, which enterprising Deputy Barney Fife picked up for next to nothing at a surplus auction in Mt. Pilot. A plaque found under the seat of that motorcycle reads: "First motorcycle to cross the Marne River, Battle of Château-Thierry, 6–12–'18, Passenger, Black Jack Pershing, driver, Corporal Nate Jackson, A.E.F." The armory also has on display a jeep from World War II and a Civil War cannon.

The folks of Mayberry are hardworking, but they also enjoy neighborly fellowship with an array of festivities. Mayberrians celebrate such events as Decoration Day, the annual county fair, a Halloween play put on by the Women's Club, the Miss Mayberry Pageant, the Ladies' Auxiliary Bazaar, the Masons' picnic, the Apricot Blossom Festival, the Opening Day Sweepstakes (a fishing contest), the annual Sheriff's Boys Day (footraces), and the Mayberry Founders' Day Picnic held at the town park. Each Fourth of July there's a picnic at the park, followed by fireworks.

The social affair of the year is Founders' Day. The agenda includes a street dance, booths, white elephant sales, a pie-eating contest, free watermelons, and a parade in which the mayor's wife will ride out on a horse and sing "opera stuff." All of these wonderful events are planned in careful detail by the Mayberry Founders' Day committee. There is even a special Founders' Day song: "Mayberry'll shine tonight, Mayberry'll shine. When the moon comes up and the sun goes down, Mayberry'll shine."

And, as if that weren't enough, Mayberry celebrates Bug Month. (That probably didn't set too well with the members of an insecticide convention that once met in town.)

Mayberry boasts a volunteer fire brigade, a public emergency committee, the Mayberry Civic League, a Chamber of Commerce, the Mayberry Good Government League, and a boosters club. It has a town library; departments of public works, gas works, and water and power; a county legal department; and a county unemployment agency. And Mayberry has its own underpass.

The good ladies of Mayberry have a Ladies' Aid Church committee, a Women's Club, a Literary Guild, and a Women's Bridge Club. For the men, there is The Regal Order of the

Golden Door to Good Fellowship, where the menfolk can play checkers and cards, swap jokes, and drink root beer. Other organizations include the Downtown Businessman's Club, the Masons, the Elks (who put on an annual High-Jinks Show), and a Kiwanis Club. Mayberry also has a Young People's Club, and Cub and Boy Scout troops.

The town was named after John Mayberry, one of the first settlers in the area and a founding father. Other prominent pioneers were James and Mary Merriweather. The Merriweathers are the main characters in the Centennial Pageant, along with the Indian chief Noogatuck. The Indians referred to Mayberry as "Happy Valley," and Noogatuck nicknamed James Merriweather "Laughing Face."

One of the town's earliest heroes was Nathan Tibbs, an ancestor of Otis Campbell's, who marched eight miles through the snow to set fire to Mayberry Bridge during the Revolutionary War. His efforts enabled General Washington's troops to capture an entire British regiment.

But the most notable event in Mayberry history is the Battle of Mayberry, described by local folks as "that glorious battle" and "a great page in Mayberry's history." The townsfolk were exceptionally proud of that historic confrontation . . . that is until the true facts were unraveled. Among the "heroes" of the Battle of Mayberry were Colonel Caleb "Stonewall" Lawson, Lieutenant Edwards (Clara's great-

great-grandfather, whom she insisted was a colonel who spurred the militia men on with his cry of "Onward, boys, do you want to live forever!"), Colonel Carleton Taylor, and Colonel Goober Pyle of the North Carolina Seventh Calvary. Carleton, by the way, was one of the first settlers, and Mayberry was almost called Taylortown. On the Indian side of this story was Chief Strongbow, a forefather of Mayberry's only Indian, Tom Strongbow. The Cherokees referred to the incident as the "Victory of Tuckahoosie Creek," where they defended their traditional hunting grounds.

The true story behind this fiasco, however, is that the battle was nothing more than a drunken brawl. (It was Lieutenant Edwards who provided the jug of corn liquor that got everybody soused.) The victims included Bessie Lawson (a scrawny cow who was accidentally shot), three deer, and one mule, which was mistaken for a deer. The infamous fight occurred in May of 1762 and was reported in a Raleigh newspaper on May 18 of that year.

Incidentally, Daniel Lawson, an ancestor of Floyd's, was Mayberry's first Indian agent and he established a trading post in what was to become the town of Mayberry.

Another page from the past in Mayberry history concerns Seth Taylor, Andy's great-great-grandfather, who operated the town's first sawmill, headed the Chamber of Commerce, and loaned the town money during the **Crisis of 1874. His cohort in crime was**

Winston Simmons, an industrialist-swindler from Mt. Pilot. It seems that ol' Seth pulled a fast one on his fellow citizens when he and Simmons saw to it that the railroad ran through Mt. Pilot instead of Mayberry; Mt. Pilot thus developed into an active and thriving metropolis, compared to Mayberry's more modest business community.

The citizens of Mayberry, in retrospect, decided that they were grateful to Seth for his actions. The Civic Improvement Committee commissioned Brian Jackson to sculpt a statue of Seth (the statue was 5'7" tall and cost $1,200), which was set up on the town square in front of City Hall.

Another infamous moment in history occurred in 1870 when "Rotten

Everybody has a big time in Mayberry

Barney shows Andy his Revolutionary family tree

Ray" Ankrum set fire to the town and burned it to the ground. He later started the Ankrum Charcoal Company.

And, reportedly, somewhere near Mayberry is buried the Ross Treasure, the lost booty of Ross's Raiders, a group of Civil War marauders who stole $100,000 in gold from Union troops. The guerrillas buried their ill-gotten gain, and now the treasure lies lost somewhere near the town.

A lot of things have happened in Mayberry over the years, but little has changed. It's still a nice, clean, small town. The citizens enjoy their gracious and warm-hearted living. And that's helped Mayberry remain "The Friendly Town."

Andy Taylor

You beat everything, you know that.
   —Andy Taylor

Andy

Andy Taylor is Mayberry County's sheriff and Justice of the Peace, but his services extend far beyond those two roles. He's a devoted father, a loyal friend, and a kind and just man whose common sense settles many of Mayberry's problems. His patience, perception, and wisdom are clearly evident as he oversees the county without wearing a gun.

The good sheriff was born Andrew Jackson Taylor and raised in Mayberry by his father's sister, Beatrice Taylor, better known as Aunt Bee. He grew up with his cousin, Barney Fife. The two have been hanging around since the fourth grade, good ol' 4-A, where Miss Moran was their teacher. (Mrs. Thickett was another teacher who they had together, as was Mrs. Von Roeder, the "beast of the fourth floor.")

Aunt Bee says that Andy was a shy boy, a stick-in-the-mud. Instead of attending his first school dance, he hid in a barn. But Andy recalls things differently and says that as a boy he was a "devil-may-care young scalawag" and that he earned his first dollar by capturing a wildcat and turning it in for the bounty the county was paying.

As a youth, Andy was at least a Second Class Boy Scout. On one occasion, he had to fight the town bully, Hodie Snitch, over his favorite fishing hole. He received a black eye but won the right to keep his place on the river bank. During his teen years, Andy earned spending money by popping corn at the Mayberry moviehouse for Old Man MacKnight. That was his first "real" job. He also earned extra money mowing yards and delivering packages.

In high school, Andy was second vice president of the 4-H Club and graduated as valedictorian of the class of 1945. He also won the county penmanship contest. Nevertheless, Andy admits that he had his scholastic weaknesses. He was never very good at spelling and, in the spring of 1938, he flunked grasshopper dissection in Mrs. Webster's biology class. Andy was also secretary of the Philomathian Literary Society (where they pasted current events into a scrapbook), and he was a member of the civics club.

Among his girlfriends in school were Alice Harper, Katherine Harney, and Sharon DeSpain. Andy and Sharon were selected couple of the year during their junior and senior years, and they even talked about marriage. This all followed his much-talked-about fling with Barbara Edwards back in the fifth grade.

Andy was an average athlete in high school. He pitched for Mayberry's baseball team. He was known county-wide for his infamous wobble ball,

Andrew Jackson Taylor—High School Graduate

which was caused by a broken middle finger. In the big game against Mt. Pilot High, he threw a no-hitter but walked seventeen batters as Mayberry lost, 10–0. Probably his biggest athletic achievement came in the football game against Mt. Pilot. On a fourth down play with four seconds left in the fourth quarter, Andy caught the winning pass. "I was fourth-string end," he modestly jokes about it now.

Andy rarely talks about his parents (he has his great-great-grandfather Seth's chin), but does keep their furniture in the attic of his house. He, Opie, and Aunt Bee live at 332 Maple Road. Their phone number is 426. The Taylor house has four bedrooms and one-and-a-half baths. There is also a cellar where Aunt Bee stores her preserves. As for Andy's room, Aunt Bee says it's like an "elephant's nest." Andy bought the house from Old Man Parmaley, and it is at least thirty-five years old.

Among Andy's other relatives are cousin Oliver Gossage in Raleigh, cousin Evin Moore, who is Grand Master of the Asheville Masons, and an Uncle Todd (actually Andy's second cousin), who is a wiper on an oil tanker.

During World War II, Andy served in France, and he still remembers a little French. He also served at one time as the head of the Mayberry Good Government League. For at least twelve years, he has served as Mayberry's sheriff.

The only thing he takes more seriously than his job is his role as father to Opie. He says to his boy: "I want to tell you something, Ope. And I want you to listen real careful because this is important. You're my young 'un, and I love you more than anything or anybody in the whole world, and nothin' or nobody can ever change that. You know, it's hard for me to tell you just how much you do mean to me 'cause you're a part of me." One of the special times father and son share together is reading the funny papers (especially "Little Orphan Annie") Sunday mornings on the front porch before church.

Still, Andy is a firm disciplinarian. He makes Opie earn his allowance by doing chores. Lest Opie get a little too far out of line, Andy believes in the biblical proverb "Spare the rod, spoil the child."

Andy usually gets up around seven o'clock each morning. The family eats supper together sometime between 6:00 and 7:00 P.M. And with Aunt Bee preparing the meals, it's amazing that the six-foot-tall Andy doesn't wind up being six feet wide. Andy drinks his coffee black (he makes a pretty good cup himself). Leg of lamb is his favorite dish, but he also loves roast beef and crispy fried chicken. His favorite desserts are pumpkin pie à la mode and blueberry and gooseberry pies. He drinks a little beer, usually when he's out of town, and occasionally sips wine. Andy even makes elderberry wine from his own recipe and he makes a delicious punch supreme. Among his more exotic tastes are a penchant for wild mushrooms, canned oysters, chocolate syrup, chili sauce, pickled avocados, and shrimp enchiladas.

Bedtime

If Aunt Bee doesn't bring lunch down to the courthouse, Andy and Barney might go over to the diner, to the Snappy Lunch, or maybe to the drugstore, where Andy might have something like this: egg salad sandwich (hold the lettuce and tomato), black coffee, and a little yellow cookie. Some days he may substitute a root beer for the coffee.

Busy as Andy is as sheriff, he still finds the time for many other activities. He's a deacon at the All Souls Church (the deacons meet on Wednesday nights) and chairman of the church finance committee. He taught Sunday school for three years and still substitutes. He bowls in the Peace Officers' League and on the town bowling team. In addition, he has served on a fund committee for the underprivileged children's charity drive. He's been in the town choir for five years, and directs and plays tuba in the town band. Andy has played James Merriweather in the Centennial Pageant. And, as if that weren't enough, he's a voting proctor and an active member in The Regal Order of the Golden Door to Good Fellowship. (The lodge also meets on Wednesday evenings.)

An avid sportsman, Andy excels in crow and skeet shooting, and he also loves to hunt quail, fish, and go frog-gigging. He and Opie frequently head for Myers Lake, where they drift along in their rowboat (named Gertrude) and fish for bass, perch, and trout. Almost every Saturday, if the weather's right, Andy, Opie, and Bar-

Andy relaxing with the *Mayberry Gazette*

ney will take off for the ol' fishin' hole. One of Andy's secret baits is the ham from Aunt Bee's good sandwiches. When it's not being used, his prized fishing rod, "Eagle-Eye Annie," hangs on the living room wall. For three consecutive years, Andy and Barney won the Opening Day Sweepstakes for the best catch on the first day of the fishing season. Andy has not missed an opening day in more than twenty years.

The right-handed sheriff loves picking the guitar, especially with the Darlings or Jim Lindsey. Andy and some of the boys in town even recorded an album, *Music From Mayberry*. He likes to play checkers and dominoes and will occasionally play a little chess or bridge. He used to play poker and was pretty good at it, but no more.

To wind down after a hard day's work at the office, Andy enjoys nothing better than to sit back in his favorite chair with a smoke and a *National Geographic*. He might also read a good mystery or work a crossword puzzle.

One of Andy's specialties is spinning tales. He's great at ghost stories and fairy tales, such as "Beauty and the Beast" or "King Arthur and the Knights of the Round Table," but he can really get into high gear when he tells some of the Shakespearean classics, like *Romeo and Juliet*.

A "one-woman man," Andy enjoys the companionship of the opposite sex. Among his various girlfriends have been Ellie May Walker, Mary Simpson, Peggy McMillan, and Helen Crump. Helen eventually becomes his fiancée. Of course, Barney Fife never helps out much in the romance department. He has skinned Andy a lot on blind dates, such as the one with a girl from Detroit, Melinda Keefer. She had fat knees and talked a lot. Then

Andy and nurse Mary (Julie Adams)

there was "that Benji girl," who looked like Benjamin Franklin. But that made up for the time when Barney was supposed to escort the queen of the State Apricot Festival around town. It was Saturday, June 23, 1952, to be exact, and Andy wound up being her escort, leaving a solitary Barney Fife standing around on a street corner.

Hobbies and romances aside, Andy is the peacekeeper of the community. Although the moonshiners and mayors sometimes are annoying, Andy has the respect of all Mayberrians. Known as "the sheriff without a gun," Andy once explained why he never carries a gun: "When a man carries a gun all the time, the respect he thinks he's getting might really be fear. So I don't carry a gun because I don't want the people of Mayberry to fear a gun; I'd rather they would respect me." (Carrying a gun also makes him too heavy on one side.) His philosophy works because he al-

Peggy McMillan (Joanna Moore)

most never resorts to violence when apprehending lawbreakers. Still, there have been times when he has been injured in the line of duty. He broke his right arm while bringing in the four Gordon boys, and he once got a black eye from Al, a boyfriend of Daphne's in Mt. Pilot.

As the high sheriff of Mayberry, Andy has many duties. He confesses that most of his and Barney's work consists of giving out parking tickets, helping kids cross the street, and putting lids back on trash cans. And there are added responsibilities, such as giving safety lectures at the high school and passing out Christmas baskets.

Andy makes music with Mary Simpson
(Sue Ann Langdon)

Andy not only acts as sheriff, he also fills in during emergency situations. He had the misfortune of umpiring a Little League game between Mayberry and Mt. Pilot in which Opie was playing. Another time he had to be the sole judge in the Miss Mayberry Beauty Pageant.

Andy gets frequent haircuts, probably because he enjoys the barbershop fraternity so much—not to mention teasing Floyd. After a trip to the chair, Andy will hop out and ask, "How much for the damages, Floyd?"

Although he rarely wears the customary tie and police hat (a habit that irks Barney), Andy is practically always dressed in his sheriff's uniform. For special events, such as church or dinner at Morelli's, Andy will slip into his blue suit and a tie, but that's about as dressed up as he ever gets. His favorite colors are brown and green.

Andy really knows how to take it easy in the evening as he lounges on his front porch. As he says, "Oh, that's the finest thing in the world, sitting on the porch on a moonlight night, staring up at the sky." He usually goes to bed between 10:00 and 10:30 P.M.

A patient man, Andy tends to keep things to himself until he reaches the boiling point. When his jaw muscles begin twitching, it's a sign that he's tense or angry. Barney and Goober are pretty good at helping Andy keep those muscles in shape.

Andy did try moonlighting once, when he purchased a franchise from Laundercoin, Inc. He was trying to

Mayberry businessman Bert Miller
(Sterling Holloway)

make some extra money for Opie's college education, so he established Mayberry's first self-service coin-operated laundry. Aunt Bee was his first customer, but after Andy saw that the business was interfering with his sheriffing duties, he sold out.

The wise sheriff has had handsome job offers in different cities (one came from hunting buddy Ed Crumpacker in St. Paul, but somebody's cousin got it; another was from Herb Mason of Hogarth Detectives in Raleigh), but Andy chooses to remain in Mayberry.

If a stranger were to ask the sheriff about Mayberry, Andy might say: "There's not much to tell. It's just a little town. We hang around. Get up in the morning and go to work and come home. For entertainment, we have television and movies, and we take rides in the car out of town on Sunday.

We have our local baseball team and we fish and we have creeks we swim in. Evenings we sit around on the porch and visit, watch the children playing under the streetlights." That sufficiently explains why he never really wants to leave Mayberry.

Andy Taylor is all things to all people. To the criminal, he is the fair but determined lawman.

Hobo (talking about Andy): You know what it is with Sheriff Taylor? Well, you see the rest of these guys, they just toss you in and you're nuthin'. Nuthin'. Makes you feel like dirt. But with Taylor, I don't know. He treats you with a little respect. Makes you feel like a regular guy. Yep. You know every time I've been in that Mayberry jail, I come walking out kind of feeling different. Makes you feel like you can be trusted.

Sheriff and deputy on the job

To the townspeople, he is a good man who has earned their highest respect. As Barney Fife will tell you: "You gotta understand. This is a small town. The sheriff is more than just a sheriff. He's a friend. The people in this town ain't got no better friend than Andy Taylor." And to his friends, he can always be counted on to come through when called upon. "The luckiest thing a man can have is friendship," he says.

Andy Taylor is not only the father of a growing boy, he is also the guardian of a charming, peaceful little town. He has been an example for his neighbors by setting one rule above all others: Andy lives by the Golden Rule. Mayberry wouldn't be Mayberry without him.

Andy and Helen

Opie takes aim

Barney Fife

Nip it! Nip it in the bud!
—Barney Fife
("Nipped i' the bud" from *The Tragedy of Brennoralt* by Sir John Suckling, 1609–1642.)

Nowhere except in Mayberry can you find a character like Barney Fife. Andy Taylor best describes Barney when he says, "He's a nut."

Barney was born Bernard P. (Milton) Fife in the month of July. He grew up in Mayberry along with his cousin and close companion, Andy Taylor. "Why, Andy's the best friend I got in the whole world," he admits unabashedly.

Court's in session

The young Barney lived a fairly normal boyhood except that he was a sickly child (his father, says Barney, was "even sicklier"). He used to get nosebleeds in school.

As a boy, Barney played such games as "Run, Sheep, Run," "Early, Early, Urchin Free," and "One, Two, Three, Red Light," racing around the streets, lawns, and farms of Mayberry. He was pretty fast, he says. He earned a medal for winning the 50-yard dash. "Barney the Rabbit" had been trained to be fleet of foot by his sickly father. Barney was a Second Class Boy Scout, just like his cousin Andy. They used to take turns spending the night at each other's house. The two boys once tried to earn some extra money by selling seeds door-to-door. Barney still has five packs of seeds. The young Fife's boyhood hero was actor Skeets Gallagher, the sidekick to "Tailspin Tommy." Barney has always been a big fan of Gabby Hayes and he likes George Raft movies.

One of Barney's talents as a painfully thin seventeen-year-old boy was the ability to slip his hand into a milk bottle and pull out an egg, but he was also an exceptional student in the classroom—or so he says.

Barney: Boy, I tell you, if I ever came home with anything less than *A*s, I just didn't dare come home.

Andy: I don't remember you getting all *A*s.

Barney: I did that once. Remember? The teacher made such a fuss about it that all the kids hated me.

Andy: I don't remember.

Barney: Well, it's a fact. I didn't want 'em thinking I was some kind of a snob or an egghead or something, so I buckled down and got bad marks.

Andy: That must have taken real effort.

Barney: You think you're kidding. Listen, an IQ can be a mixed blessing sometimes. Some people want it and can't get it. I got it and had to get rid of it. Life's funny that way, you know?

Bernard Milton Fife: Board of Directors—Tin Foil Drive, Hall Monitor, Volley Ball Court Maintenance Crew, Spanish Club

During his teen years as a student at Mayberry Union High School, Barney was involved in the usual extracurricular activities. Always one to appreciate fine literature (especially his own), "Scoop" Fife wrote a sports column, "Pickups and Splashes From Floor and Pool," for the school paper. It seems the column ran "just that once" because Barney was too far ahead of his time. The 1945 edition of the school yearbook, *The Cutlass*, credits the young Fife with taking an active part in the following: Board of Directors—Tin Foil Drive; Hall Monitor; Volleyball Court Maintenance Crew; Spanish Club.

Shy Barney had the usual problems any average adolescent boy might have with the opposite sex. Ramona Wiley, who was in Social Studies 1-A with Barney, had a crush on him and nicknamed him "Tweeky." She wrote a note to him that said, "Barney, beloved, the tears on my pillow bespeak the pain that is in my heart." Vicky Harmes was another schoolgirl enamored of Barney's charms. She used to bite off the end of Barney's raspberry snowcones (his favorite), suck all the juice out, and give Barney back the ice cone devoid of all juice. He also had a brief romance with Irene Phlogg.

Then there was the thorn in Barney's side—Jack Egbert. Jack blackballed Barney from membership in the Philomathian Literary Society. But, as Barney says, "Jack Egbert was no prize himself."

After high school, Barney entered military service as a private in the Army. During his tour of duty, he worked in the PX library on Staten Island, where he was second-in-command to a corporal in charge of three thousand books. As Barney relates, "I did my part in helping to whip the dreaded Hun." But then, also referring to his wartime experiences, he says modestly, "Of course, I would rather not talk about it."

Barney began his career as a Mayberry deputy sheriff some time in the 1950s. The exact date is questionable. It was his cousin Andy who hired him and taught him how to handle a revolver, a fact that Andy would rather forget.

Barney is zealous in his enforcement of the law. He probably knows every code, case, ordinance, and regulation on the Mayberry books. He really wants to give his chosen profession his best shot. As he said to Andy at the beginning of his career: "You see, Andy, I want the folks in this town to realize that you picked me to be your deputy because you, well, you looked over all the candidates for the job, and you judged their qualifications and their character and their ability, and you come to the fair, the just, and the honest conclusion that I was the best suited for the job. And I want to thank you, cousin Andy."

Barney is as meticulous in his personal habits as he is in his work. He always dresses sharply and in complete uniform. (He keeps his citation book in his cap.) He's as sharp as a skinny tack, all 5'7", 138 to 138½ pounds of him—right down to his size 10½ socks and his size 7½B shoes. "Us Fifes is wiry, not much flesh," as he describes himself. "All muscle." Of course, Barney is a naturally thin person. He'll tell you "that's a mark of us Fifes. Nothing goes to fat. It all goes to muscle."

Besides his uniform, Barney is especially proud of his salt-and-pepper suit. The suit is great for dancing because it "hangs just right for the dips." One color you'll never catch Barney in is black. That's because black makes him look so thin. He loves to wear a snappy hat, but if there's anything he can't stand, it's for somebody else to put on one of his hats. (His mother was the same way.)

Barney usually gets a haircut every third Monday of the month. Floyd says that Barney will never be bald: "He's got a loose scalp; there's a lot of play in it."

Barney is proud of his "21-jewel, pure-gold-band wristwatch" and his anniversary watch (that's the stainless-steel, waterproof wristwatch with the numeral 5 engraved on the back—the "5" stands for his years of service on the Mayberry police force). Although he almost never smokes, Barney carries a cigarette lighter. When he's feeling extra sporty, he might light up a cigar.

For a time, Barney resided at 411 Elm Street, where his phone number was 431 (it was a three-party line). He subsequently moved into Mrs. Mendelbright's apartments, where he initially paid a rent of $6 per week; it was later dropped to $5. For years, Barney wasn't allowed either to cook or use more than a 40-watt bulb in his lamp. He has lived at Mrs. Mendelbright's for five years. If duty calls for it, though, he will sleep in the back room of the courthouse.

Barney's mother lives in Mayberry, and he sometimes takes bus trips with her to Charlotte. There is no doubt that Barney loves his parents. For their wedding anniversary one year,

Dapper deputy

Barney gave them a new concrete, steel-reinforced septic tank. Always a bit sentimental, Barney still has the rock that his father used to keep on his desk. (Mr. Fife let young Barney strike matches on the rock and then light his pipe.)

Among Barney's other relatives are his cousin Virgil in New Jersey and his uncle, who owned a 1949 Hudson Terraplane.

Of course, Barney's closest friend is Andy, and Barney is convinced that Andy needs "Barn" to watch over him, sort of like an older brother. Barney, by the way, was the best man in Andy's wedding and he is Opie's godfather. "That darn guy," Barney says about Andy. "Somehow or other, he just brings out the big brother in me. Guess I'll just have to try and help the kid."

Barney gets a hit

Not only does he get Andy into all sorts of fine messes, Barney also believes he can be of assistance to Andy in raising Opie. "First sign of youngsters going wrong, you've got to nip it in the bud," he tells Andy.

Barney points out the price one pays for breaking the law, as he chides Opie and his young friends by giving them a tour of the jail cells: "Yes, boys, take a good look. This is the last stop on the road to crime. A man confined to prison is a man who has given up his liberty, his pursuit of happiness. No more carefree hours, no more doing whatever you want, whenever you want. No more peanut butter and jelly sandwiches."

The town deputy is quite emotional and high-strung, but it's hereditary. Barney says, "All us Fifes are sensitive." He once contradicted himself in a fit of righteous indignation, however: "Sensitive. Me! Sensitive! Boy, that's a nice thing to get started around. If there's anything that upsets me, it's having people say I'm sensitive. There's one thing I'm not—sensitive! Talk about being misunderstood."

Barney Fife is a man of his convictions. He tells his best friend: "Ange, when the ol' steel trap in here has made up its mind, there's no turning back." He displayed those convictions when he invested forty bucks in the *Music From Mayberry* album, even though Andy thought it might be a con job.

Some of Barney's sickliness from childhood still lingers. Barney is allergic to horsehair and he has low blood pressure and low-sugar blood. He soaks his feet at night and then applies a little foot powder.

A musician at heart, Barney sings first tenor in the town choir and he can play the harmonica. He also has some bongo drums and has purchased pure brass cymbals with genuine leather grips. The cymbals were Andre Kostelanetz Marchers, which Barney ordered from Cymbal City in Chicago. They set him back a pretty penny— $18.50 to be exact. He is the standby cymbalist in the town band, which has no regular cymbalist. As for his personal tastes in music, he confesses that Ted Weems' music soothes the savage

Hilda May (Florence MacMichael)

in him. He also enjoys the singing of Nelson Eddy, Tex Ritter, and Ferlin Husky.

Perhaps it is his snappy attire that makes Barney quite the man with the ladies. Andy calls him "the Adolphe Menjou of Mayberry." Barney's first serious courting experiences came with Miss Rosemary. She was followed by Hilda May. But Barney's true love is Thelma Lou. About her, Barney says, "She's my girl. Everybody knows that, for heaven's sake." Nevertheless, Barney still might slip in a date with Juanita down at the diner. And together with Andy, he is practically irresistible to the "fun girls" from Mt. Pilot. Barney has also dated a registered nurse. As he says to Andy, "Our only crime is that we're attractive to women." Yet, Barney always finds his way back into the arms of the understanding Thelma Lou. They were

Thelma Lou

classmates at Mayberry High and graduated together, but it wasn't until 1960 that they became acquainted, at Wilton Blair's funeral. Ever since that fateful encounter, Tuesday night has been "their night."

Each Tuesday at 8:00 P.M. sharp, it's Barney and Thelma Lou sitting together over at her house watching "that doctor show" on TV with a pan of cashew fudge between them. For an evening on the town, Barney and Thelma Lou might go to Mt. Pilot— strictly dutch treat, of course. Or they might just drive out to the duck pond and park. For his dates, Barney usually slaps on a little Paris Nights aftershave.

After church service on Sunday, Barney likes to take it easy. More than likely, what he'll do is "go home, take a nap, go over to Thelma Lou's and watch a little TV." Or maybe he'll go down to the drugstore with Andy to get some ice cream for later. Perhaps they'll walk over to Wally's to get a bottle of pop.

Barney is a bit vain, to say the least. He takes extra special pride in his 100 percent cotton uniform (genuine whiplash cord), which was made in Raleigh. For inspiration during grooming, Barney keeps a picture of Rock Hudson tacked near the mirror in the back room of the courthouse. Sometimes his "old baby blues" catch a glimmer of Frank Sinatra in the mirror.

But Sinatra never ate like Barney does, as his order for breakfast at the diner one morning indicates: "I'm not too hungry this morning. I'll have orange juice, bowl of cereal, stack of wheats, three eggs over (not runny), bacon on the crisp side, white toast buttered, hash brown potatoes, and coffee." And Barney can be counted on to get more than his fair share of Aunt Bee's square meals. He loves Chinese food and pizza (especially mozzarella and pepperoni). He likes his hamburgers medium rare, makes his sandwiches on salt-rising bread, and enjoys his cup of java with three lumps of sugar and a little cream. Aunt Bee even keeps a special cup with a capital *B* on it in the cupboard so that Barney can pour his own cup when he drops by the Taylor kitchen on weekday mornings.

Because of his low-sugar blood content, Barney needs lunch by noon or he gets a headache. Barney also insists that a "slender, high-spirited person

Old high school sweetheart Teena Andrews a.k.a. Irene Phlogg (Diahn Williams)

needs his sugar pick-me-up in the middle of the day." For this, Barney always partakes of his Mr. Cookie Bar. He also loves chocolate layer cake with chocolate icing. He keeps non-fat milk in his fridge and eats lots of apricots.

In his efforts to hone his singing talents, Barney takes voice lessons from Eleanora Poultice, Mayberry's renowned voice teacher. Barney's voice lessons no doubt aid his acting as well. He has played the Nelson Eddy part in *Rose Marie*, and he once auditioned for the role of Chief Noogatuck in the Mayberry Founders' Day Pageant. It's unclear whether he ever got that role.

For relaxation, Barney enjoys bridge, gin rummy, and Parcheesi, or perhaps a game of checkers or dominoes with Andy. He like to go to Mt. Pilot for war-surplus and police auctions. For hometown excitement, he might kill some time by watching the boy change the marquee at the moviehouse.

On nice evenings, he and Mrs. Men-

Undercover deputy

stairs, get his shoes shined and his hair cut, hang around the lobby, maybe watch a game or two of Ping-Pong, have the special at the Y coffee shop, then see a movie or hear a lecture on sportsmanship and cleanliness. Before bed and to cap off the evening, he might have some tapioca pudding and hot chocolate.

On the job, Barney Fife is all business. His responsibilities include manning the school crosswalk each weekday at 8:00 A.M. and 3:00 P.M. He's continually harassing jaywalkers and kids who ride their bicycles on the sidewalks. He also watches over the bicycles parked outside the moviehouse, makes a round of the town at 11:00 P.M. to check the doorknobs, is in charge of the courthouse bulletin board, and is the official starter for the potato-sack races at the Masons' picnic and the footraces at the annual Sheriff's Boys Day. He sums up his career by saying: "We're just plain simple men fighting organized crime with raw courage—strong, determined, rugged, fearless."

delbright will sit on the porch, sip cider, count the cars passing by, and make polite conversation. He might even mention the time he won the church raffle and got four free haircuts. After Mrs. Mendelbright goes to bed, Barney may read a magazine. He admits that he is something of a night owl since his head "sometimes doesn't hit the pillow till a quarter before eleven."

He likes to knit and crochet, skills he learned by watching his mother. One Christmas, he meant to knit Andy an afghan with "God Bless This House" in the North Carolina state colors, but he never got around to it.

On his vacations, Barney will generally go down to Raleigh, check into the YMCA, and try to get a corner room. He'll put on his pongee shirt, go down-

Although sleepy little Mayberry rarely has any crime of consequence. Barney is vigilant, realizing it's "a wilderness out there. And every so often a beast of prey comes sneaking in. Now, it's my job as a lawman to stalk him and run him out. That's my number one job—stalking, not fly-killing." He keeps an eagle eye out for strangers because "you just never know when another beast might come down out of the forest."

Barney lets his best girl know how he feels about his responsibility: "You see, Thelma Lou, this is what we call the deadly game. I'm in it for keeps." And when one of those "beasts of prey" does mingle in Barney's fiefdom and tangles with the dogged deputy, he tells his partner, "You know, Andy, I never thought our town would come to this. Mayberry—gateway to danger." To keep in optimum shape, Barney takes judo lessons from Mr. Izamoto in Mt. Pilot, and he practices karate.

Barney's continually looking for ways to update the Mayberry police force. If it were up to Barney, the department would have more guns, cameras for "high-speed photographic surveillance and reconnaissance," bugging devices for the jail cells, tear gas and other anti-riot equipment, more jail cells, and at least one fingerprint set. And there's no telling how many motorcycles Barney would have as part of Mayberry's rolling stock. (Barney does eventually get his official fingerprint set.) There was also the time he added Blue, a bloodhound, to the force, but Blue retired after a short, successful career in crime-stopping.

Barney keeps abreast of what's happening in the world of law and crime by reading *True Blue Detective*. He has bound volumes going back to 1959. Among his favorite articles are:"I Married a Fink," "How It Feels to Pull the Switch," and "I Picked a Pocket and Paid." He's even had one of his own articles published. He turned in a report to the state on "Safety Procedures

on Country Roads." His report featured an original jingle: "Walk on the left side after dark or you'll wind up playing a harp."

Barney reads other fine literature as well. He quotes Shakespeare *(The Merchant of Venice)* to Andy: " 'The quality of mercy is not strained. It droppeth as the gentle rain from heaven.' You're not talking to a jerk, you know."

Nevertheless, Barney is a loyal deputy and adds a lot to the sheriff's department. He celebrated his tenth anniversary as a deputy at the age of thirty-five, and has, of course, tendered his resignation many times throughout those years, even trying his hand at a couple of other vocations. He sold Miracle Sweep vacuum cleaners and moonlighted for a time by dabbling in real estate, but he always came back to his first love, law enforcement.

Barney eventually leaves the Mayberry deputy position in order to take a job with the Raleigh police department. At first he worked in state traffic, but he moved on over to the fingerprint lab, where he was in charge of N through R (Nab–Rosisky) and made $95 a week ($125 bonus at Christmas). Later, his job was expanded to include M through R, and he was promoted to staff detective.

After moving to Raleigh, Barney rented a corner room at the Y. He did board for a short time with the notorious Parker family. He also became "Mr. Independent Wheels" after he bought a blue convertible, a 1960 Edsel with a 1961 grille. Although he sometimes caught the train, he used the car to make visits back home to Mayberry.

Barney is slow to marry Thelma Lou, but that's mainly because he is married to his work. He never has any children, but he considers his side-arm an adopted child. Among his nicknames for his gun are "blue steel baby," "old Roscoe," "old persuader," "rod," and "heater." He confesses that he feels undressed when he's without his gun and holster. "Well, I ain't much of a talker," he would say. "In my business, this baby [his pistol] does my talking." And his explanation for the low crime rate in Mayberry is quite simple: "Well, I guess to sum it up, you could say, there's three reasons why there's so little crime in Mayberry. There's

The bully and Mr. Chicken—Barney snaps to attention for Fred Plummer (Allan Melvin)

Andy, and there's me, and [patting his gun] baby makes three."

Barney's beloved pistol is always close by his side, and he is ever ready to use it.

Andy: What are you doing?
Barney: Gun-drawing practice, ten minutes every day. If I ever have to use this baby, I want to teach it to come to papa in a hurry.

Barney's Nicknames

Barn
The Scamp
Barney the Rabbit
Peter Cottontail
Tweeky
Scoop Fife
Barney-Parney-Poo
Cream Puff
Reliable Barney Fife
Foxy Fife
Tiger Fife
Barney Fife the
    Bulkhead
Bernard Fife,
    M.D.—Mayberry
    Deputy
Intrepid Barney Fife
Fearless Fife
Barney the Beast
Fife the Fierce
Crazy-Gun Barney
Phantom Fife
Rifle Fife
Fast-Gun Fife
Wild Bill Fife
The Chicken
    (so-named by his
    judo class because
    "his bones snap like
    chicken")

And although Barney can make his "baby come to papa" in the blink of an eye, he is, unfortunately, too excited to aim it in the proper direction. Among the places he has planted his cherished bullet are the courthouse floor, the courthouse ceiling, Andy's front porch, and a tire on the squad car.

Mayberry has never been the same without Barney around because, let's face it, Barney Fife is irreplaceable. As Barney once expressed his biggest fear: "Swept into the dustbin of history—Exit, Barney Fife." But that's one thing that will never happen to Mayberry's legendary deputy.

Fife the fearless

Barney's Blarney

compelsions for *compulsions*
inovert for *introvert*
Smith Brothers Institution
   for *the Smithsonian*
heeliocopter for *helicopter*
kleptomenerac for
   kleptomaniac
Einsteen for *Einstein*

inarculated for *innoculated*
   (he really meant
   incarcerated)
extra-sensitive perception for
   ESP
schizofreeniac for
   schizophrenic
nave for *naive*
fire by constriction for *fire by*
   combustion or friction

viz-à-viz for *vis-à-vis* ("you
   know—hand-to-hand")
boodoor for *boudoir*
Sigmund Frude for *Freud*
demore for *demure*
noblesse oblage for *noblesse*
   oblige
therapetic for *therapeutic*

A Letter From Barney

Dear Peasants (Ha ha):

Would have written sooner but Virgil and I have been on the go every minute since we got here and checked in at the Y. It sure isn't like Mayberry, where they roll up the sidewalks every night. Ha ha.

Last night was really wild. We went to the arcade and played four games of skeeball. There was a magic store there, and I bought a tin inkblot that looks just like the real thing. Can't wait to put it on Aunt Bee's tablecloth and watch her face. Ha ha.

Next, Virgil had a tie painted for him while I shot at a tin bear with an air rifle. Let me tell you, ol' sharpshooter Barn really pinged up the place. Then we went in a booth where you get four pictures for a quarter. I was going to send you one, but it turned brown later.

After that we had supper at a waffle shop where the waitresses all dress alike in peekaboo blouses, and let me tell you . . . [Andy couldn't read this part aloud because Opie was listening].

Have to close now. Having fun but money sure doesn't last. Been here only three days and already gone through $10.

Well, see you in the funny papers. Ha ha.

Barney

Another Letter from Barney

Dear Andy:

It certainly is exciting up here in Raleigh. Really having a ball. My head hasn't hit the pillow before 11:15 since I got here. Catching all the shows. Saw that Italian picture that we read about in the paper, *Bread, Love and Beans,* and it was plenty risque, let me tell you.

The food here in the cafeteria is terrific, and I've been eating up a storm. The breakfast special is unbelievable: three hot cakes, two strips of bacon, one egg— any style, juice, and coffee, all for 35 cents. It's served only between 5:00 and 6:00 A.M., but I can't sleep anyway.

I ran into a fellow on the street the other day who tried to sell me an iron deer for my front lawn, but I don't know.

Well, it's almost 5:00, so I better get down to breakfast. Love to Aunt Bee, Opie, Floyd, Goober, and all the boys.

10–4, Over and Out,
Barney

P.S. I'm not saying anything, but there's an awful lot of pretty women up here. Ha ha.

Barney's Songs

There are also several songs by and about Barney that add to his legend. Here are two he wrote:

"The Ballad of Andy and Barney" or "The Gangster's Mistake"
(Sung to the melody of "Frankie and Johnny")

Andy and Barney were lawmen.
Bravest you ever did see.
Warned every crook in the record book to stay
*   out of Mayberry.*
They were the law (Yes, they were the law),
And they didn't know fear.

Pretty Boy Floyd come a ridin'.
Dillinger, too, big as life. They weren't alone.
There was Al Capone and in back old Mack
*   the Knife.*
They were the law (Yes, they were the law).

Then there was that ditty that someone wrote on the bank wall in Mayberry:

There once was a deputy called Fife,
Who carried a gun and a knife.
The gun was all dusty,
And his knife was all rusty,
Because he never caught a crook in his life.

"Oh, My Darin' Barney Fife"
(Sung to the melody of "Oh, My Darlin' Clementine")

In a jailhouse, down in Dixie, fightin' crime
*   and risking life,*
Dwelled a sheriff and his buddy, pistol-packing
*   Barney Fife.*
Oh, my darin', oh, my darin', oh, my darin'
*   Barney Fife.*
He's a deadly crime-stopper, what a copper
*   Barney Fife.*

One day there came a-ridin' two bad men to rob
*   a bank.*
But Fife was tricky, a dead-eye dickey. Now
*   they're locked up in the tank.*

(Andy added the following couplet.)

Oh, my Barney, oh, my Barney, had a jail and
*   couldn't lock it.*
Had one bullet for his pistol, had to keep it in
*   his pocket.*

And Barney had his own tribute to Juanita:

Juanita, Juanita,
Lovely, dear Juanita,
From your head down to your feet,
There's nothing half so sweet,
As Juanita, Juanita, Juaneet.
Oh, there are things of wonder,
Of which men like to sing.

There are pretty sunsets and birds upon the
*   wing,*
But of the joys of nature,
None truly can compare,
With Juanita, Juanita, she of beauty beyond
*   compare.*
Juanita, Juanita, lovely dear Juaneet.

What Barney Might Say
When He Gets Mad At Andy

"You're almost as funny as Floyd, you know that? Why don't you two team up? Call yourselves Frick and Frack."

"Oh, you're funny, you are. Why don't you put a flower in your lapel and squirt water?"

"You're a riot, you know that? Why don't you go some place and have it?"

"You're real funny, you are. It's too bad you're not twins. You could be the Katzenjammer Kids."

"Oh, you're a clown, you are. Why don't you put a red light on your nose and go in the circus?"

"You're a regular Felix the Cat, you are."

"Oh, you're funny, aren't you? Oh, you're real funny. You ought to get a cane and a cigar and work a carnival."

"You're funny, aren't you? Boy, you're really funny. Give you a hundred on the laugh-o-meter."

"You ought to go on the radio and be an all-night disc jockey. I could turn you off."

"You're real funny, aren't you? Laugh-a-minute Taylor. Regular Joe Penner. Hoot, hoot, yuck, yuck."

"You're funny, all right. You're a scream. You ought to get a job on one of them excursion boats."

"Why don't we go up the hospital some night and take the bolts out of the wheelchairs? That'd be funny, too."

"You belong in the funny papers, you know that? Give you a wig and dress and you're another Emmie Smaltz."

"You're just full of fun today, aren't you? Why don't we go up to the old people's home and wax the steps?"

"You're funny, you know that? You know you are as funny as a crutch."

To Andy and Opie: "You ought to go on the stage. You're a regular Burt and Squirt."

Cops and Robbers

Because Andy and Barney are law enforcement officers, much of their work involves interaction with other law officers, as well as with petty thieves, lawbreakers, and an occasional convict on the lam. Listed below are some of the more notable cops and robbers whom Andy and Barney have encountered in their glorious careers.

Mayberry Sheriffs

Sheriff Pinkley, in 1931
Sheriff Poindexter, in 1946
Fred Paley
Dale Buckley
Andy Taylor
Barney Fife, for a day

Other Sheriffs

Sheriff Jackson: the sheriff of Siler City; president of the Sheriff's Association
Sheriff Maloney: the retiring sheriff of Greendale whom Barney had the opportunity to replace
Sheriff Mitchell: Mt. Pilot
Sheriff Williams: Mt. Pilot
Sheriff Blake Wilson: apparently followed Williams as sheriff of Mt. Pilot; Andy never cared much for Wilson.
Sheriff Wilson: Marshall County
Fred: probably the sheriff in Pierce County
Monroe: the sheriff in a nearby county

Deputy Sheriffs

Bernard P. Fife, M.D.: Andy Taylor's deputy extraordinaire; the M.D. stands for Mayberry Deputy, of course
Ernest T. Bass: technically a deputy (maybe) because he is given Barney's uniform to impress his darlin' Romeena; also, he directed the school kids at the crosswalk
Otis Campbell: a temporary deputy who usually took the position for the $5 that the job pays; on one occasion, though, Andy and Barney allowed Otis to be a deputy so that Otis could impress his visiting brother
Art Crowley and **Burt:** deputized just for Founders' Day

Warren Ferguson: whether or not Warren got to be Andy's deputy because he's Floyd's nephew is not known, but he did finish fourth in his class at the Sheriff's Academy

Judd: an octagenarian called upon to serve on special occasions; likely doing it just for the $5

Floyd Lawson: a deputy on very special occasions

Jerry Miller: Robey and Early Miller's boy from West Virginia, who becomes a deputy mostly as a favor to Aunt Bee from Andy

Gomer Pyle: another temporary and even sometimes capable deputy; trained by Deputy Fife

Goober Pyle: a temporary deputy usually enlisted by Barney for special occasions or in emergencies; after Barney resigns, Goober sometimes fills in to "help out" Andy (Goober never seems to like the badge Andy gives him because it's always bent)

Bob Rogers: an apprentice deputy learning about law enforcement for his work at the State Attorney's office (his license plate is DC–269)

Other Deputies

Hanson: a deputy mentioned in passing

Joe Watson: a deputy in Siler City

Deputy's Oath

As a deputy of the county of Mayberry, I swear to uphold the laws and regulations therein, set to by statute 426 C, county rules and regulations, put there by this date, city of Mayberry, county of Mayberry, therein.

State Police

The North Carolina State Police occasionally visit Mayberry, usually either to track down suspected criminals or escapees or to drop off prisoners in the Mayberry jail. Among some of the State Police are the following:

Sam Allen: an inspector who is also a buddy of Andy's

Captain Ardell: a cynic who learns to respect Andy and Barney as they help in the capture of criminals

Captain Barker: learns that Andy and Barney are capable of catching more than "chicken thieves and such." Andy admires Barker's map with the magnetic stickers

Bob Rogers (Mark Miller)

Police Chief Benson: the probable head of the State Police, who makes a radio broadcast

Ralph Case: an over-eager inspector who is appalled by Andy and Barney's Katzenjammer Kids" approach to law enforcement; his boss is Mr. Brady

Dick: a friend of Andy's

Horton: with the State Bureau of Investigation; accompanied by Al and McGuinness

Sergeants Jacobs and Fred: another pair of troopers

Sergeants Johnson and Miller: yet another pair of troopers; they have trouble hanging on to their prisoner

Mr. Rogers: the head of the State Bureau of Investigation who just pops into the

Ralph Case (Tod Andrews)

neighborhood to say hello along with state trooper Leroy Miller

Mr. Somerset: a dog-loving inspector who has two labradors and a beagle

William Upchurch: from the state special investigation section; sent in to solve the cow thief case

Walters: a trooper accompanying Captain Barker

Federal Agents

Frank Brewster: an FBI man who comes to town to catch a payroll thief

Bowden: an agent with the Alcohol Control Bureau

Morley and partner: plainclothesmen from Memphis who stake out the Mayberry jail

Raleigh Police and Detectives

Tony Bardoli: a house detective at local hotel; a retired cop

Captain Barker (Ken Lynch)

Plainclothes detective (George Kennedy)

Miss Clark and Renee: secretaries in the Raleigh detective division

Sergeant Friendly Dean

Capt. M. L. Dewhurst: the Raleigh detective division chief; Barney's boss

Herb Mason: works for Hogarth Detectives

Sergeant Nelson

Peterson, Rayburn, and Al Jenkins: other detectives in Raleigh

Commissioner Hedges

Judges and Lawyers

Mayberry and vicinity have enough judges and lawyers. The judges are primarily around for weddings and such; the lawyers are just around. Here is a list of some of the area's more prominent practitioners of jurisprudence.

Justices

Andy Taylor: the Mayberry Justice of the Peace

Judge Branson: presides over the court in Mt. Pilot

Judge Cranston: Aunt Bee served as a juror in his court during the trial of Marvin Jenkins

Judge Parker: Mayberry's circuit judge

Other Civil Servants

Mr. Bronson: the Civil Service director in Mt. Pilot

Warden Hix: the director of the County Work Farm

Jim Peterson: a game warden in Stokes County

Attorneys

Ralph Baker: Bob Rogers' boss

Alvin Barrows: a Raleigh attorney

Myles Bentley: a reputable lawyer from Jonesboro who refuses to handle Eddie Blake's robbery case

Neil Bentley: an ambulance-chasing lawyers from Mt. Pilot who talks Otis into suing Mayberry County

George Brookfield: a Raleigh attorney

Lee Drake: a female Raleigh attorney who represents Mayberry in a case involving a county bulldozer that smashes a car

Mr. Forsythe: appears to be a partner in Lee Drake's firm

Mr. Gilbert: the prosecuting attorney in Mt. Pilot

Arthur Harrington: comes to bail out Ron Bailey

Lonas, Hill, and Davison: Mt. Pilot law partners

Mr. Milton: represents the state in the case of "Andy on Trial"

Rafe Peterson: a Mayberry attorney; also sells aluminum siding

Clarence Polk: a Mayberry attorney; also umpires baseball games

Prisons

Federal Penitentiary in Atlanta

Lintwood Federal Pen (about 400 miles from Mayberry)

Mayberry County Work Farm

North Carolina State Prison: primary residence of the Hubacher brothers

State Prison: Meehawken, South Carolina

Organizations

FBI

Police Emergency Committee: Goober is chairman; Howard and Emmett also serve

Con man Oscar Fields (J. Pat O'Malley)

Sheriff's Association

Sheriff's Safety Week (in Mayberry)

State Bureau of Investigation

State Highway Patrol

State Penal Commission

Crooks

A wide variety of crooks, convicts, criminals, and other assorted "beasts from the jungle" have wandered into Mayberry. Here are a few of the more memorable ones.

Eddie Blake: robbed a Raleigh bank of $25,000

Eddie Brooke: a three-time loser, serving twenty years in the Atlanta pen

Jack (alias George Archer) and Stella Butler: a couple who try to rob the State Mobile Museum when it stops in Mayberry

"Gentleman Dan" Caldwell: forger, embezzler, confidence man, and swindler who assures Mayberrians "on my word as a gentleman"

Tracey Crawford: about 6′ tall, 160–165 lbs.; wanted on five counts in Chattanooga

Jelene Naomi Conners: 5′4″ tall, 115 lbs., and a convicted husband-beater (No. 5831) who escapes with Big Maude

Sheldon Davis: alias Thomas A. Moody; 5′9″ tall; pickpocket who poses as a traveling salesman and becomes Mayberry's "guest of honor"

Dirkson: escaped convict (No. 7458) who is the first criminal we see Andy and Barney capture

Oscar Fields: a.k.a. Otto Feldman a.k.a. Norman Feldspar; a swindler, confidence man, and bunco artist who tries to swindle Mrs. Mendelbright out of her life's savings

Pickpocket Skip (Lee Van Cleef)

Frankie and Skip: purse snatchers at the carnival

Fred and Larry: bank robbers (they stole $6,000) whom Otis helps capture

Charlie Granger: the real burglar in the Marvin Jenkins case in Mt. Pilot

Madelyn Grayson: a con woman who corresponds with Floyd

Jed and Prothro Hanson: "Trojan horse" burglars who rob Wally's Service Station

Colonel Harvey: sells illegal alcoholic Indian elixir

Allen Harvey, Pat Blake, and Gilbert Jamel (aliases all): bank robbers posing as TV producers

Hennessey (an alias): a bank robber posing as an FBI agent

Fred Jenkins and Ray: bank robbers posing as an FBI man and a photographer (alias Joe Layton) from Intercontinental News

Luke Jenson: a hermit and cow thief; his accomplice is his dog Mack

George Jones: a swindler claiming to know the location of the fabled Ross Treasure

Ralph Kingsley and Arnold Finch: $10-bill counterfeiters who pose as printers

Henry "Shopping Bag" Leonetti: wanted for grand larceny

Mrs. Myrt "Hubcaps" Lesch (phony last name): sells stolen cars with her nephew Jake

Clarence "Doc" Malloy: with his girlfriend as an accomplice, he robs the payroll at the furniture factory and hides out at the Half-Moon Trailer Park

Bill Medwin: a bookie barber who uses Floyd's Barbership as a front for gambling (by the way, he charges eighty cents for a shampoo and $1.50 for a facial)

Mort and Ollie: bank robbers

Ralph Neal: 5'10" tall, 160–165 lbs.; escaped from Lintwood Federal Prison; a tough cookie, he encounters Barney and his part-bloodhound dog, Blue

Avery Noonan: an escaped convict whom Barney helps to recapture

Hubcaps Lesch (Ellen Corby)

Prisoner of love (Susan Oliver)

Tiny and Doc: bank robbers being held in the Mayberry jail; Pete might be the name of their partner

Pete and Charlie: operated a rigged shooting gallery at the town carnival

Sally: a blond escaped convict (No. 1000) and friend of Big Maude; Barney reminds her of ex-boyfriend Al from the Cascade Club in Toledo

George and Gladys (alias Melissa) Stevens: married but posing as father and daughter in order to try and swindle Barney with a breach of promise suit

Big Maude Tyler: 5′6″ tall, dark hair, 175 lbs.; aliases: Clarice Tyler, Maude Clarice Tyler, Annabelle Tyler, and Ralph Henderson; Big Maude (No. 38216) is the leader of three escaped female convicts that Barney and Floyd run into

Raleigh Crooks

C. J. Hasler: alias C. J. Hoffman; a jewel thief and con artist; 5′9″ tall, 132 lbs., 54 years old, brown eyes; mug shot No. 75249

The Parkers (Ma, Henny, Leroy, and Agnes Jean): supermarket burglars; they provide Barney with room and board

Others

Luke Comstock: Andy wounded him in the left leg in a 1952 gas station holdup (Luke shot first at Andy); he now owns a chain of TV repair stores in Cleveland

The Felts Brothers: two members of this notorious gang escaped from the state prison in Meehawken, South Carolina

The Hubacher Brothers: three good ol' boys in the state prison; they frequently write Andy and Barney; one Christmas they sent Andy a wallet and Barney a bookmark; Junior sings "My Little Gray Home in the West" at cell parties; Elmer is one of the brothers; Andy and Barney plan to go up there and see them some Sunday

Guest of honor (Jay Novello)

Codes and Cases

Mayberry is a town without much need for elaborate laws and regulations. Folks in Mayberry get along with each other just fine without much law enforcement. Even the sheriff doesn't feel the need to carry a gun. But when a town has a deputy like Barney Fife (and later, Warren Ferguson), well, there's going to be some enforcement of laws. The Mayberry deputies are known for their particularly strict application of all rules.

Among Barney's regulations for prisoners are two basic rules: Rule No. 1 is: Obey all rules; Rule No. 2 is: Do not write on the walls, as it is very hard to erase writing from walls. And Barney takes seriously the "Sheriff's Rules," of which Rule No. 1 is: An officer of the law shall enforce the law and order without regard to personal welfare and safety. Indeed, Barney's entire body is a weapon.

As for Andy, the rules that he follows are based on the "Mayberry Rules for a Long, Happy Life." They are: 1. Don't play leapfrog with elephants; 2. Don't pet a tiger unless his tail is wagging; 3. Never, ever, mess with the Ladies' Auxiliary.

Still, Mayberry does have its share of official codes, ordinances, and regulations. The following are the more common regulations that Mayberrians must observe. These regulations fall into a few basic categories.

Traffic and Safety

Parking on Main Street is for one hour. Parking in front of the courthouse is for official vehicles only. And there is no parking in front of Mr. Martinelli's meat market between 9:30 and 11:00 A.M. on Tuesdays and Thursdays.

Rule 8, Section B covers parking too close to a fire hydrant (too close is eight-and-a-half feet, as measured by Barney's feet). Ordinance 115 also pertains to this violation. All parking violation fines are $2.

City statute 249 A, paragraph 5, prohibits riding bicycles on the sidewalks—at least downtown. And there's a town ordinance that doesn't allow playing in the streets (it's not safe).

If you should make an illegal U-turn in Mayberry, you're subject to a "citizen's arrest" for committing a 911. The fine for that can be a whopping $5.

There are, of course, numerous restrictions on speeding. Things just can't go too fast in Mayberry. The speed limit in Mayberry is 20 mph. It's faster on the highways. For example, a section of Highway 6 around Turner's Grade is posted at 35 mph. (Andy gives the truckers a little leeway there because they need some extra speed to get over the hill.) The old dirt roads around the lake are posted at 45 mph. Speeding there, say at 70 mph, will get you a stiff $10 fine.

About the only people Andy and Barney ever allow to speed through town are the "fun girls" from Mt. Pilot. In their case, the faster, the better.

And, even in Mayberry, jaywalking is against the law. Likewise, littering will not be tolerated; it's a severe $4 if you're caught.

Alcohol

There are many regulations in Mayberry governing intoxicating beverages. They receive a regular workout from one townsperson in particular—Otis Campbell.

Mayberry is a dry town for at least part of the 1960s. Later, the town ap-

parently relaxes its restrictions. In any case, moonshining is never allowed, even though most of Mayberry's moonshiners are likeable folks.

But most of the laws concerning alcohol deal with the consumption thereof. Municipal Code 404 B governs being drunk and disorderly and public drunkeness. A 411 also covers drunk and disorderly conduct. Ordinance 502 holds "being intoxicated in a public place" to be a violation of its provisions. The penalty under this ordinance is a fine of $2 or a sentence of twenty-four hours. (Otis always takes the twenty-four hours.) By the way, Otis was first booked for intoxication on September 23, 1941.

Loitering and Disturbing

Mayberry has a variety of laws that deal with not doing enough or doing too much. Vagrancy and loitering are forbidden by Code 439, and loitering is covered again by a 63. A 317 will get you (as it did the Darlings on their first visit) for "occupancy of private property without permission."

On the other hand, being too rowdy in Mayberry is a violation of Municipal Code 721–8 and a 302—disturbing the peace. And if things really get out of control (as when a lady raised her umbrella at Barney in front of the courthouse), there's Code 421—unlawful assemblage and inciting to riot.

There are also many miscellaneous sorts of regulations, which Barney in particular is fond of enforcing. Here are just a few:

a 912—insulting an officer's intelligence (that's similar to robe-dignity insulting, an offense for which Andy once had to cite and impose a $30 fine; robe-dignity offending costs even more—$50)

a 710—assault with a deadly weapon

a 204—bribery and collusion and tampering with and/or intimidation of material witnesses

a 907—dipping a hat in a horse trough (the Darlings again)

a 785—false alarm (of which there are many)

And of course, there is a 612, which Barney will only say is "an official code." Other codes that Barney enforces are a 626, a 308, a 10–12, a 38, a 42, a 215, and a 923 and Ordinance 603. Only Barney knows what all of these are. And when Barney is suspicious of a person, he might just do a 42–J—a character report.

When Andy and Barney have "emergencies," there is the No. 2 Amber Alert—one of them staying awake at all times. We can only assume that a No. 1 Amber Alert would be both awake at all times. And if they need some extra help, they can always draft a "special deputy" under Article 156 Section 16 of the State Penal Code.

This is the essence of Mayberry law as we know it. There are other lesser known laws such as the Green River Ordinance of 1924 (Code 304), which prohibits peddling door-to-door without a license—a misdemeanor that even Barney has committed. Likewise, vending on the street without permission is prohibited by Section 17–B, Article 4. And gambling is not supposed to be allowed in Mayberry in "any way, shape, or form," but Floyd and Goober still match pennies on the street curb.

Nevertheless, there is one basic rule that all Mayberrians live by: Do unto others as you would have others do unto you.

Asa Breeney and Barney:
Double-barreled security

It's definitely no fun when that
iron door clangs shut

Cases

Over the years, the Mayberry Sheriff's department has encountered many interesting cases. Below are a few that we know by name.

Wilson vs. Thorpe's Pharmacy in Mt. Corey: Wilson bought arsenic on Tuesday, May 4; was buried on Friday the 7th

The Walker Robbery: Barney got credit for this one with a headline in the paper that read, DEPUTY SHERIFF BARNEY FIFE CRACKS WALKER ROBBERY.

Osgood vs. Welch Dispute: Ted Osgood and Huey Welch had a disagreement about Osgood's new fence blocking the sunlight from Welch's laying hens. (According to Barney, this case was similar to Willoughby vs. Perkins and could have dragged out in court for years.)

The Rafe Hollister Case: moonshining

The Emma Watson Case: chronic jaywalking (bless her heart)

The McAllister Case: this was that case involving McAllister, so Barney tells us.

The Case of the Punch in the Nose: Floyd punched Charlie Foley in the nose on August 9, 1946, at 11:25 A.M. Barney resurrected the case years later.

The Helen Crump Case: Helen Crump was arrested in Kansas City for consorting with a known hoodlum, Harry Brown, and for dealing in an illegal gambling hall and carrying a concealed weapon.

There are, of course, many other capers and criminal activities involving the folks of Mayberry, but these are the ones that are referred to by name.

Above all, Barney and Andy deal with people, not with books and legalities. Barney always tries to remember the most important lesson that Andy has taught him: "When you're a lawman and you're dealing with people, you do a whole lot better if you go not so much by the book but by the heart."

Andy explains rifle safety to temporary deputy Jerry Miller (Jerry Van Dyke)

Andy and Barney give Otis a helping hand in preparing for the arrival of his brother and sister-in-law

Opie Taylor

Can I go outside and play, Paw?
  —Opie Taylor

Red-haired Opie Taylor is Mayberry's all-American boy. He loves playing baseball, fishing, hunting frogs, and eating ice cream and his Aunt Bee's pies. On the other hand, he is not particularly fond of school, homework, haircuts, and baths.

Above all things, though, Opie dearly loves and respects his father.

Opie: Golly, Paw, you know just about everything, don't you?

Andy: Aw, I don't expect I know everything.

Opie: I mean it, Paw. You not only know everything, but you're the sheriff; you're the Justice of the Peace; you're just about the most important man in Mayberry, in the state. Why, I'll bet you're the most important man in the whole world!

And, in return, Andy thinks the world of his son. "I believe that's as good a boy as you're gonna find," he tells his friends. They wholeheartedly agree.

Floyd: That Opie is a fine boy.

Goober: Yeah, nice relationship between Andy and Opie.

Floyd: Yeah, father and son.

Opie

As for Andy's fatherly advice to Opie, he says: "You're my son, and I'm proud of you just for that. You do the best you can, and if you do that, that's all I'll ask of you."

Opie and his "Paw" have a wonderful relationship. As a widower, Andy has done an outstanding job of raising Opie. The younger Taylor knows exactly what his father expects of him, whether it be chores around the house or at the courthouse, or his conduct in the classroom or on the playground. When Opie has done something wrong, he knows that, because his father loves him, punishment will be sure and swift.

Andy has taught Opie the importance of responsibility, respect, and honesty. He told Opie: "When you make a solemn promise to a friend, it ain't right to go back on it. No. Never let your friend down, never break a trust, and when you give your word, never go back on it."

The small-town atmosphere of Mayberry serves as an ideal place for Opie to grow up in. He begins his formal schooling at the Mayberry elementary school, where his first-grade teacher is Miss Johnson. In the second grade, he has Mrs. Cox. We never hear anything about his third- and fourth-grade teachers, but his fifth-grade teacher is Mrs. Warner. She is replaced during the term by "Old Lady Crump" (Miss Helen Crump). Miss Crump is also Opie's teacher in the sixth grade and

Checking out firearms

Opie has a crush

beyond. Opie had a crush on Miss Crump and even spent his entire savings of eighty cents on a pair of nylon stockings for her. But after his dad explained that Miss Crump was *his* girl, Opie said, "As long as she's in the family, I don't care if she's my wife or my mother."

Opie's grades in school are a little above average, but he does have difficulty with arithmetic—just as his father did. He once got an *F* in arithmetic, but he usually gets *A*s in English. (He once wrote an essay entitled "What I Would Do if I Had a Tool Chest.") He tells his friends that his favorite subject is lunch, but he really loves PE. (By junior high, Opie decided that he

might like to be a dentist, and he planned to attend the University of North Carolina.) Once, when Opie and his pals were having trouble with Old Lady Crump's history curriculum, Andy got the boys interested in history by telling them about "Indians, redcoats, cannons, guns, and muskets and such." He even helped them form their own history club, the Mayberry Minutemen.

Opie is popular with his classmates. In the seventh grade, he is elected class president. One day he was washroom monitor. At one time or another, he is in several exclusive boys' clubs (No Girls Allowed). In the Wildcats, Opie is the Keeper of the Flame in charge of the Sacred Candle. (Later, his title is converted to Keeper of the Flashlight.) In that club, there looms the dreaded Curse of the Claw, which strikes any member who breaks the club oath: "I promise I will never reveal any of the secrets of the Wildcats. I will not even tell anyone there is such a club as the Wildcats and, if I ever do, I will be struck down by the Curse of the Claw." (The oath is followed by "The Growl"—"growl, growl, growl.") Along with Andy and Barney, Opie is in the Tomahawks. Later on, Opie becomes a member of the Mayberry Boy Scouts, Troop 44.

Opie loves sports. Baseball is probably his favorite sport. He plays second base for Mayberry's Little League team, the Giants. He and his teammates once reached the district finals but lost the playoff game to Mt. Pilot, 6–5, at Mayberry Field. One of Opie's prized possessions is an autographed baseball from the New York Yankees. One of his favorite baseball players is Yankee slugger Mickey Mantle.

The athletic Opie also enjoys another sport; what it is, is football. He has a prized pigskin from a State College game and he gets a lot of wear out of his jersey with the number 14 on it. He admires Baltimore Colts quarterback Johnny Unitas. That's probably because Opie is the quarterback in his neighborhood. When playing with his friends in a sandlot game, he frequently calls play No. 26. That means "everybody out for a pass." In junior high, Opie is both quarterback and captain of the school team. His coach is ex-pro Flip Conroy.

Opie has not always been so good at athletics. When he was in the first grade, he entered the Sheriff's Boys Day Races and finished last in the 50-yard dash, trudging down the track in his black, high-topped sneakers. It was a disappointing experience, but Opie learned the importance of being a good loser.

The young Taylor has taken piano lessons from Clara Johnson. During that course, he practiced two hours every day, from 3:30 to 5:30 P.M. Later, he began his piano practice at 6:00 A.M. so that he could play football in the afternoon. Opie can also play the guitar. In junior high, he joins a local rock 'n' roll band, the Sound Committee. Their first gig is at Brenda

Just a-whistlin'

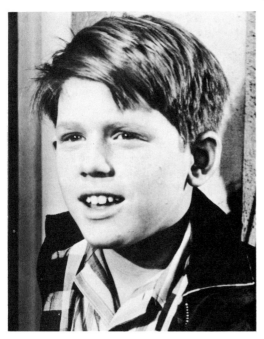

Roach's birthday party, where each band member earns $5.

While Opie plays hard, he works equally hard. He is eager to earn his allowance. Among his chores are sweeping the courthouse and the sidewalk in front of the courthouse, emptying the trash, cleaning out the garage, setting the table, taking out the ashes, keeping the woodbox filled, and mowing the lawn. For all of his efforts he receives twenty-five cents a week, although he once bucked his pa for a raise to seventy-five cents. His father thought about it and raised it to twenty-seven cents. By the time Opie is in the fifth grade, his allowance has risen to the considerable sum of $1.50 per month.

By then, Opie has a different girlfriend. Back in the first grade, his girl was Mary Wiggins (a real favorite because she had a front tooth missing). In the fifth grade, his main girlfriends are Sharon and Karen, and in junior high it is blue-eyed Mary Alice Carter.

Opie has held several part-time jobs. He worked for a while at Mr. Doakes' grocery store, where he made seventy-five cents an hour. In junior high, he works after school at Crawford's Drugs as a soda jerk and a counter clerk. He has had a paper route, sold Miracle Salve, and once set up a lemonade stand where he really pulled in the business at two cents a cup. In another enterprising venture, he and partner Howie Pruitt published their own newspaper, *The Mayberry Sun,* which they printed on the press that Howie got for his birthday. *The Sun* cost three cents for adults and two cents for students, although a few early issues were free when the boys were trying to boost circulation. He also made a little money by hunting pop bottles, which can be cashed in for two cents on the barrelhead at Foley's Grocery.

Opie, like most boys, loves to eat. He especially likes peanut butter and jelly sandwiches and milk. His favorite pie is, naturally, apple, which he loves with vanilla ice cream. As Opie grows older, his taste buds mature, and his favorite pie becomes butterscotch pecan. He is also fond of Chinese food, crabmeat, and spaghetti, but he hates carrots and spinach. His favorite after-school and before-bedtime snack is cookies and milk.

Opie enjoys an all-American boyhood. He has a clubhouse (Keep Out), a tire swing, and a basketball hoop in the backyard. In his bedroom, there's a brass bed, his father's old piggy bank, a globe, a dart board on the wall, an Indian headdress, a microscope on his study desk, and a photo of Aunt Bee on his dresser. He also has a penny that's supposed to be lucky because it was run over by a train. It must be lucky because Opie once won a bugle and ten free lessons as a door prize from the moviehouse. Of course, his father didn't feel too lucky about it.

Opie's bedtime was 8:30 P.M. in his grammar school days, but by the time he reaches junior high, he is allowed to stay up until 9:00 P.M.

Throughout his formative years (Aunt Bee says he's the spitting image

Opie and friend

of his father at that age), Opie has a number of different pets. He has a dog named Gulliver, a bird named Dickey, and a lizard named Oscar. (Oscar lives out back in his lizard house.) At one time or another, Opie also has had a pet snake, a white mouse, a goldfish, and a frog. After accidentally killing a mother songbird, Opie raised her three young chicks, which he named Wynken, Blynken, and Nod. Opie also has had an imaginary horse named Blackie.

Opie's best friends in elementary school are Johnny Paul Jason, Howie Pruitt/Williams, Whitey Porter, and Trey Bowden. In junior high, his best crony is Arnold Bailey. But his best friend is his father. Opie even tried writing a book, which he entitled *What It's Like to Be the Son of a Sheriff.* And if Opie turns out to be a pretty good

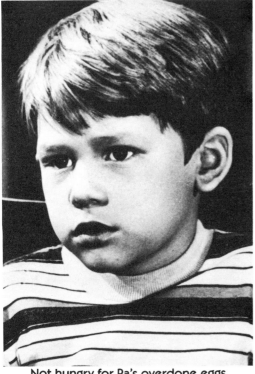

Not hungry for Pa's overdone eggs

"Don't the trees seem nice and full?"

kid—darn near too good (although he and Arnold once sneaked into the back door of the moviehouse without paying)—it's because he's got a mighty fine "Paw."

Andy usually sees Opie to bed each night with a fairytale or a story from the classics. Opie's favorite bedtime story is about the headless horseman, "The Legend of Sleepy Hollow." If there's company over and Aunt Bee needs to shoo Opie out of his room for guests, then he gets to go "adventure sleeping." That means sleeping on an ironing board between two chairs.

Andy and Opie spend a lot of time around the courthouse and, whenever possible, they go fishing down at the lake. Or maybe they'll just enjoy a quiet evening relaxing on the front porch with Aunt Bee and company.

Then there are those special talks that Andy and Opie have. Andy always takes great care in making his instructive points to Opie. As Barney has pointed out: "You just listen to your Pa, son, and you'll never go wrong."

Though Andy is rarely wrong, he can never quite evade the penetrating innocence of Opie's little-boy logic. Nevertheless, Andy has raised Opie to be respectful of his elders and thoughtful of his peers. And at night, just before he goes to bed, Opie Taylor says his prayers.

Andy and Opie have a neat time making a mess while Aunt Bee's away

Opie's Pals and Gals

Best Friends

Johnny Paul Jason: his best friend in elementary school

Arnold Bailey: his best friend in junior high

Frederick (Trey) Bowden III: has a nine-bladed knife; from Erie, Pennsylvania; born the same month as Opie; they're "blood-brothers"; he doesn't like carrots

Howie Pruitt/Williams: he and Opie put out *The Mayberry Sun*; Howie is a real monster in class, according to Helen Crump

Billy Hollander: a friend he met at Camp Winokee; lives in Walnut Hills; from a wealthy family

Mike Jones: Sam Jones' son

Whitey Porter: a good pal of his in elementary school

Girlfriends

Heather Campbell: his eighth-grade

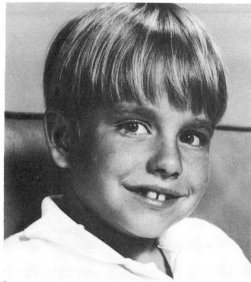

Mike Jones (Buddy Foster)

girlfriend; moved from West Virginia and became next-door neighbor of the Taylors; plays the piano

Mary Alice Carter: Opie has liked her since the first grade; she was his first "real" date; has blue eyes

Karen Burgess/Folker: a girlfriend; once fell down on the Elm Street playground; takes piano lessons

Charlotte: an early girlfriend; Opie bought her a coat

Cynthia: Helen Crump's niece

Sharon Porter/McCall: his girlfriend in the fifth grade; he gave her a new eraser; wears braces

Mary Wiggins: his first girlfriend; the prettiest girl in the first grade; has freckles, braids, a bandage on her knee, and a tooth out; Andy crowns her Miss Mayberry Junior

Schoolmates, Bullies and Rivals

Johnny Adams: the lead-off batter for the Mt. Pilot Comets

Cindy Ames: her best friend is Diana

Ralph Baker: Opie handcuffed him to a flagpole

Opie finds a baby

Opie and Cynthia (Mary Ann Durkin) get a bottle of pop

Homer Billings: male lead in senior play

Blake boy: a bully

Wilson Brown: a guitarist in Opie's band

Claudia Campbell: Heather's younger sister

Jesse Clayton: the drummer in Opie's band

Cosgrove kid: a bully

Billy Crenshaw: works at Doakes' Grocery

Estelle Evans: female lead in senior play

Devon Farley: in Cub Scout Troop No. 986

Jimmy Farrington: has a birthday party.

Howie Forman: made teethmarks on Opie's pencil

Tommy Griff: has a new driveway that's good for roller-skating

Jimmy Jackson: doesn't use the cross-walk

Clifford Johnson: a guitarist in Opie's band

Myra Lambert: played a raindrop in a school play

Betty Parker: lets Bobby Wilson carry her books home but writes sugar notes to Hector Styles

Nat Pike: the mayor's four-year-old son; says that a penny hit by lightning is worth six centers

Roy Pruitt: an underprivileged child

Steve Quincy: a bully

Jackie Simms: a boy on Opie's baseball team

Fred Simpson: an arrogant class stud

Hector Styles: gets sugar notes from Betty Parker

Sally Tums: does not have naturally curly hair

Barbie Tyler: a teacher's pet

Edgar Watson: a bully

Bobby Wilson: carries Betty Parker's books home

Tommy Wilson: a good friend who moved to Siler City

Arnold Winkler: a new kid from Raleigh; spoiled rotten; has a new Intercontinental Flyer bike worth $70

Cindy Barton

Tommy Farnell

Carter French, Jr.

Billy Gray

Aaron Harrison
Billy Johnson
Matt Merlus
Bruce Newdale
Jerry Parker
Freddy Pruitt
Brenda Roach
Fred Stevens

Arnie
Bernice
Betsy
Bruce
Charlie: a senior who works the lights for a school play
Ethel
George
Georgie: got his head stuck in a sewer
Henry
Hollis

Iris: the best friend of Mary Alice Carter
Joey: on the football team
John: loses baseball in the Remshaw House
Joy
Leon: loves peanut butter and jelly sandwiches
Pete
Phoebe
Ralphie
Sheldon: a bully who gives Opie a black eye
Sonny
Steven
Tim: the back-up quarterback behind Opie on the football team
Tom
Tommy: his father is the chief accountant at the shoe factory; he has a walkie-talkie set

(Courtesy Rance Howard)

Quick draw experts (real-life brothers Ron and Clint Howard)

Mayberry Menagerie

Matching Quiz on the Animals of Mayberry

Match items from the numbered list with the correct answers from the lettered list.

The Loaded Goat

1. Bessie Lawson
2. Emmett
3. Dogs, dogs, dogs
4. Shep
5. Mack
6. Gulliver
7. Fido
8. Dickie
9. Great big collie dog
10. Oscar
11. Blackie
12. Pink elephant
13. Owl
14. Baker and Charlie
15. Jimmy
16. Fluffy
17. Dolly
18. Sport
19. Spot
20. Hazel
21. Old Sam
22. Louise
23. White mouse, snake, and frog
24. Queenie
25. Cat that died
26. Blue
27. Bo (Beauregard)
28. Mrs. Snyder's cat
29. Crow
30. Mosaic cow
31. Hoot owl

32. Raccoon and a possum
33. Muskrat
34. Hawk
35. Turkey
36. Wild pheasant
37. Fish
38. Web-footed, red-crested
39. Old Man Davis' cow
40. Wynken, Blynken, and Nod

AA. Mrs. Peterson's cat
BB. Frank Myers' chicken
CC. Luke Jenson's dog
DD. Annual shoot held in Mt. Pilot
EE. Possibly the most difficult wild bird to ensnare
FF. Omen of the _____
GG. Opie's lizard
HH. Mule
II. Owned by Clint Biggers
JJ. Gomer's childhood dog
KK. What Andy shoots and occasionally eats
LL. Opie's dog
MM. Goober's childhood canary
NN. Arnold Bailey's

A. Mrs. Cruteck's cat
B. Tree-filling orphans
C. Sheds hair on Al Becker
D. Opie's unnamed pets
E. Scrawny cow
F. Star dog of TV show
G. Mr. Frisby's rooster
H. Opie's imaginary horse
I. Dynamite-eating goat
J. Legendary silver carp
K. Barney's bloodhound
L. Dogwood Farms' dairy mare
M. Opie's bird
N. Type of pie the Darlings like
O. What Otis the artist creates
P. What Mayberrians love to do
Q. Howard Sprague's childhood pony
R. Possible threat to Wynken, Blynken, and Nod
S. Otis's colorful pachyderm
T. Weddy Huff's stolen cow
U. Goober's talking dog or Otis's invisible dog
V. Creatures Ernest T. lived with in a cave
W. What Skinny Griffin says will bite
X. What Otis buys thinking it's a horse
Y. Talked to by Andy
Z. Lake loon

The Omen of the Owl

Answers to the Animal Quiz

1. E	21. J
2. HH	22. MM
3. II	23. D
4. F	24. A
5. CC	25. NN
6. LL	26. K
7. Q	27. G
8. M	28. R
9. C	29. KK
10. GG	30. O
11. H	31. N
12. S	32. V
13. FF	33. W
14. T	34. Y
15. I	35. DD
16. AA	36. EE
17. L	37. P
18. JJ	38. Z
19. U	39. X
20. BB	40. B

Well, I'll be doggone!

Aunt Bee Taylor

Aunt Bee

First and foremost, Aunt Bee Taylor is a homemaker. She takes pride in caring for her nephew, Andy Taylor, and his son, Opie. Their home is neat and clean, and the pantry is always loaded with good things to eat. Andy's aunt, nevertheless, is quite an individual, and, if she sets her mind to something, she can be extremely feisty.

Beatrice Taylor raised Andy after his parents' deaths. Although never stated, it is most likely that she is the sister of Andy's father. She came to stay with Andy and Opie in 1959, when Opie was only five, right after their housekeeper, Rose, left to be married.

At first, Opie shunned Aunt Bee's attention, but when it looked as though she would be leaving, he decided that she would be better off staying with him and his father. Opie once said: "Well, if she goes, what'll become of her? She doesn't know how to do anything: play ball, catch fish, or hunt frogs. She'll be helpless."

Bee is originally from West Virginia. She lived in Morgantown for five years, and when she was eighteen, her family moved to Peoria. Her birthday is March 17.

Bee has three sisters, Florence, Ellen (who lives in Raleigh), and baby sister Nora. Nora and her husband, Ollie, live in Lake Charles, Louisiana. They have two sons, Roger and Bruce, who are about Opie's age. Bee also has a brother. Her cousin, Edgar, resides with his wife, Maude, in Mt. Pilot. (Maude has "the versitas.") Another cousin, Bradford J. Taylor, came to visit once. Aunt Bee's niece, Martha (Andy's second cousin), and her husband, Darryl, have also visited. They left their six-month-old baby, Evie-Joy, with the Taylor household for a week. That's because Martha and Darryl were going to the wedding of Martha's sister, Grace, in Jersey City, New Jersey. Aunt Bee has an Aunt Louise and she confesses that she had a great-uncle who was a cattle rustler.

Clara Johnson is Bee's closest friend. They went to school together at Sweetbriar Normal School. Bee and Clara were on the school's basketball team, where Bee was the backbone of the squad. Bee made almost all *As* in high school and was an exceptional chemistry student, but she never went to college—perhaps because she was not very good in arithmetic. Bee and Clara both still remember their school song:

Sweetbriar, oh, Sweetbriar, where hearts are
young and gay,
Sweetbriar, oh, Sweetbriar, forever and a day.
Sweetbriar, oh, Sweetbriar, where hearts are
young and gay,
Sweetbriar, oh, Sweetbriar, forever and a day.

It is rare when Aunt Bee reminisces with Andy and Opie about her childhood. She has told them how she and Florence used to entertain visitors in the parlor by reciting poetry such as "Fading Flower of Forgotten Love" by Agnes Ellicot Strong. As a girl growing up in West Virginia in the early 1920s, Bee played Alice in a church production of *The Little Princess*. That production was directed by the Reverend Dargood. In Sunday school, she played the queen in *Six Who Pass While The Lentils Boil*.

She once told Andy and Opie that when she was Ellie Walker's age, she used to enter beauty contests. She remembers her first blind date with Orville Buck: they went ice skating. Orville was later killed in an explosion. Among her longtime friends are Mabel Pollock, Billy Sensible, and Charles Humbolt, and she has corresponded with Rita Akin in Raleigh and a lady in Buffalo for years.

Beatrice Taylor (Beatrice means "she who makes happy" in Latin) never married, but she has raised a lot of children. Naturally, she's a great cook, and, although Andy doesn't always show his gratitude in words, you'd better believe he knows it.

Bee: Did you like the white beans you had for supper?

Andy: Um huh.

Bee: Well, you didn't say anything.

Andy: Well, I ate four bowls. If that ain't a tribute to white beans, I don't know what is.

Bee: Well.

Andy: Eatin' speaks louder than words.

Bee: You know, your education was worth every penny of it.

Andy once told his aunt that she should be called Miss Fried Chicken of Mayberry. Every Sunday, she prepares either fried chicken or roast beef for dinner. Among her specialties are rhubarb pie and homemade strawberry ice cream (from an old family recipe), both of which have won blue ribbons at the county fair. But her top dish is tuna. She can do amazing things with it and she generally serves it at least once a week. Another of Aunt Bee's special dishes is ham loaf with green beans Chinese style. She got that recipe from the *Mayberry Gazette,* but because she lined the garbage pail with the newspaper, she had to guess about the final ingredients.

Miss Taylor is great at many other dishes: rib roast beef, beef casserole, potatoes, muffins (from an old family recipe), and cakes and pies of all kinds (mouth-watering best describes her pecan, Nesselrode, banana creme, chocolate, and blueberry pies). And Andy always says she has a green thumb with apple pies. For special occasions, she'll fix crabmeat, a delicacy that all the Taylors enjoy. She also does a lot of canning and preserving. But woe unto the man who bites into one of her homemade pickles. Andy and Barney can tell you that they're horrendous (like kerosene cucumbers). The same goes for her homemade marmalade.

Aunt Bee's culinary skills have reached further than the table of the Taylor house. Of course, many days around noon she carries a wicker basket down to the courthouse for Andy and Barney's lunch. That earns her the nickname of "Miss Luncheon Tray." Her recipes have been featured in the *Mayberry Gazette,* and she was once on a Siler City television program as the "Mayberry Chef." Another time she invested $400 in a Chinese restaurant with Charlie Lee as her partner. They called it Aunt Bee's Canton Palace. She served as hostess, while Charlie handled the cooking chores. She sold her interest in that venture after a short while.

Once, her cold leftovers served as a midnight feast for visiting American and Russian dignitaries who were in Mayberry for a summit meeting. It was her handsome victuals that paved the way for peace. As the diplomats prepared to leave, it was only natural for Bee to give them some leftover fried chicken in a brown paper sack for the road.

Beatrice Taylor is a romantic soul, and she has had her share of suitors. One whom she prefers not to have had is Briscoe Darling. Roger Hanover is one of her old beaus who came to call, but he proved to be an irritating bore. There were also brief romances with Henry Wheeler, the Reverend

Leighton, and Professor Hubert St. John. There was a more serious courtship with ex-Congressman John Canfield. But Bee always nixes the idea of matrimony and remains the delightful and unencumbered lady she is. She even spurns the amorous advances of Fred Goss, Mayberry's top man in the cleaning business.

Bee has had an exciting life. When the Taylors visited Hollywood, she won $4,850 worth of prizes on "The Win or Lose Show." The family had to sell most of the gifts in order to pay off the $1,138.72 in taxes they owed. (She did keep the garbage disposal and the TV set.) While in the movie capital of the world, Bee saw lots of famous celebrities, but unfortunately didn't get to meet her favorite star, Rock Hudson.

Another highlight was being chosen to appear on television as the Foster Furniture Polish Lady. This experience brought back memories of girlhood when she used to watch actress Clara Kimball Young from the second-floor balcony of the local theater. She even wrote a jingle for Foster Furniture Polish: "Shine on Foster's Polish; that's the one to buy; you ain't had such shining since January, February, June, or July."

Aunt Bee learns to fly

And then there was the time that Bee and Clara wrote the tune, "My Hometown," for Flag Day. Pop singer Keevy Hazelton recorded the song, and Bee and Clara had a hit on their hands. Of course, it was a once-in-a-million happenstance, but that didn't keep the duo from trying again with another song, "Venice," which never got off the ground.

One of the most exhilarating events in Bee's life was winning the Tampico Tamale Contest. The grand prize was a ten-day, all-expenses-paid trip for two to Mexico. Another high spot in Bee's life was taking flying lessons. No one in Mayberry would have believed it possible, but she came through like an ace pilot at Mr. MacDonald's Flying School. She even flew solo while family and friends watched.

Goober taught Bee how to drive, which is one thing Andy could bless Goober for. She hates to drive in the rain because storms make her nervous. She drives a Ford Sunliner convertible and buys super gas at Wally's.

There was another time, other than the restaurant business, that Bee attempted to work outside the home. She was a secretary at what was formerly Hanson's Print Shop at 177 Main Street. She earned $30 a week, working from 1:00 to 4:00 P.M. passing out business cards printed in green ink. The job ended when the owner-operators were busted for counterfeiting ten-dollar bills.

Aunt Bee's primary concern is taking care of Andy and Opie. They pay heed to what she tells them because she won't put up with any excuses. "Fiddle-faddle," she might say to Andy or Opie if they try to get out of a chore. She keeps Opie in line, and as Opie's told his dad: "She sure can kick up a fuss when a fellow gets his clothes all tore and messy." She doesn't allow him to take food up to his room, either. Still, Opie really appreciates his aunt's tender loving care.

Opie: 'Course, there's one thing Aunt Bee's awful better at.
Andy: Don't say "awful better," just say better.
Opie: Oh, well, then there's one thing Aunt Bee's better at.
Andy: What's that?
Opie: She's better at hugging.
Andy: Yeah, she sure is that. That kind of hugging money can't buy, right? Why don't you run upstairs and collect one?
Opie: Guess I will, Pa.

Next to her family, Bee loves her friends and neighbors. She relishes discussing the social life of Mayberry, perhaps over a cup of coffee (she likes hers with cream, no sugar), or while snapping green beans on the front porch. She might even try to pass a little gossip on to Andy.

Bee: Well, don't you want to hear what she said?
Andy: I thought you said you weren't gossiping with her.
Bee: Well, I wasn't gossiping. She was gossiping. I was just listening.
Andy: Oh, oh, you were just listening. Oh.

Aunt Bee gives Warren an earful

Bee: Well, I couldn't walk away. That would be rude.

Andy: Oh, I see. It's ruder to be rude than to be gossiping.

Bee: Well, Sarah knows that anything she tells me doesn't go one bit further.

Andy: Good for you again, Aunt Bee.

Bee: Well, don't you want to hear what she said?

One of Bee's hobbies is gardening. Roses are her favorite flower. She has even developed her own rose, Bee Taylor's Deep Pink Ecstasy, which is a cross between a Mrs. Pinkney Variegated Pink and an Alma Swapout Sunset Pink. She also grows Peabody roses in the front yard. Beatrice has been treasurer and president of the town's Garden Club (meets on Thursdays), and she and other members sometimes drive down to Raleigh for the state flower show.

Bee Taylor, like most Mayberrians, is civic-minded. She once headed a committee for the beautification of Elm Street. The group planned to replace all the elms with magnolias and change the name to Magnolia Street. She was chairman of the Greater Mayberry Historical Society and Tourist Bureau. She has been in the town choir ("My Chinatown" is probably her favorite song), has served as a juror, is in the Mayberry Women's Club, and has served as head of the Civic Improvement League. She even ran for a seat on the town council, but was unsuccessful in her bid against Howard Sprague. Clara was her campaign manager. Aunt Bee is also in the Ladies' League. For a while, she took art classes on Wednesday nights and polished up on her water color skills.

One of the most distressing incidents in Aunt Bee's life was the time she misplaced her antique gold-and-pearl pin (worth $275) that had been given to her by Aunt Martha, who was the best friend of her grandmother on her mother's side. Of course, most of the time she wears just an ordinary string of pearls.

Among other things, Aunt Bee is an excellent knitter and she enjoys quilting with her friends. She crochets doilies for the jail cells. She plays the piano, but not too often, and only rarely wears her glasses. She has occa-sional back trouble. (Her back can go out on her at any time.) She usually goes to bed after the ten o'clock news.

Bee Taylor is a warm and gentle lady. She has been baptized. She is Mayberry's Good Samaritan, and it is her tender heart, which is as wide as her kitchen, that makes everyone love her. It can truly be said that a stranger has never entered the Taylor house, because Aunt Bee makes all feel right at home immediately. Bee takes mighty fine care of Andy and Opie by nourishing them both physically and spiritually. The coffeepot is never empty, and the cookie jar is always full in Aunt Bee's kitchen. And there's plenty of homemade loving to go around.

Aunt Bee compliments Goober on his beard

Clara Edwards Johnson

And will you look at that—mildew! You can't expect me to do anything about mildew.
—Clara Johnson

Clara Edwards Johnson

Clara Edwards Johnson is the best friend of Bee Taylor. Their common interests include baking, gardening, sewing, and church work. They also love to gossip, as likely as not over coffee in Bee's kitchen. (Clara has always enjoyed "a little sweet tea and spicy talk.")

Clara is a widow and has a son, Gale. A number of years after Mr. Johnson's death, Clara reclaimed her maiden name of Edwards. Her irregular beau is Clark Cooper, who has the unbecoming habit of slitting his shoes.

Clara is a bit vain. She dyes her hair. Her idea of a dreamboat is Cesar Romero. For the last twenty-five years, she has suffered with neuralgia.

In her youth, Clara was a talented athlete. She and Bee went to school together, and Bee admits that Clara was the best dribbler on the basketball team at Sweetbriar Normal School. Many years later, Clara and Bee remain the best of friends, even though

Clara tends to be a busybody.

She has a sister who lives in Saber and an uncle who was a sailor. Her brother Claude is a musician and plays with Hippy Harrison's group. Clara's musically gifted family is further evidenced by her nephew, Ferdie, who plays the accordion. Clara herself plays the piano and she is the organist for the All Souls Church. Because music is Clara's forte, she takes great pride in her playing, and she gives piano lessons (she offers a twenty-lesson course) to young Mayberrians, including Opie Taylor and Arnold Bailey. She hoped to inspire Opie to piano greatness when she said: "It is only by dedicating ourselves completely that we can hope to achieve a degree of excellence. And I, who have devoted my life to music, can attest to its rewards." However, when Opie and some of his friends formed a rock 'n' roll band, Clara became their manager and treasurer.

Clara is not only a gifted instrumentalist, she also enjoys singing. One of her favorite songs is "Some Enchanted Evening," and she attends choir practice on Wednesday evenings. On top of all this, Clara is also an accomplished actress: she has played Lady Mayberry in the Centennial Pageant. And, as is fitting for someone as cultured as she,

Clara is a member of the Album of the Month Club.

Baking, cooking, and canning are among Clara's other skills. Her pickles are famous county-wide. For twelve consecutive years, she has won the blue ribbon at the county fair (allspice is her secret ingredient). She also bakes delicious apple pies. For those, she adds just a pinch of nutmeg (while the ingredients are simmering) to bring out the flavor.

Besides her music and her cooking, Clara is recognized for her gardening skills. For seven straight years, she has won awards at the flower show for her Clara Edwards Snow Valley White roses. Clara has also served as president of the Garden Club.

Clara's address is 516 (we don't know for sure which street, but it's probably just several houses down from the Taylors). She sometimes gets a lift to church with Bee, Andy, and Opie if she isn't driving her own automobile (license plate DF–183). When not playing the organ, she shares a pew seat next to Bee.

Though she can be meddlesome, Clara is a kind-hearted soul. She is a lady of many talents. Most of all, she is the dedicated friend of Aunt Bee. That in itself is special.

Mayberry Morsels

Food is a popular topic in Mayberry, probably because there are so many good cooks around—most notably Aunt Bee and Clara Edwards Johnson. Besides all that delicious home cooking, there are such fine eating establishments as Morelli's, the Bluebird Diner, and the Junction Cafe. And let's not forget the Snappy Lunch.

Most townspeople will recommend Morelli's if you're looking for a quality meal. Morelli's which is about halfway between Mayberry and Mt. Pilot, serves its own standard deluxe special: minestrone and pounded steak à la Morelli. It's only $1.85. (The shrimp cocktail is extra.) From your dining room seat, you can even look through a window to the kitchen and see the cook pounding the steak.

If you don't care to try their steak, each Monday, Morelli's serves chicken in its own sauce, and they prepare pizza late almost every night. As an added bonus, Morelli's has a gypsy violinist who performs on some enchanted evenings, and the tables are decorated with candles and red-checkered tablecloths.

But back in town, the Bluebird Diner is probably the most popular place for a quick, hot meal. Barney is generally more partial to the diner than is Andy. (That's because a visit allows him to flirt with Juanita.) He especially likes to eat there when the special is three Vienna sausages, succotash (heavy on the tomato puree), and a slice of bread and butter, on a paper plate—all for just eighty cents. (How do they do it?) And, by the way, the diner serves enriched bread.

Other diner specials include: the Breakfast Special for seventy-nine cents; corn beef and cabbage on Tuesdays; chicken croquettes (they're terrible, according to Opie), and catfish casserole on Fridays. Then there is the meatloaf plate; the pot roast plate; chicken à la king; steaks; chops; macaroni surprise; blueberry, peach, and apple pies; and the waffle special—forty-five cents (and that includes the syrup). Other items on the diner menu include: roast beef—$1.35; roast pork—$1.25; chicken-fried steak—$1.35; hamburger steak—$1.25; steak sandwich—$1.25; ham and lima beans—$1.30; malts—59 cents; soft drinks—5 cents. Goober Pyle, the town's biggest eater, thinks the diner makes the best mashed potatoes around.

Barney usually goes for fast foods, especially at night. One evening he ordered the following for himself and Andy: two "chili-sized" burgers with chopped onions, ketchup, piccalilli, and mustard; a side of french fries; a slab of rhubarb pie; and a chocolate malt. "The diner guarantees their food to stay hot—hours after you've eaten it," says Barney. Not only that, but the diner delivers.

If the diner isn't your cup of tea, try the drugstore for lunch. The businessman's special there includes a hollowed-out tomato stuffed with avocado and raisins. The lemon phosphate costs extra. And for dessert, over at Crawford's Drugs you can get a banana split for thirty-five cents. Yet another option remains the Mayberry Hotel, which serves breakfast from 8:00 to 9:30 A.M.; lunch from 12:30 to 2:30 P.M.; and dinner at 7:00 P.M.

For beverages, Andy and Barney are big ones for drinking coffee. When they aren't enjoying it from Aunt Bee's big coffeepot in her kitchen, they make their own in the back room of the courthouse. Of course, on a hot summer day, they might stroll down to Wally's for a bottle of pop. After all,

he's got the best selection in town, and it only costs a dime. And there's always a chance Opie might have his lemonade stand open.

Mayberry was a dry county for a long time, but eventually it allowed the sale of wine in some of its finer restaurants, such as Morelli's. Of course, if a Mayberrian wants beer or hard liquor, he'll still have to go to the County Line Cafe or find a friendly moonshiner (for more information, just ask Otis).

Foreign cuisine is also available in Mayberry. Originally, Mayberry's first Chinese restaurant was called Aunt Bee's Canton Palace, but she turned the operation over to Charlie Lee. Customers there have their choice between two chow mein dinners, the $1.65 meal or the $1.95 one. But for most Oriental-food lovers, Mt. Pilot is the place to go. Barney has taken Juanita there for dinner. It only costs $2.75 for the family dinner for one. There are at least two Chinese restaurants in Mt. Pilot, Dave's Hong Kong and Ching Lee's. And should a visitor ever get lost and wind up in the mountains of Mayberry County, the charitable Charlene Darling Wash might offer up a sumptuous meal of hog backbone or fish muttle.

No matter where you slice it, Mayberry's got good eating.

Floyd Lawson

Oh . . . well, what *did* Calvin Coolidge say?
—Floyd Lawson

Floyd

Town barber Floyd Lawson was born and raised in Mayberry. For nearly thirty years, he has cut hair in his one-chair establishment, which also provides a haven where the men of Mayberry can relax, play checkers, tell jokes, and swap hunting and fishing tales. Floyd's Barbershop is a town tradition.

Aunt Bee: You know, that place has become an institution. It's been the center of the town's activities for years.
Opie: Say, Pa, when I get older can I loaf around the barbershop, too?
Andy: Well, I wouldn't call if loafing, Opie.
Opie: Gee, Pa. You don't do anything there. You just sit around and play checkers and talk and grunt.

The bespectacled Lawson is a nervous, fluttery fellow with a dusty sense of humor. Floyd's idea of a hot joke: "Say, have you heard the one about the zebra who fell in love with a pair of pajamas?" Another time, when Andy's leaving for vacation, Floyd tells him: "Hey, Andy. Don't take any wooden nickels." It's hard not to like Floyd; he's popular with everyone.

Floyd is married (at least part of the time we know him). His wife's name is Melba, and they have a son, Norman. Floyd is proud of his son's talent on the saxophone and just loves that "Saxomania." Norman plays outfield in the Little League. Floyd also has a sister, a niece named Virginia Lee, a nephew (Warren Ferguson), and a shaggy dog named Sam.

One of Floyd's ancestors, Daniel Lawson, was Mayberry's first Indian agent. Daniel had a trading post where the town now stands. Floyd himself is named after his mother's brother.

Public-spirited Floyd served on the town council for four years. "Four of the stormiest years in Mayberry's political history," he says. "It was just a constant battle against corruption." The council could count on Floyd to voice strong opinions, even on the minor issues. He was really up in arms about the famous drinking fountain scandal that occurred when someone ran a hot water line to the fountain. "Somebody tried to cover up," he recalls.

Floyd was a founder of the Mayberry town band and he plays the trombone. He once offered a tour of the town to unwary visitors. It was a service of the Greater Mayberry Historical Society and Tourist Bureau Limited. The cost of the tour was a bargain at two bits.

Floyd has served as secretary of the Downtown Businessman's Club and he's a member of The Regal Order of the Golden Door to Good Fellowship.

When Andy ran a write-in campaign for sheriff, Barney appointed Floyd to be the precinct head of the blocks that went from Main to Maple, from Maple to Elm, and from Elm to the fire hydrant.

Floyd has also been a deputy. He assisted Barney on one case in which they nabbed three notorious female convicts. The next edition of the *Mayberry Gazette* carried a banner headline that read: LOCAL BARBER CAPTURES ESCAPED CONVICTS. Another official duty of Floyd's is to carry the flag in the Veterans' Day Parade.

For twenty-eight years, Floyd rented his shop from the Robinson family (they live in California) at $50 a month. Later, Howard Sprague bought the barbershop property and raised the rent to $65. After a brief quarrel, Floyd and Howard compromised at $57.50.

In the sidewalk outside the barbershop is the inscription: "Bobby Gribble hates Emma Larch." (Emma later became Mrs. Bobby Gribble.) Young Bobby wrote that in the cement in 1954, when the sidewalk was first laid.

Floyd attended barber college, which is where he learned a little Latin. His biggest dream is to have a two-chair shop. Floyd did get two chairs, if only temporarily, when Bill Medwin came to work for him. Floyd put a new sign in the window: Two Chairs—No Waiting. But that all fell through when Medwin was arrested on charges of booking bets on horse races.

Although sometimes troubled by rheumatism and sinus problems, Floyd stays quite busy with a number of hobbies. He raises prize-winning pansies and he loves to fish. (Check out his hat with all those fishing lures sometime.) He would even let Barney drive his jalopy (license plate RD–757) when they went fishing. Later, he purchased a convertible.

The blue-eyed barber is an experienced actor and writer. He was in *The Mikado* in high school, where he was "the backbone of the dramatic club," or so Floyd says. He also portrayed John Mayberry in the Mayberry Founders' Day play. Floyd even wrote his own ad for the Founders' Day program: Best Clip Joint in Town.

He composed "Hail to Thee, Miss Mayberry" for the Mayberry Beauty Pageant. It was an appropriate composition for the event.

"Hail to Thee, Miss Mayberry"
(sung to the tune of "O Tannenbaum")

Hail to thee, Miss Mayberry,
All hail to thee, all hail,
Your loveliness, your majesty,
Brings joy to every male,
All hail, all hail, all hail, all hail,
All hail, all hail, all hail, all hail,

He also wanted to write a book, and had a great opening sentence: "The sun is dropping lazily down behind the purple hills in the western sky." But that is as far as he ever got.

On a typical day in the barbershop, Floyd is likely to be matching wits with Barney or Goober while attempting to give Andy a haircut.

Andy: Floyd!
Floyd: What's the matter?
Andy: My sideburns.
Floyd: Your sideburns. What's the matter with your sideburns?
Andy: Why, they're both even.
Floyd: Why, I'll be dogged. How'd that happen?
Andy: I declare, Floyd, I believe you're getting the hang of it, and looka there. They're the right length and everything.

Floyd owns two acres of land on the north side of the county. "Fill in that swamp, it'd be a paradise," he says. He'd be willing to sell it at $200 an acre, or for a friend, $150 an acre.

In the early 1960s, Floyd charged a dollar for a haircut, 75 cents for a shampoo, 35 cents for a shave, and a quarter for a shoeshine. Floyd later upped his prices to $1.75 for a haircut, $2 for a butch or a flattop, 75 cents for a shampoo, 50 cents for a shave (it costs Floyd 20 cents per towel to have them washed), and two bits for tonic. His special scalp treatment is just $3. The largest tip he ever received was from a Raleigh fertilizer salesman. Floyd probably got to be such an outstanding barber from practicing on cats when he was a boy.

Floyd: I always did want to be a barber, even when I was a little kid. I used to practice on cats. I'd catch them in the alley and then I'd clip them. We had the baldest cats in the county.

Andy: That's a fact, and folks still say

that Floyd ain't much with people, but he's a great cat barber.

Some folks disagree over Floyd's skills.

Barney: Next time I want a haircut, I'm gonna stick my head in a pencil sharpener.
Floyd: Sure, and it'll fit, too.

Floyd appreciates a fine head of hair. He commented about Andy's hair once, when he thought Andy might be leaving town: "Sure gonna miss cutting his hair. Oh, he's got nice hair. It's soft but it's strong. It's easy to clip. He sits real still in the chair, too. He doesn't fidget one bit."

The Mayberry barber remembers cutting Andy's hair when the sheriff was a boy. Andy wanted to eat the shaving cream, Floyd recalls, because he thought it was ice cream. Floyd doesn't allow the youngsters to read

Inside Floyd's Barbershop

comic books while in the chair. Their heads swivel, he says.

Floyd's Barbershop is always open, if not for business, then for fellowship. The boys might have their guitars and banjos out for picking and grinning, or it might be just Andy and Floyd indulging in a game of checkers. Occasionally, someone will come in the shop to tack a note to the community bulletin board. If business is slow, Floyd may be sitting in the barbershop chair himself, reading the newspaper and licking a lollypop.

Floyd loves lollypops and tapioca pudding. Of course, for a real treat, Floyd likes nothing better than a nectarine crush and he tells Wally, "You've got the best pop in town." Floyd generally has one cup of coffee for breakfast and then another cup at 10:00 A.M. He usually takes an hour for lunch.

Floyd's best friends include Andy ("You're a prince of a fellow. A real prince," he tells Andy), Barney, Goo-ber, Howard, and Otis. In addition, grocer Charlie Foley and Floyd have been friends for more than twenty years, but they have had their spats. When Floyd was just beginning business in 1946, he gave Foley a shave as Foley slept. After Foley awoke, an argument started. Foley called Floyd a crook, and Floyd punched Foley in the nose. It ended up with Sheriff Poindexter arresting them both for assault. Andy even has it in the records. It occurred on August 9, 1946, at 11:25 A.M.

Floyd's personal hero is President Calvin Coolidge. He thinks that old Cal said everything memorable that was ever said. It is usually up to Andy to tell Floyd that "Calvin Coolidge didn't say that."

If anyone epitomizes Mayberry's easy-going, carefree lifestyle, it has to be Floyd Lawson. None of Mayberry's folks is more endearing than the beloved barber.

"Andrew Paul Lawson" helps Floyd pose as a wealthy widower for his first meeting with his Lonely Hearts Club pen pal

Dreaming of a two-chair shop

Otis Campbell

I'm dead sober, Andy, but I expect I'll get over it.
—Otis Campbell

(Courtesy Hal Smith)

Otis Campbell

Otis Campbell is Mayberry's most spirited citizen. He is Mayberry's distinguished town drunk. Although Mayberrians don't approve of heavy drinking, Otis is an extremely popular man-about-town. Even by Mayberry's standards, Otis is an easy-going, happy-go-lucky soul. Because of Otis's genial nature and impeccable integrity, Sheriff Taylor entrusts Otis to incarcerate himself after a night on the town. Almost every Friday and Saturday night, Otis stumbles into the courthouse (he has his own key to the front door), totters over to his favorite cell (Cell No. 1), and locks himself in. He then returns the key to its place on the wall just outside the cell and settles down for a solid night's sleep on his cot.

On some nights, when Otis is really gassed, Andy and Barney will chase the pink elephant from his cell, hum a few songs to quiet Otis's nerves, and maybe get him a glass of water (one sip is usually all that Otis will want). "You fellas actually drink this stuff?" he asks. Gin seems to be Otis's preferred beverage, but most of the time he guzzles Mayberry County moonshine.

When Otis is in the jail, he frequently becomes the subject of Barney's interrogation. The well-meaning deputy thinks he can crack Otis with one of his sophisticated methods of questioning. The Barney Fife Subconscious Prober-Primer (so named by Andy) is one of Barney's most famous and least effective attempts. Otis refuses to budge. As he says, "Us town drunks have a code we live by." Tick-a-lock.

And if there's any doubt whether Otis is sober enough to be released from jail (even if his twenty-four hours are already up), Barney is always eager to test Otis for sobriety. Most famous of these examinations is the Barney Fife Nose-Pinching Test for Drunks (again, so named by Andy). It is usually Barney, though, who can't endure the simple rigors of his own tests. Any efforts to rehabilitate Otis are miserable failures. As Otis notes, "I seen temptation coming, but it seen me coming, too." Andy says, "In a way, that drinking does a good service for the town. Otis laps it up so fast that the other folks can't get to it."

If anyone ever came close to rehabilitating Otis, it was Aunt Bee. Andy turned Otis over to his aunt one day, and she put him to hard labor cleaning rooms, filling the woodbox, mowing the yard, washing windows, chopping wood, scrubbing floors, washing dishes, and vacuuming the hall. Otis, in turn, nicknamed her "Bloody Mary" and called her little workhouse "The Rock."

On Friday and Saturday nights, Otis will often play rummy over at Charlie Varney's house. (One way or another he usually gets gin.) When intoxicated, Otis is prone to do any number of things. Once, he bought a cow for $20 from Old Man Davis. Otis thought it was a horse. Sometimes he is accompanied by his invisible dog, Spot. But one thing Otis will never do is drink and drive.

Otis is usually in need of a shave and is almost always wearing his trademark white suit—complete with suspenders, white hat, and necktie. He has glasses but never wears them. Awaiting him in his cell is his own light blue terry cloth bathrobe.

Otis's fine for public drinking is $2 or twenty-four hours. He always takes the twenty-four hours since he wouldn't waste $2 on something that doesn't have a cork in it. If Barney and Andy are at the courthouse when Otis locks himself up, he might ask them to "please wake me up at eight o'clock." And in the morning, if Aunt Bee hasn't brought him breakfast, Barney will fix him two soft-boiled eggs (four minutes), one piece of toast, and black coffee with one sugar. If Otis doesn't get his full eight hours of sleep he may wake up grouchy and say something like: "Whoever said that dawn comes up like thunder sure knew what he was talking about."

Otis has a wife, Rita, and a brother named Ralph, who is also a famed drinker. Ralph and his wife, Verlaine, once visited Mayberry on their way to

Memphis. Otis is also a distant relative of Charlie Foley's, the butcher, and he has kinfolk in Siler City. Otis apparently has an Uncle Nat who resembles Jimmy, the dynamite-eating goat.

The most famous of Otis's relatives is probably Nathan Tibbs. Otis received a plaque from the Women's Historical Society signifying that Otis was the closest living descendant of Tibbs, a Revolutionary War hero who marched eight miles through the snow to set fire to Mayberry Bridge.

But Otis is noted mostly for his free-spirited drinking. "I don't trust my own judgment when I'm sober," says Otis. He always seems to be able to find a still—even when Andy and Barney are positive that they have "licked moonshining in Mayberry once and for all." For some reason, Otis does most of his drinking in Mt. Pilot in later years, perhaps because Andy had indeed cleaned up the stills in Mayberry County.

For a while, Otis was in the town choir. He smokes. And he has a recurring ailment, a trick knee, which he says he injured while playing football with his wife. He also says that spicy food is bad for his liver. And even though Otis shows potential as a deputy sheriff and talent as an artist (who can forget his nice mosaic cow), he really has only one interest: "I got a hobby—drinking." He seems most at

"Pipe down, Otis!"

home in his familiar cell on his familiar cot. Even his job as a glue-dipper at the furniture factory doesn't keep Otis from his regular visits to the court-house. His cell is his "home away from home," and according to Andy, he is always welcome.

Barney describes Otis: "His silly round face, his wrinkled tie, little pot belly. He really is a good fellow. Never hurt anybody. Never said a mean thing."

The courthouse always seems a little warmer when Otis is around.

Moonshiner Jubal Foster (Everett Sloane, who wrote the lyrics to "The Andy Griffith Show" theme song, "The Fishin' Hole")

Mayberry Moonshiners

Big Jack Anderson: had a still in the old Remshaw place
Jubal Foster: burned his barn down while tending his still
Mr. Frisby: butter-and-egg man who did serious moonshining on the side
The Gordon Boys (Billy, Ike, Junior, and Sherman): had a still in Franklin Hollow
Rafe Hollister: had a still near Willow Creek Road; doesn't mean any harm
Jess Morgan: "A little moonshinin' never hurt no one."
The Morrison Sisters (Jennifer and Clarabelle): had a still in their greenhouse; made home brew for special occasions
Sam Muggins: just made a little for Christmas cheer
Luke Reiner: takes pot shots at total strangers
Rube Sloan: had a still on Furnace Crick
Ben Sewell: lives on Ash Road; a potato farmer; had a still near Council Flat

Rafe Hollister

But I done my time. And I ain't been moonshinin' since . . . well, I mean, not so as you could notice.
—Rafe Hollister

Rafe Hollister is one of Andy Taylor's best farming friends. Rafe and his wife, Martha, raise cattle, chickens, and various crops such as hay, beans, and corn. They also raise children.

Rafe is especially careful about his corn crop since his second career depends upon the success of the corn harvest: Rafe moonlights as a moonshiner. Even though he and Andy are good friends, Andy once had to lock Rafe up for ten days for operating a still up on Willow Creek Road (case No. 68456735).

Rafe is short and stout. He generally wears a hat, overalls, and sometimes a work vest. He usually needs a shave. Rafe drives a truck, is a good shot with a rifle, and can be mulely stubborn. These qualities make him a natural leader of the farmers in his neck of the woods.

Although Rafe hates Sunday-go-to-meeting clothes, he did once allow Andy to get him slickered up for a singing contest. The new suit prompted his wife to say, "Sure is something, Rafe. You look good enough to get buried." Rafe retorted, "I feel like I'm fixing to."

Even if the clothes did make Rafe feel uncomfortable, they didn't prevent him from winning the Ladies' League Musicale. Among the songs he sang were "Believe Me if All These Endearing Young Charms," "Look Down That Lonesome Road," and "Riding on That New River Train."

Rafe doesn't hold much with doctors. Since his daddy lived to be a hundred without ever seeing one, Rafe says he doesn't plan on breaking the family tradition. "I ain't never been to a doctor in my life. When I was born, I had my mama. When I die, I'll have the undertaker. I don't see no sense in cluttering up things in between." He got his tetanus shot anyway.

Ellie May Walker

I'm a pharmacist and there are certain prescribed rules I'm sworn to follow.
—Ellie Walker

Elinor May Walker (everybody calls her Ellie) came to Mayberry to help her Uncle Fred run his drugstore. She is well qualified since she holds a freshly earned Ph.G. degree (that means graduate in pharmacy—not pharmacy gal) from Bernard University.

Ellie is a lovely, pleasant girl. Aunt Bee says, "She's as pretty as a peach. Why, the boys ought to be buzzing around her like flies 'round a spoonful of honey." Ellie has a bright smile for all who enter Walker's Drugstore. She has a wonderful sense of humor and loves children. Ellie has a bit more of a formal education than most Mayberrians, but she is still able to learn a lot from the natives. The pert pharmacist lives across the street from the church and she drives a station wagon. She and some of the other people in Mayberry once invested in a folk music album.

For reasons unknown, Ellie doesn't stay in town very long, but while she is in Mayberry, she accomplishes a lot. For one thing, she instigates the women's liberation movement in Mayberry. She is the first female to run for public office and she surprises folks when she actually wins a seat on the Mayberry Town Council. Ellie also confronts several rigid traditions while in Mayberry. Sometimes it takes a little elbowing into Andy's ribs to get her point across. And even Andy confesses that Ellie is a sharp cookie when he says, "Why, Ellie May, I say, behind that pretty face you've got an awful handsome brain."

Ellie is Andy's steady girl. They enjoy church socials, picnics, and town dances together. Aunt Bee tells Andy, "Ellie's a wonderful girl, and if she's gonna have a husband, it ought to be you." But things never get too serious between Andy and Ellie, even though Andy once made a hasty proposal to her. She turned him down.

Though Ellie doesn't make Mayberry her permanent home, she is the prettiest dispenser of medicine the town has ever had.

Ellie Walker

Thelma Lou

That Barney's really quite a guy.
—Thelma Lou

Barney and Thelma Lou

Thelma Lou (we're never told her last name) is Barney Fife's regular girl. That's all there is to it, and everybody knows it.

Thelma Lou is an attractive girl with pretty, auburn hair. She has a wonderful personality and a heart of gold. It takes a girl like that to endure some of Barney's antics, not to mention his cheap dates.

Thelma Lou graduated from high school in the class of 1945 with Barney and Andy. She works in an office in town (we're never told exactly where she works or what she does). Her home phone number is 247, her phone number at work is 596, and her house number is 830.

Thelma Lou has at least one brother and two cousins, Mary Grace Gossage ("She's a dog," says Barney) and Karen Moore. (Karen is the female skeet-shooting champion of Arkansas who beat Andy in a contest with a perfect score.)

Thelma Lou is in the town choir and she plays the piano. She is also a good cook and loves spaghetti. She prepares a mean leg of lamb, makes fried chicken, bakes fudge brownies with walnuts and pecans, and has a delicious recipe for homemade peach ice cream. (She goes to the dentist in Mt. Pilot.)

Barney and Thelma Lou have had some interesting dates. They always go dutch treat because Barney is a cheapskate. He keeps telling Thelma Lou that the best things in life are free. In any case, every Tuesday night at 8:00 sharp, Barney will go over to Thelma Lou's house to watch "that doctor show" on TV. There they will sit on the sofa in Thelma Lou's living room and munch away on a pan of cashew fudge.

If Barney is feeling really romantic, he might put on some Cole Porter music, which he says has a "certain effect on Thelma Lou." On a warm summer evening, they might smooch a little while sitting in Thelma Lou's front porch swing.

Their courtship follows a regular routine: they go to church on Sunday; Tuesday nights it's her place for television; Thursday nights it's the diner for the special; and Friday nights, when Barney is on duty, it's coffee at the courthouse.

Theirs is one of the great romances in Mayberry history. Thelma Lou fervently hopes that Barney might one day pop the big question. There is no doubt that she loves him dearly.

Thelma Lou: Barney is going to be in the choir? My Barney?
    Andy: That's right.
    Thelma Lou: But Barney can't sing.
    Andy: I know.

Mary Grace Gossage (Mary Grace Canfield)

Thelma Lou: He's a warm, wonderful person and I love him dearly, but he can't sing.
    Andy: That's true.
    Thelma Lou: He's kind, considerate, good-hearted, the most gentle person I've ever known, but he can't sing.
    Andy: You're right.
    Thelma Lou: He's the man I want to marry, the man I want to be the father of my children.
    Andy: But he can't sing.
    Thelma Lou: Not a lick.

Barney truly loves his sweetheart, but for years he was just never quite ready to tie the knot. He does tell her how he feels about her. "Hi, pussycat," Barney whispers over the phone. "I want you to know that you're the only one I ever gave a hoot for."

"She's mad about me," Barney confides to Andy, and he tells Thelma Lou, "You know I'm crazy about you. You're the only girl for me." He means it. And he shows it.

Among Barney's gifts to Thelma Lou are a fur stole that fell apart (set him back $13.25) and a $2 pineapple skinner. He once bought her a half gallon of West Indian Licorice Mocha Delight ice cream (cost him forty cents). The nicest birthday gift he ever gave her was dinner at Morelli's, where they had the deluxe special.

Barney's thoughtfulness is matched by Thelma Lou's concern for him. She does, though, love to tease Barney, and she enjoys trying to make him jealous by flirting with the likes of Gomer, Andy, and even Opie Taylor.

Thelma Lou's best friend is Helen Crump. When they're together, they can be a real force to deal with. Andy and Barney never have a chance when it comes to quarrels or making decisions with the girls.

About a month after Barney moved to Raleigh, Thelma Lou left Mayberry. She settled down in Jacksonville, where she married Gerald Whitfield, the foreman of a wrecking crew. Thelma Lou's marriage dashed all of Barney's dreams, including "the ivy-covered cottage, the patter of little feet. Pfftt!" When he found out, a forlorn Barney Fife said, "She was the only girl I ever loved, Ange. She's the only girl I ever *will* love."

Around Mayberry, Thelma Lou is remembered as a kind person and a good friend, but for Barney, Thelma Lou will always be "the cat's."

It's a bit of a stretch for Barney to meet the state's new height and weight requirements for law enforcement officers.

Sharp shoppers

Helen Crump

All right, class. Class, you have your
homework assignment. Class dismissed.
—Helen Crump

Helen Crump

Miss Helen Crump is Andy
Taylor's sweetheart and
Opie Taylor's school-
teacher.

Helen grew up in Kansas. She was a
skinny kid. In the eighth grade, she
was the state spelling bee champion.
She majored in journalism in college
and, while working on her master's
thesis on organized crime, she went
undercover as a crook's moll.

That incident made the August 4
issue of the *Kansas City Chronicle* (page
seven) along with a picture of her being arrested by the police (she was
arrested on August 3, 1959, and ar-
raigned on August 4). She was charged
with having a .38 caliber revolver in
her possession, for dealing cards in an
illegal card game, and for consorting
with a notorious hoodlum, Harry
Brown. She was, of course, acquitted
of all charges.

Helen came to Mayberry from Kansas City in the early 1960s. She rents
her house (No. 895) from a landlady
whose movie idol is Dale Robertson.

Andy's first encounter with "Old
Lady Crump" came after Opie and

some of his pals complained to Andy about their history lessons. Miss Crump became angry because Andy had told the boys that history wasn't all that important. Andy managed to straighten things out, and later he and Helen began courting. Their first "date" was set up by Barney and Thelma Lou, and they dined at Thelma Lou's. Their first real date was dinner in Mt. Pilot for Chinese food.

Helen and Andy frequently double-date with Barney and Thelma Lou. They'll usually take in a movie at The Grand or maybe go to a dance. They sometimes go to dinner at the diner or over to Morrelli's (there's dancing there, too).

Helen enjoys picnicking and bowling. She and Andy like to play Scrabble, too. Helen enjoys playing the piano and singing in the town choir. She has a pet cat. She is a terrible cook, but she can make apple crumb pie. She uses Blue Moonlight perfume, and after the Taylors' trip to California, Andy gave her a pillow from Hollywood and a pearl necklace.

Some of Helen's relatives who come to visit include her Uncle Edward, and Cynthia, a niece from Wheeling, West Virginia (Cynthia's favorite subject is history). Helen keeps the love letters from an old sweetheart, Maynard Meyers. Maynard is married now and has six kids.

Mostly, though, Miss Crump loves her teaching. At one point, she tells Andy that she won't be interested in getting married until she has had a chance to teach for a while. Miss Crump understands and genuinely cares for her students. As she explains to her principal, Mr. Hampton: "I'm trying to say that this period of life which we all go through, the teen-age period, is a very frightening time. It's got its fears and its doubts and its curiosities. And they come to us and they say, 'I want, I need to express myself in my own way.' And we continue to say to them, 'Why, certainly, if you have some little thing you want to express, you go right ahead and tell me. But you tell me in my language and what I want to hear.'

"Well, Mr. Hampton, I think it would be very good if occasionally we said to them, 'Yes, you can do it in your own way, and I'll help.' And I contend, Mr. Hampton, that those youngsters are every bit as moral and sane and stable as we adults feel ourselves to be."

Miss Crump teaches Opie in the fifth and sixth grades. Her classroom is No. 10. Because she had acted in some college plays, she was once the director of Mayberry High's senior play. Helen also develops a second career as a writer. She wrote a book for children, *Amusing Tales of Tiny Tots,* under the pseudonym of Helene Alexion Dubois. The book was contracted by Roger Bryant at the Bryant Publishing Company in Richmond (Miss Fain is his secretary). For her work, Helen received an advance of $1,000. Robling Flask did the cover design for the book, and Harold Mosby was the promotion man.

Sweethearts

But, really, the only man in Miss Crump's life is Andy Taylor. The two enjoy a relaxed courtship. They don't rush into romance, although Barney Fife does everything in his power to get them hitched. Helen eventually becomes Andy's fiancée, and they live happily ever after.

Mayberry Media

The Mayberry Nielsens

1. "The Manhattan Show Time": a popular TV talent show
2. "The Jerome Sanger Show": Andy, Opie, and Aunt Bee enjoy this
3. "Shep & Ralph": "The story of a man and his dog"
4. "The Mayberry Chef": Aunt Bee was the original
5. "Rudolph Rabbit": a cartoon show that Goober enjoys
6. "Travelogue": Aunt Bee's favorite TV show
7. "The Rex Benson Show": "Featuring Rex Benson and the Singsongers, presented to you by Foster's Furniture Polish"
8. "The Win or Lose Show": hosted by Jack Smith. Aunt Bee was a grand-prize winner
9. "Colonel Tim's Talent Time": on WASG (CBS affiliate) in Raleigh; "Well, it's 'bye for now, and bless you all." Colonel Tim's show has launched the talents and careers of such show business greats as Ozzie Snake, Rosamae Johnson, and Jughead Peters and his Aristocrats
10. "International Secret Agent F45": starring Michael Glendon; Warren Ferguson's favorite show; he once watched the episode entitled "Mission Istanbul"
11. "Jim Apache, Indian Spy": one of Opie's favorites
12. "The Twilight Zone"

TV Stations

WZAZ—in Siler City

WASG—in Raleigh

KNC—in Raleigh; broadcast live the opening night of the world-premiere movie starring Mayberry native Teena Andrews

Radio Stations

YLRB—Mt. Pilot

WMPD—"The Voice of Mt. Pilot"

CQL—advance weather station in Greenland

Local Newspapers

Mayberry Gazette—a weekly; comes out on Wednesday; Farley Upchurch is the publisher

Regular *Mayberry Gazette* columns include:

"Mayberry Marry-Go-Round"—the engagement column

"Mayberry After Midnight"—by Red Akin

"Longitudes and Latitudes"—a travel column by Lonnie Ladner

a garden column by Howard Sprague

a society column by Ella

The Mayberry Sun—Opie and Howie's student newspaper

Magazine And Book Matching Quiz

Match the proper Mayberrian to the magazine or book that he or she subscribed to, read, or wrote. Some answers may be used more than once or not at all.

Magazines

1. *Aviation Journal*
2. *Boating*
3. *Law & Order Magazine*
4. *Learn-A-Month Magazine*
5. *Love Magazine*
6. *Mechanics Monthly*
7. *Nation's Industry*
8. *National Geographic*
9. *New Features Magazine*
10. *Police Gazette*
11. *Sheriff's Magazine*
12. *Thrilling Stories*
13. *True Blue Detective*

A. Andy
B. Aunt Bee
C. Barney
D. Gomer
E. Goober
F. Floyd
G. Opie
H. Howard Sprague
I. Warren Ferguson
J. Otis

Books

1. *Amusing Tales of Tiny Tots*
2. *The Art of Judo,* by Professor Matzamota
3. *The Cutlass*
4. *From the Cradle to Junior College,* by Dr. Walker; has sold more than 65,000 copies
5. *The Fundamentals of Extrasensory Perception*
6. *Jokes for All Occasions*
7. *Moon Men Invade Venus on Giant Bats*
8. *Penetentiary*
9. *Poems of Romance,* by T. Jonathan Osgood
10. *Psychological Aspects of the Law*
11. *Roses Are the Backbone of Your Garden,* by Mabel J. Mosley
12. *Twenty Scientific Tricks a Boy Can Do at Home,* by Seymour Shreck, who also wrote *Fun in a Garage on a Rainy Day*
13. *Superstitions, Signs, Omens, Portents, and Charms To Ward Off Bad Luck;* belonged to this Mayberrian's grandmother
14. *Psychic Phenomena,* by Dr. Merle Osmond, who is the head of the College of Psychic Phenomena in Boise, Idaho; Dr. Osmond used to teach the guitar
15. *Ivanhoe*
16. *Watkins Grading Manual*

A. Andy
B. Aunt Bee
C. Barney
D. Barney and Warren
E. Opie
F. Howard Sprague
G. Helen Crump
H. Warren Ferguson
I. Warren gives this to Goober
J. Tillie Kincaid
K. Goober and Opie
L. Andy and Barney

Answers

Answers to Magazine Quiz

1. B
2. A
3. A
4. C
5. C
6. D
7. E
8. A
9. E
10. A
11. A
12. E
13. C

Answers to Book Quiz

1. G
2. C
3. L
4. B
5. H
6. F
7. I
8. C
9. C
10. C
11. J
12. E
13. C
14. C
15. K
16. G

Other Newspapers

The Mount Pilot Times
The Mount Pilot Bugle & Sun
Mount Airy News

Goober's Comic Book Literary Guild

"Crab Monster"
"Grunge Monster"
"Space Phantom"
"Spiderman"
"Purple Avenger"

Coming Attractions At The Mayberry Grand

G-Men
Two in Love—starring Ed Olson and Viola Kern
Something About Blondes
Sheriff Without a Gun—starring Bryan Bender and Darlene Mason

The Monster That Ate Minnesota—Goober's watched this one ten times
House of Blood
The Beast That Ate Minnesota
The Monster From Out of Town
The Monster From Mars
The Monster From the Moon
The House Without Windows—rated "3½ clovers" by the *Mayberry Gazette*
The Anteaters From Outer Space

Now Showing In Mt. Pilot

Raiders of Tripoli
La Vie de Femme

Now Showing In Raleigh

Bread, Love and Beans—"risque," according to Barney

Gomer Pyle

Goober says hey, Andy.
—Gomer Pyle

Gomer Pyle

Gomer Pyle may not be exactly what you would think of as a good ol' boy, but he is a good boy. Although Gomer is naive and innocent and not too bright, he is nonetheless good-natured and always eager to please.

For years, young Gomer has worked at Wally's filling station as a gas pump boy. He tells Andy: "Me, I don't do no engine work. Just gas and oil, water and air. Water and air is free. We don't make no charge for it. Now you take gas and oil. That is a different proposition entirely. We make a charge for that . . . depending on how many times the pump out there goes ding-dong. It's thirty cents a ding."

Later, Gomer becomes a pretty good mechanic, though never quite as proficient as Wally or cousin Goober Pyle. He learns the tricks of the trade, such as pouring soda pop on batteries to clear the corrosion around the terminals. And when a visitor's car conks out, Gomer will try to get to the source of the problem right away: "Could be your gauge," he says. "Sometimes she'll tell you *F* when you really got yourself an *E. E* means that it's empty. *F* means that it's full."

While he's working at Wally's, Gomer lives in the back of the station. He is saving up to go to college. He wants to be a doctor. His room in the rear of the station is a pretty nice setup. He's got a kitchenette, complete with a one-burner stove, a wooden egg crate, forks, and salt and pepper. Later on, Wally really spruces up the place by painting it and adding an icebox and an extra burner.

Gomer's everyday wardrobe consists of his work clothes, baseball cap, greasy rag, and a loaded keychain that hangs from his belt. Gomer's personality might best be summed up by the words "Aw, shucks." He isn't exactly a sparkling conversationalist, especially on dates, but he does try hard. For his first date with Thelma Lou's cousin, Mary Grace Gossage, Gomer wore his best suit, yellow socks, new shoes with brass buckles (the shoes cost $8), and his purple tie with acorns on it. He also wore a new brown belt with a horseshoe buckle (imitation mother-of-pearl). Gomer worried that his socks were too porous because the little hairs on his legs popped through.

Gomer's best friend is his cousin Goober. Both Gomer and Goober love movies, and Gomer's favorite actors are John Wayne and Preston Foster. Gomer counts Andy and Barney as

A growing boy's gotta eat

Gomer Pyle, U.S.M.C.

two close friends, although at times he can be annoying to both of them. Still, Barney believes that Gomer has the raw talent to make a good deputy (after all, Gomer is "the cream of the crop") and he regularly recruits Gomer to be a temporary deputy.

In addition, Gomer can do a few other things. He drives the tow truck for Wally and he can operate an acetylene torch. He can do an amazing imitation of a hoot owl and is an extraordinary dancer. Most surprisingly, Gomer is a wonderful singer. He has been called upon to sing as a special soloist with the town choir. His rich, deep singing style is a startling contrast to his boyishly twangy speaking voice.

Gomer is six feet tall, dark, and nice. He has a scar on his right hand from the time his house caught on fire. He once had a dog named Sport ("sweet but dumb"). Among his acquaintances, other than the many friends who stop by the station to hear him tell tall tales, are Birdie Blush and Skinny Griffin. Gomer and Birdie fish together in the lakes and streams of Mayberry County. Gomer's special bait for trout is Limburger cheese and a slice of onion.

Gomer is a healthy young man, but he does get carsick. Every night, he gargles before settling down in bed with his comic books. He always carries an extra shoelace with him.

The only time anyone can remember the genial Gomer getting angry was when he had that string of bad luck at Pearson's Sweet Shop. It seems Gomer bought ten lucky peppermints, and they all had white centers. He bought a dozen more, and they were all "whities," too. That irritated Gomer because if he had gotten at least one with a pink center, he would have won another free candy. Had he bitten into one with a green center, he would have won a flashlight!

Eventually, Gomer decides to join the U.S. Marine Corps, but he never does get the eagle tattoo with "Mother" written on it. (He had always dreamed of getting one.) Upon entering the Marines at Camp Wilson near Wilmington, North Carolina, Gomer immediately hits it off with Gunnery Sergeant Vincent Carter. Sergeant Carter becomes Gomer's best friend, but that's another story, and another television series. ("Gomer Pyle, U.S.M.C.," a spin-off of "The Andy Griffith Show," first aired on CBS on Friday, September 25, 1964, at 9:30 P.M., EST. It ran for six seasons and 230 episodes.) Colonel Watson is the commanding officer of Gomer's battalion.

While a resident of Mayberry, Gomer provides the townsfolk with true friendship. He is always sincere, with his big grin and his wish of "Lots of luck to you and yours!" And, well, that's Gomer—*Shazam!*

Sgt. Carter (Frank Sutton)

Goober Pyle

Three hours is a long time to go without eating.
　—Goober Pyle

Goober Pyle

Goober Pyle is one of Mayberry's most talented citizens. In addition to being good with cars, he can impersonate Cary Grant ("Judy, Judy, Judy") and Edward G. Robinson ("Okay, you guys; come on, you guys; all right, you guys; beat it, you guys"), and he can limp like Chester of "Gunsmoke" fame. It's a thrill to see Goober's trick of sewing his hand together. As his cousin Gomer says, "Goober, you really got talent."

Goober was born and raised in Mayberry and was a bully as a child. Among the things he was good at as a boy were making friends with a skunk, catching flies bare-handed, and drinking the most water without taking a breath. For pets, he had a skunk and a canary named Louise. He now has a dog, Spot (so named because he doesn't have any spots), who can be seen lounging around the filling station.

As a lad, Goober earned a quarter a day by chopping wood for the neighbors, feeding their chickens and slopping their hogs, delivering groceries for a general store, and then working at his dad's gas station. He quit after the first day. As Gomer says, "My cousin Goober ain't stupid. He's ugly, but he ain't stupid."

After graduating from high school, Goober went to auto training school in Raleigh. He worked there for a while and also served in the National Guard before moving back to Mayberry. He says that the two things he knows are cars and guns.

Perhaps the best mechanic in town, Goober once hopped up a rowboat with a V–8 engine so that it could do 80 mph on water. He takes the boat out on Sundays, after he washes his mother's car. After all, he wouldn't put his mother in a dirty car. Goober has a 1958 convertible for sale for $600, but it's not the same one whose V–8 engine he removed.

Goober is one of Mayberry County's best athletes. He played on the high school football team, and at the county fair one summer, he hit the bell eighteen times in a row. He's also been the arm wrestling champ for four years running and he once ate fifty-seven pancakes (with syrup and butter) to win the pancake-eating contest at the county fair. Goober considers the pancake-eating honor his highest individual achievement. Nowdays, he just eats a normal portion of twelve or fifteen pancakes.

The Goob is also a terrific sportsman. As a marksman, he has won the turkey shoot in Mt. Pilot for two consecutive years. He likes to crow-shoot

and he's a pretty fair fisherman. His secret bait is banana peel with red yarn. On his best weekend of fishing, he caught seven perch and six large-mouth bass. He and Floyd often talk about Old Sam, Mayberry's legendary silver carp.

Floyd: I got a feeling this may be the year I catch him.
Goober: The only way you'll catch Old Sam is if he comes in here for a shave and a haircut.
Floyd: There's one thing for sure. You'll never catch him, and you know why? To catch Old Sam, you gotta be smarter than he is. Ha, ha.

Like father, like son, Goober's dad used to operate his own garage. Goober worked for Wally for eleven-and-three-quarter years before finally buying the station from Wally at the age of thirty-six. While working for Wally, Goober earned $1.25 an hour.

After Goober became proprietor of the station, he changed the name to Goober's Service. He hired a kid named George to man the pumps and he came up with some clever mottos: Free air with a smile; Free water with a smile; and, The only thing we don't wipe clean is the smile on our faces.

Goober's filling station is located at the intersection of Main and Garden Road. The phone number there is 363. He sells about eighty gallons of Acme gasoline (regular and super) per day. During his biggest week one year, he changed three flat tires. He is also proud that he can take a carburetor apart in thirty-eight minutes and twelve seconds. Among the people who have pumped gas for Goober are Spooky Benson, Harvey, Rodney, and that Norris boy.

Goober once took off from work for three weeks to go on a hunting trip. When he came back, he had a beard— the first one in Mayberry in ten years. The beard made Goober feel like an intellectual, but he shaved it off when people became bored by his "wise" remarks. That didn't stop him from reading seven comic books per week.

Goober is almost always wearing his work clothes: his beanie, which keeps

"Service with a smile"

the oil out of his hair; his service shirt (complete with ballpoint pens, pencils, and a tire gauge), and work pants, with a greasy rag in the back pocket. He drives around Mayberry in his red pickup truck (license M37905) but later gets a baby blue one.

The friendly Pyle is a member in good standing of The Regal Order of the Golden Door to Good Fellowship, where he has served as an officer (Keeper of the Door). During the summer, he is manager of the Giants, Mayberry's Little League baseball team. "Hit one for the ol' Goober" is one of his famous sayings. Goober also bowls on the town bowling team, is in the town choir, and likes to play checkers.

Goober's close friends, besides Andy, Barney, Floyd, Howard, Emmett, and Wally, are Earlie Gilley, Gilly Walker, Shorty Watson, and Lou Jordan. The shy Goober is a bit awkward with girls. Thanks to Barney's tutoring, he finally gets up the nerve to

Goober the intellectual

court Lydia Crosswaith, but that affair doesn't last too long. He later dates Dr. Edith Gibson, Gloria (Andy's "cousin" from Siler City), and a girl on the softball team, but his true love is Flora Malherbe, a waitress at the diner. About Flora, he says, "Some girl, huh?" Floyd agrees, "She's a lulu, all right."

Goober takes art class in Bible school and he plays the harmonica. He owns a pair of truck-tire cufflinks, which he wears with his "Ivory League" coat, and he still has his favorite toy, a teddy bear named Buster. His phone number is 371J. Fall is Goober's favorite season, except for summer and spring.

Goober, who loves to hang around the courthouse, can always be counted on to fill in as a spare deputy, though he's not always as dependable as he is eager. Nevertheless, as Andy says to Goober, "You know, Goob, sometimes you really get a line on things." Sometimes.

There are times though when he gets on Andy's nerves.

Andy: Goob, did anybody ever tell you you've got a big mouth?

Goober: Yeah, but I don't pay no attention to 'em.

Goober's law enforcement duties include guarding the town cannon on Halloween. And once he filled in when Andy was ailing and gave out fourteen traffic tickets in a single day.

His childlike characteristics make Goober one of the most-liked personalities in town. You can tell when he's really excited because he'll be yelling "Woo, woo" just like Daffy Duck.

Goob loves to read and swap comic

Nothing like a good comic book

"Hit one for the ol' Goober"

books with Opie, and he likes to go to scary movies. He's seen *The Monster That Ate Minnesota* ten times. His favorite actress is Maureen O'Sullivan (Jane in the *Tarzan* flicks). "She sure can swim," he says. He never misses a Cary Grant movie and he likes to watch "Rudolph Rabbit" cartoons on TV.

Goober is Mayberry's top gourmand. That simply means he eats more than anyone in town. His tastes in food are unusual. He's game for such culinary treats as a strawberry ice cream sundae with pickles on top, or a peanut butter and tuna sandwich with ketchup and a chocolate milkshake. His favorite vegetable is corn on the cob.

Mr. Darling nicknamed the loveable Goober "Big Ears," but it's really Goober's heart that's big. Goober, like his cousin Gomer, is willing to do anything to help someone. Whenever anyone in Mayberry asks a favor of Goober Pyle, the answer always comes up "Yo!"

Howard Sprague

(Courtesy Jack Dodson)

Mother likes me to get plenty of vitamin C during flu season.
—Howard Sprague

Howard Sprague

One of Mayberry's most intellectual citizens is its articulate civil servant, county clerk Howard Sprague. As clerk, Howard has his mind sharply tuned in to everything that is happening in Mayberry. His speciality is statistics.

Howard: I'm making a chart on the relation between accidents and population growth.

Andy: Oh.

Howard: It's a sort of statistical study. I'm doing it on my own time as sort of a hobby.

Andy: It would seem to me that accidents would increase in direct proportion to the population.

Howard: Yes, you would think that, wouldn't you?

Andy: Yeah.

Howard: Well, my figures up to now indicate there's a 1.7 differential.

Andy: No kiddin'.

Howard: That's rather surprising, isn't it?

Andy: Yeah.

Howard: I was flabbergasted.

Andy: You must have been. I guess all this is sort of in line with your work.

Howard: Oh, yes, yes. Facts and figures, facts and figures. Births, deaths, marriages, property ownership. I have my fingers on the pulse of whatever happens in the county.

Howard studied at the Bradbury Business College, on the third floor of the Essex Bank Building in Mt. Pilot. He took the full one-and-a-half year course.

As clerk of Mayberry Township's license division, Howard is in charge of handling such matters as business licenses, building permits, dog licenses, sales tax permits, marriage licenses, and bicycle licenses (fifty cents). And no one in town will ever forget that he single-handedly reorganized the entire sewer system of Mayberry—a task no ordinary man would have tackled.

Although Howard is a personable fellow, his widowed mother refuses to cut his social birthcord, preventing Howard from truly becoming one of the boys. Andy says, "She's got him tied to her apron strings, and there's very little slack," while Aunt Bee says that Howard "has a ring in his nose, and his mother pulls him around by it."

Still, Howard tries awfully hard to fit in with Mayberry's "in crowd," but as he himself admits, "I never done much horsing around myself." The amiable Sprague always was a little bit different. As a youth, Howard had a pet horse whom he named Fido. That was because the animal thought it was a dog.

Howard graduated from Mayberry Union High with Andy Taylor, but at

Howard catches Old Sam

Howard for town council

the time they didn't really know one another very well because Howard always sort of kept to himself. During his high school days, he had a crush on one of Andy's sweethearts, Alice Harper, but he was too shy to ask her for a date. After graduation, Howard got his first job as a truck driver for the Mayberry Transfer Company. "To this day, I still have a soft spot in my heart for ton-and-a-half trucks," he says. However, he's now comfortably settled in his natural niche, Room 203 of City Hall.

Howard and his mother eat out every Wednesday night, usually at Ching Lee's or at an Italian restaurant. Howard loves Oriental cuisine, especially water chestnuts.

The Spragues enjoy going to the movies and they play bridge frequently with the Albrights. Howard's mother was adamant about his not joining The Regal Order of the Golden Door to Good Fellowship, but eventually she gave in and allowed him to become a member. One year he was even toastmaster of the lodge banquet.

After his mother remarried and moved to Mt. Pilot, Howard remodeled his "pad," complete with a bearskin rug, pillows on the floor, and a bar. He invited his friends in for a drink. "Hey, what do you say to a little drinkee, boys? Huh? Name your poison, gents: grapefruit, lemon-lime, orange, or, if you prefer some of the hard stuff, I've got a little cider that's starting to turn. What do you say, a bit of the bubbly, boys?"

The six-foot-three-inch-tall Howard is by nature quite shy with the ladies. Among his infrequent dates have been county health officer Irene Fairchild (she moved into his old office, Room 201), Alice Harper (the girl he had a crush on in high school), and Betty Parker. As shy as Howard is, it really surprised some folks when he began courting regularly. The woman in his life was Millie Hutchins. She used to be the steady girlfriend of big Clyde Plaunt in Mt. Pilot, and when Clyde came to plant a few fisticuffs on Howard, the mild-mannered city clerk showed the stuff he was made of.

One year, Howard ran against Aunt Bee for a seat on the town council. Floyd's Barbershop served as his campaign headquarters. He won that race quite handily. He also serves his fellow citizens as a member of the school board and of the Community Church's building and safety committee. In addition, he is chairman of the Mayberry Civic Improvement Committee.

Among Howard's hobbies are music and dancing. He loves the music of the Silver Herringbones. He used to be a poor dancer but has vastly improved. Andy claims that Howard is the best dancer in town. The dancing clerk especially enjoys "those Latin rhythms." Howard sings high tenor for the Mayberry Barbershop Quartet, too. That's appropriate because he purchased the barbershop from the Robinson family in California with a $1,500 down pay-

ment. He then became Floyd's landlord. "I've always sort of kind of had a yen to own a piece of the good earth," he said.

Howard loves to read, especially psychology books, and he can quote Charles Cotesworth Pinckney. He's also handy with a pen. He writes a garden column for the *Mayberry Gazette*, and he fills in as a sportswriter, covering such events as the fishing derby and Little League baseball games.

Howard's favorite beverage may be root beer, but he also enjoys a nice malted. He's allergic to penicillin (among other things), and he drives a

Two of Mayberry's finest citizens

nice, conservative eight-cylinder car. His phone number is 397. And he still throws a baseball like a girl.

He's especially proud of his mustache. He's had it for about thirteen years. His father, grandfather, and great-grandfather all had one, too. It's a Sprague family tradition, and Howard believes it gives him an air of distinction. In fact, some people have told him that the mustache makes him look like a young Tom Dewey.

Howard usually sleeps on his stomach and he snores so loudly that he sometimes even wakes himself up. He is an impeccable dresser (he loves bow ties) and a firm believer in personal hygiene. He brushes his teeth fifteen minutes every morning and fifteen minutes before bedtime. "Oh, I know there are lots of toothpastes that prevent cavities," he says, "but I like to wage my own battle."

Once, Howard tried to cast off his buttoned-down image and deserted Mayberry for St. Benedict's Island, the "Pearl of the Caribbean." As he said just before making his bold move: "Andy, some men are talkers and some men are doers, and I've discovered that I'm a doer. Being a doer, well, the time comes when a man's just got to follow his rainbow."

St. Benedict's turns out to be a beautiful and serene place, a seemingly ideal tropical paradise for Howard's beachcombing. There are few people on the island. One of the first natives Howard meets is a boy named Sebastian, who shows Howard around the island. But mostly, Howard just skips rocks, thumps on his bongo drums, lounges in his hammock, and tries a little surf casting. Later, he meets a few more island inhabitants such as Wes, Norm, Grover (once a big lawyer in Detroit), and the unnamed proprietor of the island's general store.

Even though St. Benedict's is beautiful, and Howard's rent is inexpensive ($10 per month), he begins to yearn for his friends and the rewarding job that he had back in Mayberry. He returns to his hometown more appreciative of how special Mayberry is, realizing that time is not forever. Upon his return, Andy asks him, "I thought you wanted to follow your rainbow and everything." Howard answers, "Yeah, well, I guess I just followed it to the wrong end. My pot of gold is right here in Mayberry."

Howard was never much of a sportsman, but he astounded everyone in Mayberry the day he caught the famous silver carp, Old Sam. "I consider it a triumph of science over animal cunning," he said. (Potato salad was the potent bait that did Sam in.) Old Sam was taken to the Raleigh Aquarium, where a bronze plaque credited angler Howard Sprague with the catch. After Howard realized that Old Sam was a legend around Mayberry, he brought the fish back home and released it in its native waters.

Howard's favorite sport seems to be bowling, and he's on Mayberry's bowl-

Mayberry bowling team

ing team. Even though he's uncoordinated, Howard bowled a perfect game against the Trucker's Cafe team from Mt. Pilot. He was the first Mayberrian to perform that feat.

Showing a comic flair like his Uncle Carl, Howard appeared as a small-town joke-teller on "Colonel Tim's Talent Time" TV show on station WASG in Raleigh. Goober called him "Mayberry's No. 1 comedian." He was the toast of Mayberry for a short while, but his jokes became a little too personal. He eventually retired from the limelight. Nevertheless, Howard remains as endearing as the smile behind his mustache.

Emmett Clark

You know the things that ruin these irons—women use too much starch.
  —Emmett Clark

Emmett Clark

Emmett Clark is Mayberry's top handyman. He runs the Fix-It Shop, located next door to the sheriff's office in what used to be Floyd's Barbershop. Emmett has been in the fix-it business for more than thirty-eight years. He operated from his house in Mt. Pilot for a long time before moving to Mayberry. He earns close to $7,500 annually. Speaking of his station in life, Emmett philosophizes: "As one with experience, I've said to myself a thousand times, I've said, Emmett, why don't you forget big business? Why don't you pull out when you've still got your health? I've said it a thousand times."

But Emmett can't leave his work. His life is built around his friendships with the townspeople. His shop replaces Floyd's Barbershop as one of the most popular gathering places for the menfolk, particularly Andy, Goober, and Howard. At Emmett's, they find a relaxed, comfortable environment where they can chat about politics or the weather over a cup of coffee, and they also share lively discussions that sometimes have a way of evolving into arguments.

Emmett is quite a fixer-upper. He

makes keys, and he can mend just about anything from radios to electric guitars, but his specialties are cuckoo clocks and toasters. "The problem in toasters is usually the timing device," he says with a voice of authority. (He has made a professional study of timers.) And although he is quite adept at his vocation, his temper can get away from him. His impatience causes him to get upset over little matters, and he will sometimes almost throw a screwdriver or hammer to the floor in disgust.

Emmett realizes the value of having a good set of tools around. The sign on the wall of his shop reads: We Don't Loan Tools. Mayberry's handyman drives a Ford pickup truck around town. After all, he does make house calls. He also has a car.

Emmett and his wife, Martha Beecham Clark, are very happy living in Mayberry. They celebrated their twenty-fifth wedding anniversary there. Emmett gave Martha a mink coat on that special day along with a genuine thermal-weave woolen bathrobe. (Goober had suggested Emmett get her a new set of nylon tires.) The Clarks have taken trips to Akron, Ohio, and to St. Petersburg, Florida, where Emmett landed a 361-pound blue marlin.

Emmett's brother-in-law, Ben Beecham, has an insurance agency in Raleigh and offices all around the state. Ben drives a 340-horsepower Continental, which sports a "Support Your Local Police" bumper sticker. Ben

eventually talked Emmett into selling for him, but Emmett was out of his natural environment. That didn't stop him from selling policies to Andy (for Opie), Goober, and Howard, but after a short time, he returned to his Fix-It Shop, where he was more at ease and a happier man.

Emmett sponsors the town bowling team. He spent his entire advertising budget ($24) to buy three bowling shirts. He bowls when his back problem isn't bothering him. Emmett is also a superb dancer, evident in the fact that he made it to the finals of the Harvest Ball one year. He is a member of the church's building and safety committee, as well.

Martha loves gardening, especially growing begonias, and she's a member of the Garden Club and the Bridge Club and is on the church's finance committee. She enjoys Greer Garson movies, and her best friend is Mrs. Edith Pendleton. Martha suffers occasional bouts of bursitis.

Being civic-minded, Emmett once ran for head of the Mayberry Town Council. He conducted a spirited campaign but nevertheless lost to the worthy Sam Jones. He was even a temporary deputy once, until he wrecked the squad car.

Emmett is an A-okay guy. Andy and all the fellows think highly of him. Not only that, Emmett has a cousin who is a personal friend of the chairman of the Liquor Control Board in Nebraska. Emmett Clark is a man who can count his blessings.

Warren Ferguson

As Andy Taylor says, "Warren's not a rare case—a rare bird, maybe, but not a rare case." Like his predecessor, Barney Fife, Deputy Warren Ferguson has everything and everybody analyzed and he'll be happy to tell you all about it.

Warren Ferguson

Warren hails from Boston, where he probably acquired his distinctive manner of phrasing things. He has a sister who lives in Moline, California, with her husband (a former serviceman and now a Lions Club member) and their four kids. Warren's uncle is none other than Mayberry's town barber, Floyd Lawson. The smooth-talking, suave Ferguson says that the girls "were all over him" back home. In fact, that was one of the reasons he had to leave. As it turns out, he is very shy with women, and they make him nervous.

Warren has been a deputy in several towns and graduated fourth in his class at the Sheriff's Academy, which he attended for sixteen weeks. He studied ballistics there. It seems slightly possible, however, that Warren's Uncle Floyd had something to do with his gaining employment on the Mayberry police force.

Before law enforcement, Warren was in the wholesale fish business for three months. "If you don't make your deals quick enough, nobody has to tell you when you're taking a loss," he says. "You can smell it." A man of unseeming strength, Warren won first place in the arm wrestling contest at the Founders' Day Picnic. For that feat, he won a month's supply of mint jelly.

Warren's favorite hobby is mosaics. He's even lectured on "The Fascinating World of Mosaics." Warren sleepwalks, and he thinks he has powers of extrasensory perception. He loves Chinese food and he has a fabulous hangover cure: hot sauce, sassafrass root, sorghum molasses, and a raw egg. He is an avid reader, but he hates for people to dog-ear the pages of his magazines. He especially enjoys Perry Mason stories, and Fred Astaire is one of his favorite actors.

In the field of law enforcement, Warren's personal hero is Barney Fife. He calls Barney a living legend. Unfortunately, Warren is never quite capable of filling Barney's size $7\frac{1}{2}$B shoes. While Warren is extremely diligent in his efforts as deputy ("He tries hard," says Andy), he never learns the lesson that sometimes you have to go "not so much by the book but by the heart." That was at least one lesson that Barney was able to understand after serving under Andy's tutelage. This trait is probably the major characteristic that separates Barney and Warren in the performance of their duties. And Warren, like Barney, has high praise for his superior, Sheriff Andy Taylor. He tells Andy that in the vast universe, "You're nothing but a tiny dot, a speck, a minute insignificant nothing. But I'm proud to call you my friend."

In a lot of ways, Warren displays the familiar habits of his Uncle Floyd. "He's a winner," Floyd says of his nephew. "He's a real Lawson. He's the image of my sister. Same high forehead, same pointy nose." Warren has a tendency to rattle off meaningless phrases, just as Floyd does. Of course, Warren always thinks he is saying something profound, whereas Floyd doesn't say much of anything. Warren even came up with a slogan for the Mayberry Founders' Day Committee: "May Mayberry never founder."

After his tenure in Mayberry, Warren probably went on to become a deputy in yet another town. Even though he wasn't in Mayberry long, Warren Ferguson remains memorable.

Taking care of business

Ernest T. Bass

You ain't heard the last of Ernest T. Bass.
—Ernest T. Bass

"How do you do, Mrs. Wiley?"

Ernest T. Bass is Mayberry's wild man from the mountains. In general, he is a loveable nuisance, not just for the Darlings but for Andy and Barney and just about anybody who has a glass window. That's because Ernest T. is a chronic window-breaker. Sometimes he throws rocks; sometimes he throws bricks; but he's breaking windows all the time. After his first confrontation with Bass, Andy said, "If you were to ask me, this Ernest T. Bass is a strange and weird character."

"Just plain ornery is what he is," responded Briscoe Darling.

"He's a nut!" Barney concluded.

Ernest T. wears a worn-out hunting cap, a long-sleeved cotton undershirt, trousers, and a black vest. Bass is not really a mean person, but he did try to kill a mockingbird once. Andy tries to teach Ernest T. the ways of society, but it all comes to naught at a party where Andy passes Ernest T. off as his cousin Oliver Gossage from Raleigh. At least Mr. Bass learned how to say, "How do you do, Mrs. Wiley?"

While attempting to court Charlene Darling Wash, Ernest T. brags that he

---

is the best rock-thrower in the county and that he's saving up for a gold tooth. He plans to knock out the three teeth in front and put the gold one in the center and "leave space on each side so it'll stand out better that way, 'specially when I'm dancing." Eventually, he does get a gold tooth, but it's just gold leaf that he has done by the sign company (it costs him $1).

Ernest T. gets his chance to sweet-talk and woo Charlene with his charming ways, but he never does win her heart. Later, he comes down to Mayberry to join the Army. Andy and Barney try to warn the recruiter. "He's

Ernest T. gets an education

(Courtesy Howard Frank Archives)

curious," says Barney. "He's a trouble-maker," says Andy. The 112-pound Bass impresses the sergeant with his feats of strength: "I can do twenty chinups with one hand. I can dip into a barrel of water and fetch out a watermelon with my jaws, and I can chuck a full-growed sick jackass over my shoulders and tote him five miles to the doctor."

Ernest T. never does make it into the Army, but at least he does get a uniform—Barney's. Ernest T. needed it to impress the girls back home. He confesses to Andy: "As clever and as good-looking as I am, I just can't get a girl. I got looks, brains, personality; I kiss good. The only thing standing 'twixt me and sweet romance is a uniform." For a while, Ernest T. courted Hogette Winslow, the daughter of Hog Winslow, but he hit her on the head with a rock. She needed seven stitches. (She wound up marrying the taxidermist who sewed her up.) Ernest T. eventually finds sweet romance with Ramona Ancrum, his "Sweet Romeena." He also refers to her as "My darling Romeena."

If romance had never come to Ernest T., he planned to "hermitize" himself. In fact, he once lived in a cave for six months with a possum and a raccoon. That's when he learned to wash his food before eating it. Ernest T. has a cow now.

Another time, Ernest T. Bass came to town to earn his diploma. Helen Crump, his "mother figure," gave the diploma to him in a short but sweet ceremony, saying, "This is to certify that Ernest T. Bass has achieved a special award for learning." Yet another time, he came to town to find gainful employment. He needed $12 to buy a tent and a lantern for his honeymoon with Ramona. Andy gave Ernest T. a job as a temporary deputy and had him working the school crossing. Andy had to fire him for throwing rocks at the cars that wouldn't stop.

This kind of commotion riles Barney, who says, "Ernest T. Bass is a first-rate, grade-A, number-one nut." The deputy tells Andy, "Just give me five minutes behind the barn with him."

"He'd kill you," is Andy's reply.

Ernest T. often speaks in rhymes. Among his favorites are: "I don't chew my cabbage twice"; "You ain't heard the last of Ernest T. Bass"; "I ain't talking, I ain't talking, the more you ask, the more I'm balking"; "Wrong or right, I'm here to fight and if you're wondering who I be, it's me, it's me, it's Ernest T."

After his problems are solved by Andy, Ernest T. always heads back up to the hills.

Andy: "There goes a happy man."
Barney: "There goes a happy *nut*."

The Darlings

That one makes me cry.
—Briscoe and Charlene Darling

Charlene Darling

When the Darling family comes rolling down from the mountains in their old flatbed Ford, a good time is raring to be had by all—all the Darlings, that is.

Andy has his hands full keeping the Darlings out of trouble and trying to fend off the amorous advances of the pert Charlene, who is forever moonstruck by Andy's charms. And the Mayberry sheriff continually has to fight the superstitious nature of this backwoods family. He generally handles the Darlings by resorting to their own customs. (And pity poor Aunt Bee. She winds up with the enormous task of feeding the entire famished lot. Her muffins, from an old family recipe, are particularly appealing to the Darlings.)

Briscoe Darling is the outspoken patriarch of this fun-loving, amusing, and music-making clan, which is composed of his daughter and four sons. Briscoe's musical instrument is the jug; Doug, also called Jebbin, plucks the banjo; Rodney picks the guitar; Dean, also called Other, plays the mandolin; and pipe-smoking Mitch plays the bass fiddle. Charlene sings and sometimes dances mountain jigs.

Briscoe probably described the Darlings best when he said, "We're knowed as a family of hearty-eating men and beautiful, delicate women." He omitted the fact that they are extra-heavy snorers. Papa Darling refers to himself as "Briscoe Darling, tiller of soil, feller of trees," and his main philosophy in life is "got time to breathe, got time for music."

The Darlings live in a cabin in the mountains, not far from the Robert E. Lee Natural Bridge (an oak tree that fell across the creek). Mr. Darling's wife is deceased. Briscoe was her second husband. (Her first one got run over by a team of hogs.) Briscoe married at the age of thirty; his wife was seventeen.

Charlene's husband is Dudley (Dud) D. Wash. Their betrothal had been pledged when they were five years old. Dud served three years as a private first class in the U.S. Army before being honorably discharged. In his moneybelt he kept all of Charlene's letters, her hair ribbon, and the remainders of a mountain gladiola she had given him. On his return from the service, he gave Charlene a tiger-eye ring from Spokane. Dud now makes his living hunting beaver and possum.

Charlene and Dud eventually have a child, little Andelina, whom they name after Sheriff Taylor. After all, it was Andy who married them. They had to be remarried later by a preacher in order to suit the whims of Ernest T. Bass.

(Courtesy Doug Dillard)

The Darlings

The Darlings came down to Mayberry once looking for a boy to betroth to Andelina but had no luck. That's kind of hard to imagine, considering the dowry consisted of an eight-by-ten cottage (minus the roof) on the back twenty, a cow, and two acres of side hill with good strong boulders.

When the clan comes to visit Andy and Aunt Bee, they usually have to make a stop at the David Mendelbright Memorial Horse Water Trough in order to fill up their truck radiator. Mr. Darling uses his hat to fill 'er up. And, speaking of hats, all the Darling menfolk wear them.

The family once took a room at the Mayberry Hotel (Room 27), but when their merrymaking got too loud, Andy put them up in the jail, where Aunt Bee provided the victuals. It was Aunt Bee's good home cooking that got the boys to speak. After one of her meals, Mitch was overheard to say, "About to pop," while the talkative Doug remarked, "Great beans, Aunt Bee." And as Aunt Bee left the courthouse that night, they all chimed in unison, "Good night, Aunt Bee." Aside from their singing, the boys are never again heard to speak.

Briscoe, like the boys, also compliments Bee on her cooking. "Eatin' speaks louder than words," he tells her and Andy. And after dessert one evening, he tells her, "Three cuts of pie is my high-water mark."

Briscoe appreciates Andy's kindness to his family. "You know something, Sheriff?" he said once. "That haircut of yours may be city-style, but your heart was shaped in a bowl." Still, Mr. Darling possesses a great deal of mountain pride. He tells Andy, "If it's charity, we want no part of it because we aim to hang on to our position in the community." (Briscoe is a volunteer fire ranger.)

When the Darlings came into a small fortune of $300 after selling a parcel of land to the Mayberry County government, they headed to town looking for wives for the boys. And they almost got one—Miss Helen Crump. It was on account of the Omen of the Owl, which is the most powerful omen there is to mountain folk. The omen holds that if you see an owl in daylight, the next female you see will be your bride. Helen almost became Rodney's (he's the fun-loving one) wife. Lucky for her, the Darlings saw a second owl in daylight, which is a counter-omen to the first one. So the Darling boys went home empty-handed, which is kind of hard to figure since Mitch, according to Briscoe, "is as strong as an ox and

Mountain Neighbors of the Darlings and Ernest T. Bass

Widow Bradshaw
Idelle Bushy: used to date Dud Wash
Hasty Burford: fox hunts with Dud
Widow Hastings
Old Man Kelsey: has vast real estate holdings
Jailsick Sturman: used to be in the service
Hog Winslow daughter, Hogette

almost as bright. And he can do his sums up to and including three, and he's pretty."

Charlene has also had matrimonial troubles. She used a spell once to divorce Dud. The proceedings included burying an owl's beak, a piece of pork, four tail feathers from a chicken hawk, and a broken comb, and saying, "Beak of owl, strip of swine, tooth of comb; take mine from thine. Kinaba in, kinaba out, kinaba in and 'round about," and then waiting until the next full moon.

Music by the Darlings

The Darlings are actually The Dillards, a bluegrass quartet from Salem, Missouri, composed of Doug (on banjo) and Rodney Dillard (on guitar), and Mitch Jayne (on bass fiddle) and Dean Webb (on mandolin). (Mr. Darling accompanies the boys on the jug.)

Songs Performed by the Darlings

"Old Joseph"
"Doug's Tune"
"Dooley"
"Cold Trailin' "
"Hickory Holler"
"Banjo in the Holler"
"Salty Dog"
"Cindy"
"Leaning on the Everlasting Arms"
"Anniversary Waltz" (also called "Dance Till You Stockings Are Hot and Raveling")
"Sinkin' Creek"
"Jamboree"
"Duelin' Banjos"
"Low and Lonely" (a solo by Briscoe)
"Shady Grove"
"John Hardy"
"Ebo Walker"
"Stay All Night, Stay a Little Longer"

Songs That Make 'Em Cry

"Slimy River Bottom"—makes Charlene cry
"Keep Your Money in Your Shoes and It Won't Get Wet"—makes Charlene cry (never played)
"Never Hit Your Grandma With a Great Big Stick"—makes Charlene cry (never played)
"There Is a Time"—makes Briscoe cry
"Dirty Me, Dirty Me, I'm Disgusted with Myself"—makes Briscoe cry (never played)
"Boil Them Cabbage Down"—makes Charlene cry
"Will You Love Me When I'm Old and Ugly"—makes the baby, Andelina, cry (never played)

Songs Mentioned But Not Played

"Tearin' Up Your Old Clothes for Rags"
"Wet Shoes in the Sunset"
"Tow Sack Full of Love"

Sweet on Miss Rosemary (Amzie Strickland)

Savvy salve salesmen Trey Bowden, Opie Taylor, Johnny Paul Jason, and Howie Pruitt

Mayor Roy Stoner

Rocky romance

Otis shines as he and his wife Rita arrive to receive his plaque from the Women's Historical Society

Barney takes Andy "sidecar express" to the diner

Goober and Floyd drive Andy crazy in Gilly Walker's car

Sign of the times: Andy's not happy with Barney that word leaked out about the gold shipment coming through town

Two credits to Mayberry

Barney and the choir—somebody must have hit a sour note

A singing Rafe Hollister shines with a fine set of pipes

Barney gets a little help with his boarder patrol

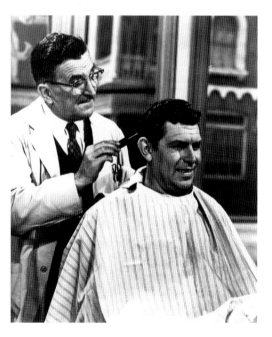

Andy and Floyd—a cut above

Opie welcomes Aunt Bee home

Jim Lindsey plays his best with Andy

A winning grin

Mayberry bric-a-brac—Andy, Goober, and Floyd are careful to keep an eye on Ernest T. Bass, who's as ornery with bricks as with rocks (Courtesy Steve Cox Collection)

Mayberry pair admires lake

Mayberry men in uniform

Good friends

"Judy, Judy, Judy, Judy, Judy"

Glad in plaid

Just hanging out at Floyd's

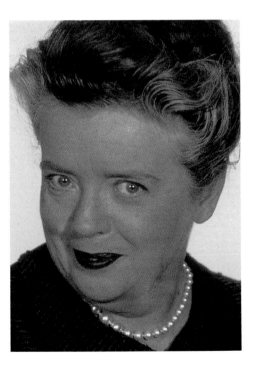

Sweet Bee

Mayberry favorites

Watermelon time

Heartfelt love

"Shazam!"

All-American boy

Justice of the Peace

Proud father and son

(Courtesy Doug Dillard)

The Darling boys (Doug Dillard, Dean Webb, Rodney Dillard, and Mitch Jayne)

Fortunately, Andy discovered the counter-omen for that predicament (a rider dressed in black on a white horse and riding from east to west), and all worked out well, with Dud and Charlene being reunited.

Among Mr. Darling's favorite sayings are, "More power to you" and "Everybody on the truck." Once everybody is back on the truck, the Darlings head back home. If it is nighttime, Doug will sit on the front fender, holding a lantern so Briscoe can see where he's going. Things then settle back down to normal in Mayberry.

Music From Mayberry

Mayberry band members

Music is big in Mayberry. Real big. Just about every fan of the show can whistle along with "The Andy Griffith Show" theme, "The Fishin' Hole."

"The Fishin' Hole"*

*Well, now, take down your fishin' pole and
    meet me at The Fishin' Hole,
We may not get a bite all day, but don't you
    rush away.
What a great place to rest your bones and
    mighty fine for skippin' stones,
You'll feel fresh as a lemonade, a-settin' in the
    shade.
Whether it's hot, whether it's cool, oh what a
    spot for whistlin' like a fool.
What a fine day to take a stroll and wander by
    The Fishin' Hole,
I can't think of a better way to pass the time
    o'day.*

"The Fishin' Hole"

We'll have no need to call the roll when we get
    to The Fishin' Hole,
There'll be you, me and Old Dog Trey, to doodle
    time away.
If we don't hook a perch or bass, we'll cool our
    toes in dewy grass,
Or else pull up a weed to chaw, and maybe set
    and jaw.
Hangin' around, takin' our ease, watchin' that
    hound a-scratchin' at his fleas.
Come on, take down your fishin' pole and meet
    me at The Fishin' Hole,
I can't think of a better way to pass the time
    o'day.

A favorite Mayberry song is "My
Hometown," which was composed by
Bee Taylor and Clara Johnson. It was
recorded by pop singer Keevy Hazelton.

My Hometown

My hometown is the greatest place I know,
Where the neighbors I find are gentle and kind,
And the living is easy and slow.
My hometown is the only place to be,

Here the worries are small, and the kids grow
    tall and healthy and free,
It's my hometown, my hometown, Mayberry,
    Mayberry.

And all Mayberrians enjoy singing
the Mayberry Union High Alma Ma-
ter.

Mayberry High Alma Mater

Mayberry Union High,
Victory is yours well nigh.
We'll hit the line,
For points every time,
The orange and blue will try, try, try, try.
And when the victory's won,
You'll be our favorite son,
Proud waves your banner in the sky,
Mayberry Union High.

Even Ernest T. Bass can sing. He
tried serenading Charlene Darling
Wash with the folk song "Old Aunt
Maria."

Old Aunt Maria, jump in the fire,
Fire too hot, jump in the pot,
Pot too black, jump in the crack,
Crack too high, jump in the sky,
Sky too blue, jump in the canoe,
Canoe too shallow, jump in the tallow,
Tallow too soft, jump in the loft,
Loft too rotten, jump in the cotton,
Cotton so white, stay there all night.

Mayberry loves music. Among the
musical organizations in town are a
drum and bugle corps, a drum and fife
corps, a town marching band (one of
the worst in the state and particularly
bad at "The Stars & Stripes Forever"
and "The Skater's Waltz"), a town chorus, and a church choir. Songs that the
town chorus performs include "O Sole

Mio," "Santa Lucia," and "Welcome, Sweet Springtime" (that one is on page 14 A of the hymnal).

The Mayberry town dances are many. They include the Women's Club Dance, the annual Harvest Ball (with music provided by Casper Tice and his Latin Rhythms), the annual Chamber of Commerce Dance (the biggest dance of the year, with music by Freddy Fleet and His Band with the Beat), street dances, and church dances (square-dancing, naturally). Another popular local group is the Original Carl Benson and His Wildcats (Carl's mother handles the sax), who play at a lot of high school class reunions.

Mayberry can also be proud of its barbershop quartet, which won the Mt. Pilot Sheriff's Barbershop Quartet Contest for three consecutive years, thus retiring the trophy. The quartet is comprised of Andy, Burt, Wally, and Howard Sprague. Jeff Nelson substituted for an ailing Howard the third year. The quartet won with "In the Gloaming" and "Beautiful Isle of Make Believe."

Some of the boys from Mayberry had their music recorded on an album, *Music From Mayberry*, with such tunes as "Whoa, Mule," "Cripple Creek," and "The Crawdad Song," which is one of Andy's favorites. He and Opie even team up on it occasionally, as well as on "Old Dan Tucker." Andy also likes "On Jordan's Stormy Banks," "The Fox," "The Midnight Special," "John Henry," and, when he's serenading a girlfriend, he might strike up "I Wish I

Choir members: Andy, Sharon (Barbara Griffith), and Barney

Was a Red Rosy Bush." Andy and Barney can harmonize beautifully on such songs as "Sunshine," "When Sinners Lose All Their Guilty Stains," "Church in the Wildwood," and "Go Tell Aunt Rhody." When townspeople get together, they might sing "Liza Jane," "Old MacDonald," "Seeing Nellie Home," "She'll Be Coming 'Round the Mountain," "Sourwood Mountain," "Get Along Home, Cindy, Cindy," or "Down in the Valley."

Andy and Barney sometimes tease their prisoners. They've sung "The Vacant Chair" to Otis and "Dig My Grave" to Rafe Hollister. Barney once teased Andy about his love life with "For It Was Mary" when Andy was dating nurse Mary Simpson. Favorites at the All Souls Church include "Bringing in the Sheaves," "Leaning on the Everlasting Arms," and "Love Lifted Me" (that's on page 256 in the church hymnal).

There's no doubt about it. Mayberrians are music lovers. Amen.

Folks Around Town

Mayberry may well be the friendliest town in all of North Carolina. That's primarily because there are so many friendly folks living there, and each one of them possesses unique characteristics that add to the homemade flavor of the community. Some of the more familiar acquaintances of Andy, Barney, Aunt Bee, and Opie are described in the following paragraphs.

We never see **Sarah,** the telephone operator, but if there is anyone in town who knows what is going on, it's Sarah. She listens in on all calls. She's on top of all the latest gossip and she's not afraid to share it with others. Because Sarah is so loyal to her job, she practically never gets out of the house. She also has lots of ailments, and she has the habit of dipping snuff. Her athletic mother enjoys bowling.

Juanita Beasley is another local citizen we never see, but she is the most renowned waitress in Mayberry history. Originally she worked tables over at the Junction Cafe (phone number 142R). That's where all the truckers stop. But she is now serving a loyal clientele at the Bluebird Diner (phone number 242). Juanita may very well be the most popular gal in town. "She's everybody's Juanita," says Andy. And she does have a multitude of admirers, not the least of whom is Barney Fife. She loves Chinese food and enjoys going parking up by Myers Lake.

Mayor Pike is "our fat little mayor," according to Orville Monroe. He has a high voice and can never make up his mind, as he always goes along with the vocal majority. The little mayor usually wears a white hat, string bow tie, and a black coat, and he uses suspenders to hold up his trousers. The mayor and his wife have three daughters; two of them are Josephine and Juanita. Josephine is the youngest, but Juanita can sing. (Her version of "Flow Gently, Sweet Afton" will amaze you.) They also have a son, Nat. The mayor's wife is fond of opera, while the mayor prefers rabbit hunting.

Mayor Roy Stoner succeeds Mayor Pike. The balding politician is a real believer in making Mayberry as up to date as any other town in the state, but he has a tough time convincing Andy of that. "I am trying to make something out of Mayberry. Why, with that new underpass we could be a real metropolis." He doesn't like to mention that the new underpass goes by his brother's gas station. Mayor Stoner's wife's name is Mabel. He claims that he knows the governor, and when he approves of something Andy has done he calls him Andrew. The mayor carries a pocketwatch, enjoys fishing, and has visited Hawaii. His office is right above the courthouse. He usually wears a hat.

Jim Lindsey no longer resides in Mayberry, but while he did he was the best guitar picker in the county. With Andy's prompting, he joined Bobby Fleet's Band with a Beat (he makes $75 to $100 a week). Jim had a big hit with "Rock 'n' Roll Rosie from Raleigh." In

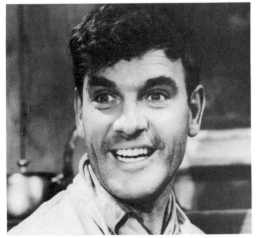

Jim Lindsey (James Best)

fact, he earns enough to purchase a little red sports car (Mercedes 190SL), three guitars, and a fancy set of threads. Jim's favorite meals are chicken-and-dumplings and fried chicken and cornbread. Aunt Bee calls him Jimmy.

Emma Watson (Cheerio Meredith)

Emma Brand Watson is one of the top gossips in town, but she sees it a little differently: "We don't gossip; we just pass along the news." She is also a chronic hypochondriac: "Did I have a pain? Started right here in the side and shot down my leg, rared up the other side and around my back, and then went clean on up my neck." She has been arrested for jaywalking. Emma bakes pies almost every day, and suffers from sciatica, among other ailments. She buys her special pills (they're just sugar) from Walker's Drugstore for ten cents a pack. For a short time, she was the manicurist at Floyd's Barbershop.

Judd Fletcher is over seventy years young and can generally be found

Judd (Burt Mustin)

lounging around the Mayberry square, sitting on a bench, whittling, playing checkers with crony Chester Jones on the porch of the Mayberry Hotel, or visiting in Floyd's Barbershop. Judd is a skilled raconteur and loves better than anything else to tease Barney Fife. The old geezer torments Barney unmercifully, and Barney can only come back by calling him a "Wisenheimer." Judd has blue eyes. He wears a white hat, overalls, and a sweater most of the time. He sings in the town's barbershop quartet, is in The Regal Order of the Golden Door to Good Fellowship, and once was deputized by Barney.

Asa Breeney is another old-timer in town. Not believing in retirement, Asa holds down three jobs. He is the guard at the Mayberry Security Bank, night watchman at Weaver's Department Store, and part-time desk clerk at the Mayberry Hotel. The only way he can manage all three jobs is by sleeping a little during each of them. Barney re-

fers to him as Rip Van Winkle. He has misery in his back. Asa's awfully proud of his pistol, even though a few screws are missing and the bullets have turned green with mold. His hobby is collecting tin foil in a ball.

Wally is one of the best mechanics Mayberry ever had. Gomer says, "When it comes to motors, he's sure got a green thumb." Wally can diagnose what's wrong with an engine by simply listening to it run. Or, if the owner can just imitate the sounds, Wally may be able to tell what the problem is. He can take a car apart and put it back together right before your eyes. Wally owns the town gas station and he has a great set of tools. Wally's Service Station is open from 7:00 A.M. to 7:00 P.M. and offers gasoline, oil, lubrication, tires, accessories, car repairs, candy, gum, and cold drinks. The filling station has the best variety of pop in town; huckleberry smash and nectarine crush are just two of the many flavors available. Eventually, Wally sells the station to Goober, but he also runs a laundry. Wally loves reading "Moon Mullins" in the Sunday morning paper as he rocks on the front porch of his house. Wally won't work on Sundays, but he does allow Gomer to sell gasoline then. His phone number is 363 down at the station, which also boasts a public telephone. He has a married daughter named Verdi.

Ben Weaver could be the richest man in town. He's certainly Mayberry's most relentless businessman. Ben

Ben Weaver (Tol Avery)

store 150 pounds of beef in his freezer. Even though he and Floyd Lawson are good friends and have their places of business side-by-side, Foley will never forget the day that Floyd punched him in the nose. Charlie is married, and one of his habits is falling asleep in the barber chair. Floyd says of Foley: "He's a nice guy, but he's a cheapskate."

Charlie Foley (Frank Ferguson)

not only owns and operates Weaver's Department Store, he also rents houses and he's pretty strict about folks paying their bills on time. "I don't know how a man can be so ornery," Andy says of Ben. Some people might call Ben a skinflint or a tightwad, but beneath his rough exterior is a pretty fine fellow. He has the reputation of being a gruff old Scrooge, but when it comes down to it, he is another warm and caring citizen of Mayberry. Ben is a real church-goer and he knows every song in the hymnal (except for "Leaning on the Everlasting Arms," which he mouths). Ben often wears a black suit and black hat and he's had his store in town for nigh unto twenty-five years. His is the only store in town that can legally sell spirits.

Charlie Foley is another independent businessman. He runs Foley's Grocery & Meat Market and keeps pretty busy minding the store. Foley's grocery features farm fresh vegetables. A kind man, he once let Aunt Bee

John Masters is the musical mastermind of Mayberry. He directs the town choir and selects Mayberry's representative for the annual musicale. (Mr. Masters refers to Barney's singing as "a caterwauling tenor.") He is also the coordinator and director of the Centennial Pageant. He is a sharp dresser (always in tie or bow tie) and makes his living as sometime reservations clerk at the Mayberry Hotel. He usually steps out at 8:00 P.M. to eat. When he gets upset, Mr. Masters breaks out in hives. He lives on Elm Street.

Orville Monroe is the town mortician and TV repairman. Be sure and ask him about his free estimates and layaway plan. He sometimes uses the hearse to pick up spare television parts. At least for a while, his business is next door to Floyd's Barbershop, and Andy says, "Folks claim he charges less to bury you than to fix your set." Orville is a member of the town council, and his daughter plays the accordian.

Johnny Paul Jason is quite a kid. He's one of Opie's closest pals, and he knows a lot of old wives' tales. Among them are: tar is real good for the teeth; if you lick indelible ink, you die in a minute-and-a-half; if you touch a bird, the bird is going to die; a horsehair put into stagnant water will turn into a snake. Andy says, "Johnny Paul sure is a gold mine of made-up facts," but Opie explains that Johnny Paul reads in bed with a flashlight. Johnny Paul is Charlie Foley's nephew, and he has a sister and a No. 1-size chemistry set.

John Masters (Olan Soule)

Arnold Bailey is another of Opie's close friends. Arnold has the knack of getting Opie into trouble. Arnold's dad is a doctor, and he has a little brother. He once wrote a paper on his most unforgettable character, Sheriff Andy Taylor. Arnold Bailey is also the football team's manager and he can play the piano.

Millie Hutchins (Arlene Golonka)

Millie Hutchins came to Mayberry from Mt. Pilot. She works behind the counter at Boysinger's Bakery. Millie dates Howard Sprague. They courted for three months and during the last month they were together every night (except for the nights she washed her hair). Howard then proposed, and she accepted, but the engagement was only temporary. They had asked Andy and Helen to be best man and maid of honor. Howard planned the honeymoon: first day in Morgantown and the King Arthur Pageant, and then off to see Blue Rock Caverns on the second day. Millie's parents live in Wheeling, West Virginia, as do her Uncle

Phil and Aunt Hannah. Millie hates schedules and loves to do things on the spur of the moment. She wanted Howard to shave off his mustache because he reminded her of a Keystone Cop.

"Bernie" and Skippy (Joyce Jameson)

(Courtesy Joyce Jameson)

"Hello, doll!"—Andy gets snuggled by Daphne (Jean Carson)

Skippy and Daphne are from Mt. Pilot, but they drive over to Mayberry quite frequently to surprise Andy and Barney. Their phone number is 327MP. The "fun girls" love to dance, especially at the Kit Kat Club, where beer is served. Daphne thinks Andy is a doll, but her boyfriend, Al, disagrees and once gave Andy a black eye. Skippy plays the ukelele, snorts when she laughs, and is crazy about "Bernie." Daphne favors polka-dot blouses. These two wild and crazy gals like to speed their convertible through the streets of Mayberry, hoping that Andy and Barney will chase them in the squad car and take them to jail.

The Reverend Hobart M. Tucker, D.D., is minister at the All Souls Church, later called the Community Church. He lives on Maple Road. Andy says, "I hold with Reverend Tucker. He's good enough for me. We been taking from Reverend Tucker a good many years now, and I ain't about to change." But then again, Andy has said, "Sometimes he can be as dry as dust." Andy also says, "I believe Reverend Tucker's sermons on happiness are the best things he does." Among the preacher's top sermons are "Seek and Ye Shall Find" and "The Dice Are Loaded Against the Evil-Doer." Some Sundays there is an early service, and don't forget, preaching starts at 11:00 A.M. The reverend sometimes wears glasses and he enjoys bowling.

Leon is a familiar sight on the sidewalks of the town. He is about four or five years old and he always wears a cowboy hat, a bandana, blue-jean jacket, cowboy boots, and cap pistols. His other trademark is a peanut butter and jelly sandwich, which he has with him at all times and which he is always most happy to share. ("No thanks, Leon.")

Fred H. Goss is the top tailor-cleaner in town. Fred smokes, is haphazard, and dresses rather sloppily, but he's good at his work. The sign in his shop says "When You're in a Rush, Call Us—special three-hour service." Fred can tell what people have been up to simply by examining their clothes, and he's usually up on the latest gossip. Fred really knows his business: "Like I say, it always pays to look your best." And he tells Otis: "Got the spots off,

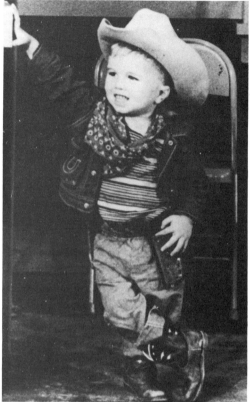

(Courtesy Rance Howard)

Leon (Clint Howard)

(Courtesy William Keene)

The Reverend Hobart Tucker (William Keene)

Otis, but it might save us all a lot of trouble if you just got yourself a whiskey-colored suit." He also says, "Gravy is no joke, no sirree; takes a lot of work to get it cleaned off proper, lots of good spottin'." Of course, wine stains are almost as bad, and "there ought to be a law against paper taffeta." Fred also hates rhinestone buttons. Fred has an eye for Aunt Bee and courts her for a short while before moving on to date Clara Johnson.

Mrs. Mendelbright ("Bless her heart") runs an apartment house (No Children, No Pets, No Cooking, No Vacancies). Barney resides under her roof for five years. She once received a

Mrs. Mendelbright (Enid Markey)

white Bible from the church for being its most faithful member. She is particularly proud of the dresser her mother shipped to her from Ft. Lauderdale; it's in Barney's room. Among other enterprises, she plans to grow mushrooms in her basement, and she once bought a machine that tore car tires into long shreds of rubber. She used those to weave floor mats, seat covers, and purses.

Edith Pendleton is a busybody and a meddler, but she never really means to do anybody any harm. She is on the Mayberry School Board and a member of the PTA. She's a good cook, and when Aunt Bee was out of town once, she kept house for Andy and Opie. She likes to play dominoes.

Lydia Crosswaith may be a hopeless case. Her name meant "Native of Lydia" in ancient Greece. Barney says she's an albatross. She's a friend of Thelma Lou's. Lydia likes people, but has problems relating to others. "I don't mind ordinary conversation,"

she says, "but I hate to chitchat." She also gets carsick, doesn't know how to play bridge, and can't bowl because of a bad back. The sunlight causes her to break out with herpes, and pretzels lay on her chest. She doesn't gamble or play Go Fish. She hates the guitar but enjoys the clarinet and saxophone, and she can play the piano. She is originally from Greensboro and now works in Mt. Pilot. Her dad used to work at the lumber plant. (He hates his work.) Her address is number 598 on some best-forgotten street.

Flora Malherbe is a healthy young blonde who works at the diner and is Goober's steady girl for a while. Once, when Goober took a week's vacation, she filled in for him at the station and sold record-setting amounts of gasoline. She has a good friend, Bernie, who runs a fur business in Mt. Pilot.

Mrs. Sprague proves a pain for poor Howard, who dearly loves his mother. She mollycoddles him to death and won't let him out of the house after

Edith Pendleton (Ruth McDevitt)

dark. "Oh, Howard," she says to her son as they wash and dry the dishes, "you've gone back to your father's old habit of not rinsing the backs of the plates." She is a member of the Garden Club; she calls Andy, "Andrew"; and she tends to exaggerate. She once told Goober that Howard's late father was a compulsive gambler, when all he ever did was play gin rummy. She has a secret ingredient for her spaghetti sauce (oregano), which has been handed down through the family for five generations. Mrs. Sprague eventually marries George Watkins and moves to Mt. Pilot. Their courtship was a whirlwind six-month affair, and George proposed to her at Morelli's over candlelight and rice pudding.

Malcolm Merriweather is what you might call a naturalized Mayberrian. He never really lives in Mayberry, but Mayberry accepts him as one of its own anyway. He even fills in as director of the crosswalk down by the school. Malcolm is from Heckmondwike, England. Malcolm's mother was born just two blocks off of Piccadilly Circus. He was a gentleman's gentleman for Colonel Chumley for eleven years and was a member of the Coldstream Guard. Malcolm was bicycling across America when he stumbled into Mayberry by colliding with Fletch Roberts' truck. Because the accident caused about $40 damage, Andy let Malcolm work the damages off at his house. Malcolm cooked and cleaned for Andy and Opie while Aunt Bee was out of town. He also taught Opie about proper eti-

quette. He is a good cook, paints faces on boiled eggs, makes delicious roly-poly pudding, and does magic tricks. Malcolm was the one who found Andy's police cap in the back of a cupboard. He even made Andy wear a tie to work. On one occasion, Malcolm almost came to blows with Ernest T. Bass. His experience as a falcon-keeper wasn't much help then.

Just Passing Through

Throughout the years, numerous visitors have come to Mayberry. What follows is a list of some of Mayberry's more prominent guests.

Teena Andrews: native Mayberrian Irene Phlogg becomes a movie star and returns to her hometown for her world-premiere movie, accompanied by her manager, Harold Carson, and her secretary, Harriet

Ron Bailey: a smart-alecky rich kid who learns responsibility by observing Andy's disciplining of Opie

Ben Beecham: Emmett Clark's brother-in-law; owns the Ben Beecham (Insurance) Agency in Raleigh

Harriet Bixby and Mrs. Wicks: from the Women's Historical Society; they present Mayberry with a plaque

Jean Boswell: a reporter for publisher J. Howard Jackson who does an under-cover job on Andy

Dr. Harrison Everett Breen: of New York City; he preaches a sermon on "What's Your Hurry" at All Souls Church

Ellen Brown: a manicurist who works temporarily at Floyd's Barbershop before deciding to marry big-city barber Pierre

David Browne: a hobo with the magical

Andy and the Woman Speeder (Jean Hagen)

word "Tuscarora"

Ralph and Verlaine Campbell: the brother and sister-in-law of Otis Campbell

Mr. Clark: a likeable "pickup" man of counterfeit money being printed in Mayberry

Mr. Coefield: owns a barbershop chain; offers to rent Floyd's Barbershop from Howard for $75 a month

Roger Courtney: an Esquire club member who fishes with Andy

Elizabeth Crowley: a woman speeder from Washington, D.C., who apparently hasn't seen any photos of Frank Sinatra in a while

Don: a friend of Peggy McMillan's from college, where he was a straight-A student; now a pharmacist

Uncle Edward: Helen Crump's uncle who makes spaghetti

Wilbur Finch: a salesman with the Manhattan Shoe Company; his boss is Mr. Simms; Finch sets a company record by selling sixty-seven pairs of shoes in one day while in Mayberry

Bobby Fleet and His Band with a Beat: a popular band that visits Mayberry sporadically; Freedy Fleet visits, too; band members include Phil Sunkel on trum-

pet and Carl on clarinet

Flossie: a dancer with the carnival

George "Tex" Foley: an eight-year-old runaway from Eastmont

Willard Foster: the owner of the Foster Furniture Polish Company; lives at 403 Elm Street in Raleigh; car phone number is KG-62114

Foster Furniture Polish Show crew members: the talented crew includes director Jim Martin; assistant director Bob Saunders; makeup woman Eva Kryger; cameraman Sid Hickox; and crewman Burt

Fred Gibson: brings Gibson's Wild West Show to Mayberry; the show features Clarence Earp, who is billed as the great-nephew of Wyatt Earp.

Mr. Giddings: sells a Laundercoin franchise to Andy

"Cousin" Gloria: the daughter of Aunt Bee's friend Minnie in Siler City; Frank is Gloria's fiancé

Mary Grace Gossage: Thelma Lou's cousin who dates Gomer

Governor Ed: an early governor whose car is ticketed by Barney for a parking violation; he has a chauffeur

Governor George C. Handley: came to Mayberry for Founders' Day one year; also commented Opie for his enlightening essay on the Battle of Mayberry

Mr. and Mrs. Garland: she leaves baby on the stoop of the sheriff's office

Gypsies: Murrillos, Silvio (Grecos), Sabella, and La Farona (the gypsy queen)

Roger Hanover: an old beau of Aunt Bee's who is intent upon freeloading on the Taylor's goodwill; Andy tells him, in effect, to "hang it on the wall."

Mr. Harmon: a Hollywood movie producer

Keevy Hazelton: famous pop singer; records "My Hometown"; he's accompanied by manager Bill Stone

Mr. Heathcote: a fatherly federal revenue agent (government license plate 51957)

Mr. Higby: a piano tuner

Bill Hollenbeck: just passing through

Count Istvan Teleky: the spirit of the gypsy lamp and fortune-telling cards who grants Opie three wishes

J. Howard Jackson: a vengeful publisher who is fined for speeding in Mayberry

The Reverend Leighton: fills in for the Reverend Tucker for a few weeks; preaches the sermon "Be Yourself"; later he is called to fill the pulpit in Mt. Pilot

The Great Mandrake: a carnival personality

Cousin Martha: she and her husband Darryl, leave their baby, Evie-Joy, with Bee for a week

Ralph Mason: an antique dealer who buys the town cannon

Edgar J. Masters: a speeding trucker nipped in the bud by Barney at Checkpoint Chickie

Mr. Maxwell: a New Yorker who puts together a folk album featuring the boys from Mayberry; sells the album to the National Record Company in Richmond

Mr. McBeevee: a miraculous telephone lineman; truck license plate number is J86449

Fred Michaels: the vice president for regional sales in northeast North Carolina with the Emblem Oil Company

Newton Monroe: a bumbling traveling salesman who discovers that he is "ept"; his cousin Gilbert is a dental technician; eventually lands a job as a salesman at a hardware store in Mt. Pilot

Karen Moore: Thelma Lou's champion skeet shooting cousin from Arkansas

Mr. Murray: a repairman; also does knife-and-scissor sharpening

Uncle Ollie and Aunt Nora: relatives of the Taylors from Lake Charles, Louisiana; they have two sons, Roger and Bruce

Carl Philips: owns the TV station in Siler City

Sergeant Pratt: earliest Army recruiter

Ed Sawyer: comes to Mayberry, hoping to make it his hometown

Frank Smith: visiting from the Raleigh School Board to help Helen with the Watkins Grading Manual; he is Jesuit-educated and has a degree in history

Professor Hubert St. John: a visiting lecturer who wrote *I Know South America;* Aunt Bee reminds him of his late wife, Ethel Montgomery St. John; he has a son, Jonathan

Bradford J. Taylor: Aunt Bee's highfalutin' cousin

Mrs. Rose Temple: a little old lady who wants to sell her 1959 Ford to Barney; her nephew, a minister, escorts her to Mayberry

Malcolm Tucker: with Tucker Enterprises in Charlotte; he's in a hurry when his car breaks down; it's doubtful that he is related to either the Hutchinson, Kansas, or Buffalo Tuckers

Mr. Vasilievich: a Russian diplomat who comes to Mayberry for a summit meeting with Mr. Clifford of the United States; Mr. Ruskin is the interpreter

Virgil: Barney's sensitive cousin from his mother's side of the family in New Jersey; the son of a cabinetmaker; he discovers his true talents, one of which is not telling crab jokes

Mrs. Margaret Williamson: a reporter who writes the "Meandering with Margaret" column for the Raleigh paper

Major Jim Wolpar: with the Twenty-Second Armored Division of the U.S. Army; stopped in his tank by Andy on Highway 6

Mayberry, R.F.D.

Sam Jones

Sam Jones is the leader of Mayberry's farming community. His farm is one of the most productive in the county as it has corn and other crops. The farm has been in the Jones family for more than one hundred years, and Sam inherited it from his father.

Like Andy Taylor, Sam Jones is a widower. He has a son, Mike (Michael is his real name), who is a few years younger than Opie Taylor. For twelve years, Mrs. Fletcher was the housekeeper and cook for Sam and Mike, but she abruptly departed with the arrival of the Vincente family.

Mario Vincente is an Italian who befriended Sam while he was stationed overseas in the service. Mario came to Mayberry to work for Sam on the farm. He also brought his sister, Sophia, and his father with him. It takes a while for Sam and the Vincentes to grow accustomed to one another (we're not sure if Papa ever did learn to drive Sam's automatic, three-speed Model D432X blue tractor, but the friendliness of Mayberry makes the adjustment easier).

Aunt Bee, Mike, and Sam

Clark and wins the election by 405 votes. He makes an excellent leader.

For entertainment, Sam enjoys music. He plays the piano and sings, and it's probably safe to assume that he is a superb dancer. He dates a girl named Doris. Overall, Sam Jones possesses many wholesome qualities that allow him to follow in the distinguished footsteps of Andy Taylor. Sam continues the tradition of leadership without a gun, but just in case, it's comforting to know that Sam does have a sharpshooter's medal.

Aside from farming, Sam is very active in Mayberry civic affairs. He is a member of the school board and, persuaded by Andy, Howard, and Goober, agrees to run for head of the town council (replacing Herb Bradshaw). Sam winds up running against Emmett

("Mayberry R.F.D." replaced "The Andy Griffith Show" on CBS, Monday nights at 9:00 P.M., EST, on September 23, 1968. It ran for three seasons and seventy-eight episodes. It was on "Mayberry R.F.D." that Andy married Helen Crump, and later had a son, Andy Taylor, Jr.)

Mayberry R.F.D.

Away from Mayberry

Raleigh

Raleigh is the "big city" located about fifty miles southeast of Mayberry. The capital city of North Carolina, Raleigh hosts numerous events of particular interest to Mayberrians. Among these events are the annual marching band festival, the annual flower show, the Strawberry Festival, and an auto show. Raleigh also has a zoo.

Among the businesses with Mayberry ties in Raleigh are the R & M Grain Elevators (owned by Peggy McMillan's father), the Super Bargain markets, the Foster Furniture Polish Company, Shebab's Hogarth Detectives, and Amalgamated Motors. Hillside University and Mrs. Wellington's School for Girls are also located in Raleigh.

One of Raleigh's television stations is CBS affiliate WASG, from which "Colonel Tim's Talent Time" is broadcast. The "Foster Furniture Polish Show" also originates in Raleigh. One of the nicest hotels in town is the Commodore ($15 per day), and the Golden

People in Raleigh

Veeda Aiken: a pen-pal of Aunt Bee's

Agnes Jean Babcott: she twirls batons to the tune of "When the Saints Come Marching In" while on "Colonel Tim's Talent Time" TV show

Roger Courtney: a fishing buddy of Andy's and a member of the Esquire Club include Tom Wilson, John Danby, George Bronson, Cliff Britton, and Jim Baker

Mrs. Deacon: member of auxiliary

Miss Fenwick: the secretary to publisher J. Howard Jackson

Ernie Lewis: has his own gas station; was in trade school with Goober

Oldfield: the manager of the Super Bargain Market

Roy Swanson: a friend of Goober's from trade school; his wife is the former Ruthy Matthews

Mr. Twyford: a member of the Raleigh School Board

Palace is the city's finest restaurant. The prestigious Esquire Club is also in Raleigh.

Being the state capital, Raleigh is the center of law enforcement for the state. The state prison is in Raleigh, and the Policeman's Ball is held there, too. The opportunities in law enforcement eventually lure Barney Fife to Raleigh, "the asphalt jungle." Of course, Barney always did like going to Raleigh on his vacations anyway. He would invariably check into his beloved corner room at the YMCA and then hit the town for a "big" time.

Mt. Pilot

Mt. Pilot is Mayberry's sister city to the east. With a population of about thirty thousand, Mt. Pilot is much larger than Mayberry and is a city of hustle and bustle. It is located in Pilot County.

Mt. Pilot is a favorite place for Mayberrians to shop and eat out; they especially enjoy Chinese dinners there. The city is a popular place for Mayberrians to bowl, go to the drive-in movie, dance, or just have a night on the town. Although it's a nice place to visit, most Mayberrians are glad they live in the much more serene Mayberry.

Siler City

Siler City is in Stokes County. It's about a twenty-five minute drive from Mayberry. The WZAZ (Channel 12) television studio is here. Charles Phil-

ips owns the station, and among the employees are Dick, the stage manager, Charlie, the director, and Mr. Sable, the announcer.

Siler City is on the same bus run that goes through Mayberry and Mt. Pilot, and the town hosts the Fisherman Derby. A man named Fitz lives here. He once got Barney's salt-and-pepper suit from the dry cleaners by mistake.

Walnut Hills

Walnut Hills, not far from Mayberry, is a wealthy community with its own golf course. Among the inhabitants are George and Laura Hollander (George is on the boards of five corporations) and their son Billy; Frank Glendon (owns a grocery store chain) and family; and the Martin Breckinridges (he is the biggest real estate developer in the state).

Hollywood

A big event for the Taylor family was when they traveled to Hollywood to see the filming of *Sheriff Without a Gun,* the movie based on Andy's career as sheriff of Mayberry. The movie was produced on Stage 4 of Art Spiegel's Belmont Pictures under the direction of A. J. Considine. Al Saunders was his assistant director. Bryan Bender was the actor who portrayed Andy, while Darlene Mason co-starred as Andy's girlfriend.

Miss Mason resides at the Hollywood Marquee (her phone number is Hollywood 2-7399). She and Andy become

Jack Smith

Opie obtains a number of auto-graphs, too. Among them are those of Doris Day, Kirk Douglas, Cary Grant, and necktie salesman Dave Snyder (he fooled 'em because he was wearing sunglasses). The Taylors even get their own chauffeur, an out-of-work actor named John (his real name is Bob).

Even with all the glamor that Holly-wood has to offer, the Taylors retain their fondness for simple pleasures. On their last night in Tinseltown, the family stayed in their suite (No. 403) at the Piedmont Hotel and watched "The Jerome Sanger Show" and "Jim Apache, Indian Spy" on TV. And Aunt Bee wrote a letter to one of the Smed-ley sisters back home.

acquainted (why, she is even from near Whitewater Creek in Kansas) and later have dinner at the Marciet, an elegant restaurant. It is Miss Mason's publicity man, Pat Michaels, who suggests that Andy and Miss Mason pose together for photographs by Lou, her publicity photographer. When one of the pho-tos makes the newspaper, Helen Crump is not exactly thrilled.

While the Taylors are in Hollywood, they visit some of the typical tourist attractions: Schwab's Pharmacy, Dino's, the Brown Derby, the LaBrea Tar Pits, Grumman's Chinese Theater, and the corner of Hollywood and Vine. They also see the homes of movie stars Debbie Reynolds and Jack Benny. At Cesar Romero's house (ad-dress 505), the maid even tells Opie to get off the grass, but not before he gets to hold Mr. Romero's newspaper.

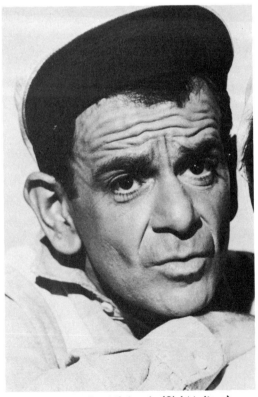

P.R. Man Pat Michaels (Sid Melton)

Darlene Mason (Ruta Lee)

Trip to Mexico

One of the most exciting events in Aunt Bee's life was her trip to Mexico. She won a ten-day, all-expenses-paid trip for two to Mexico City simply by having the lucky number in the Tampico Tamale Contest. Clara and Myrtle each paid half of their expenses so they both could go with Bee.

The traveling trio arrived in Mexico City on TWA flight 17 (Gate 12). While there, they saw many sights, including the floating gardens, Aztec pyramids, a bullfight, Carlotta and Maximilian's palace, and a genuine Mexican farmacia. And they rode a donkey. The highlight of the trip was probably their dinner at a Mexican restaurant, where they sipped sangria while being serenaded. They then witnessed a real Mexican floor show, flamenco dancer and all.

Although Bee and her friends didn't think so at the time, they later realized what a wonderful time they had had on the trip. They definitely got their twelve-pesos-per-dollar's worth.

Contradictions

Throughout the course of "The Andy Griffith Show" there were a few inconsistencies or minor contradictions that, while inconsequential to the quality of the series, are nevertheless of great interest to many fans.

Some of these contradictions are listed below:

1. Three middle names are given for Barney: Oliver, P., and Milton.
2. Miss Clara Edwards is also called Mrs. Clara Johnson, and in one early episode she is called Bertha.
3. Goober Pyle was once called Goober Beasley by Andy.
4. In one episode, Floyd Lawson is called Floyd Colby.
5. Asa Breeney is also called Asa Bascomb.
6. Jud is referred to as Jubal; in one episode he is called Burt (the actor's real first name).
7. Dudley D. Wash is also called Dud A. Wash.
8. Howie Pruitt, Opie's friend, is also called Howie Williams.
9. Opie's girlfriend, Sharon McCall, is also called Sharon Porter, Karen Burgess, Karen Folker, and Ethel (all were played by the same actress).
10. Town loafers Chester Jones, Jase, and Choney are played by the same actor.
11. Three different addresses are given as the home of the Taylors: 14 Maple, 24 Elm, and 332 Maple.
12. Barney's length of service as a deputy: he was sworn in on August 1953, yet in another episode, he celebrates his fifth anniversary on May 16, circa 1963.
13. Goober's age: he was born in 1941, but he buys Wally's Service station in the mid-1960s at the age of thirty-six; later he is said to be thirty-three.
14. Floyd Lawson has a son and wife in a couple of episodes, but he is a widower with no children in one episode.
15. Barney buys his first car from Mrs. "Hubcaps" Lesch, but in some early episodes, he already had a car.
16. Gomer Pyle is not much of a mechanic in early episodes: he just pumps gas. Later, he can diagnose and fix all sorts of mechanical problems.
17. When Barney was locked in the bank safe, he escaped by busting through a wall into a beauty parlor. In a later episode, Andy states that the bank vault has not been opened in fifteen years and that it has a back door.
18. Since the battle of Mayberry was fought in 1762, Mayberry's Centennial Pageant should be a Bicentennial Pageant.
19. On several occasions, Barney says it's twelve miles to Mt. Pilot, but Andy says it's an hour's drive; Emmett once said it was about a thirty-minute drive.
20. Raleigh is said to be fifty or sixty miles from Mayberry, but it once took Emmett five hours to drive from Raleigh to Mayberry.

21. There is supposed to be only one hotel in Mayberry, the Mayberry Hotel, but later the Blu-vue, the Gibson, and the Palmerton hotels are mentioned, and a sign on one building says Gem Hotel.

22. Goober locks up the station at 6:00 P.M., but the sign says open 7:00 A.M., closed 7:00 P.M.

23. Barney's car from Raleigh (a 1960 Edsel), Aunt Bee's convertible and Otis's jalopy all have the same license plate, AY-321. Other license plates appear on more than one car—GP-780, DC-269, VT-772, and RD-757 in particular.

24. In one episode, the licence plate on the squad car is not JL-327. It is DC-269.

25. Barney's weight is given as 100, 132, and 138 pounds.

26. Aunt Bee says there is only one train a day into town, but there are at least three, according to the timetable at the train depot.

27. Various structures in town seem to float from location to location, especially the church building. Almost all of Andy's girlfriends seem to have lived across the street from the church.

28. In the first class reunion, Barney and Andy were graduates of the Mayberry Union High class of 1945, but in the second reunion episode, a banner reads "Class of '48."

29. Mayberry Union High is also referred to as Mayberry Central High.

30. One of the popular bands to play at Mayberry dances is Freddy Fleet and His Band with the Beat, but it is also called Bobby Fleet and His Band with a Beat.

31. Mt. Pilot is sometimes mentioned as if it is in the same county as Mayberry, but it is usually said to be in another county, Pilot.

32. Aunt Bee sometimes cooks her rib roast at 300 degrees and sometimes at 350 degrees.

33. Helen indicates in 1968 that she had been in Mayberry for eight years, but it is unclear where she was hiding the first three years.

34. Poindexter was sheriff in 1946, but Andy didn't mention him when he once gave a complete rundown of all the sheriffs since 1941.

35. The show's credits once listed William Keene's character as the Reverend Martin instead of Tucker. (No reference was made to the reverend's last name during the episode itself.)

36. Emma (Brand) Watson's house is near the lake in one episode and in downtown Mayberry in another episode.

37. Andy once commented that pork chops, green beans, and chocolate pudding were his favorites, but earlier Barney said his favorite dish was leg of lamb.

38. Frank Myers is said to own a medallion from the St. Louis World's Fair of 1906. The fair was in 1904.

39. Sometime between his dinner in Raleigh with Peggy McMillan and his dinner with Darlene Mason in Hollywood, Andy apparently forgets what escargots are. ("I believe I'll let the snails go by.")

40. Barney says it's unusual for his head not to hit the pillow before "quarter till eleven," but one of his deputy duties is to make the 11 P.M. rounds to check the doorknobs of businesses.

Odds and Ends

1. When Andy and some of the boys from Mayberry record a folk song album, they receive a $5,000 advance. (The group Andy played with was portrayed by The Country Boys, better known as the Kentucky Colonels.)
2. There is a rocking chair in one cell, and fresh flowers are kept in both cells at the courthouse.
3. There is a Mayberry phone book, but folks almost never use it (it's not needed with Sarah around).
4. A bus leaves Mayberry at 4:00 P.M.
5. A garbage truck and a hook-and-ladder wrecked at Fourth and Main once.
6. The drugstore is open on Sunday afternoons.
7. The license plate number of bus No. 75 from Macon, Southern Bus Lines, is RH-572. That's the same bus that brought Dud Wash home to Charlene Darling.
8. A carnival man once brought a stuffed whale to town, and a big crowd went to see it.
9. The church bells ring on Sunday morning.
10. The Sunday paper is delivered to the courthouse.
11. Mayberry has a stoplight.
12. There are usually six guns in the rifle rack in the courthouse.
13. The squad car is a Ford Galaxie and later a Ford Custom.
14. It was on March 3, 1951, that Ed's Service serviced the freezer that Aunt Bee had purchased at an auction.
15. When the 3:45 train stops for water, you can hear its whistle in the courthouse.
16. Midnight Madness is the brand of perfume that Ellie sprays on Andy. Walker's Drugstore also stocks Twilight Blush, Shimmering Rose, and Frosted Cherry Bon-Bon (nail polish).
17. Jail visiting hours are 2:00 P.M. to 4:00 P.M.
18. Yakamoto is the brand of razor that Newton Monroe gives to Barney.
19. The numbers of the Scout Troops in Mayberry are 44, 138, and 986.
20. A man in Mt. Pilot had his house stolen. (That would never happen in Mayberry.)
21. The train from Raleigh arrives in Mayberry at 4:00 P.M., the one from Asheville at 6:00 P.M.
22. According to Dr. Pendyke, Miracle Salve is good for poison ivy, prickly rash, athlete's foot, the complexion,

spring itch, and crow's feet.

23. Parker Creek, on Old Ranch Road, needs a new bridge. It is one block from Baker Street, which also crosses Parker Creek. Howard has figured out that it would save $3,628 to build the bridge on Baker Street, plus $468 to repair the old bridge for pedestrians. It would cost $57.60 a month for ten years, and would be 30 percent deductible, so the net cost to the city would be $140.

24. New sewers are not needed on Main Street.

25. When the Mayberry barbershop quartet sang in Mt. Pilot, they used dressing room F and went on last, at 8:30 P.M.

26. Andy's house has three problems: the roof leaks, the water pipes in the kitchen make loud noises, and there is a crack in the kitchen ceiling.

27. There are rooms for rent over the Mayberry moviehouse.

28. When Clara won the pickle contest at the county fair for the twelfth year in a row, her jar was No. 4. (Aunt Bee's losers were No. 11).

29. There are 145,000 miles on Aunt Bee's car.

30. Aunt Bee took flying lessons at MacDonald's Flying School in plane No. N59558. It was a single-engine plane, and her first flight cost $5.

31. Aunt Bee paid $4.50 for some gypsy earrings and got gyped, just as Clara did.

32. Four ounces of Blue Moonlight perfume cost $64.

33. The ad for the car that Barney bought from "Hubcaps" Lesch read: "Aged widow must sell beautifully maintained low-mileage car, one owner, 1954 Ford sedan. Has been driven only to church on Sunday and once a year to Aunt Martha's for Thanksgiving. No dealers. Any reasonable offer. The good Lord willing, you'll call MP-3791."

34. Barney paid $297.50 for his car and told Mrs. Lesch to give $2.50 to Mr. Lesch's favorite charity.

35. What Wally found wrong with the car Barney purchased from the "aged widow": plugs, points, bearings, valves, rings, fuel pump, starter switch, ignition wires, water pump, oil pump, clutch, clutch bearings, clutchplate, brake lining, brake shoes, radiator hose, brake drums, radiator hose cover, sawdust in the transmission. And it could stand a good wash.

36. Written inside of Barney's eighth-grade history book: "Bernard P. Fife. This book belongs to Bernard P. Fife. If lost or stolen, please return to Bernard P. Fife, signed Bernard P. Fife." And the title page reads: " 'A History of the U.S. of America,' by Bernard P. Fife."

37. Andy and Barney once tried to drive to New Orleans in an old Model A that Andy had, but the bearings burned out, and he sold it for $12.

38. When Andy wants to mow the lawn, he borrows a mower from his neighbors, the Wilsons.

39. According to Andy, the area of Mayberry County is about 266 square miles.

40. The Taylors once took a trip to Parkinson's Falls.

41. Andy once sprained his left wrist in a canoe accident.

42. Edgar Beasley is an old friend of Andy's.

43. The stop sign on Spring Street is prone to falling down.

44. Barney attempts to rehabilitate the four Gordon boys by giving them a choice between woodcarving, leathercraft, metalcraft, and Mr. Potato sets. ("I'll take the Mr. Potato set.")

45. Barney pays twenty-five cents an issue for *Learn-A-Month* magazine. One issue is "Odd Facts Known by Few."

46. Barney once charged Andy with "Seventy-six documented cases of malfeasance."

47. When Barney ran for sheriff, his election poster stated: "Fife for Sheriff, Honest, Fearless, Incorruptible."

48. Barney plays the stock market. He owns one-eighth of a share of stock with Wally, Floyd, and the boys, and he has received a check for twenty-seven cents as a dividend.

49. The results of the 50-yard dash at the annual Sheriff's Boys Day: first place—Billy Johnson; second place—Aaron Harrison; third place—Freddy Pruitt; last place—Opie Taylor.

50. When Opie worked at Crawford's Drugs as a soda jerk, he saved $70 in the first three weeks.

51. For a week of feeding Dolly, the horse that pulled the milk wagon, Opie was paid $5, but he had to give Arnold sixty-five cents for going out to check on Dolly one afternoon.

52. According to Howard, 90 percent of lake fish are caught when the water temperature is between 60 and 68 degrees.

53. Andy and Opie have seen at least three Gregory Peck films together.

54. Aunt Bee once purchased 150 pounds of beef at Diamond Jim's.

55. Aunt Bee won $5 at the filling station's Grab-Bag for Cash contests.

56. The only time we ever see Barney's mother (portrayed by Lillian Culver) is when he frisks her at a roadblock ("The Manhunt," Episode 2).

57. Andy found out about Helen's past from Miss Blanchard of the *Kansas City Chronicle*.

58. There are thirteen members in the church ladies choir: twelve singers and the organist. Their robes cost $37.50 apiece.

59. It's two steps up to the Taylors' front porch.

60. It's six steps up to the church house door.

61. Sunday School starts at 9:00 A.M. at the All Souls Church, and preaching is over at noon. The church is not air-conditioned.

62. There are at least two other Darling menfolk who live in the mountains, besides Briscoe and his four sons. Andy once had to go up and settle a fight that started when Jed Darling told Carl Darling that there was no Santa Claus.

63. Mayberry has an athletic team called the Mayberry Bears, which is probably a baseball team.

64. Andy's Aunt Nora from Lake Charles, Louisiana, wants to set him up with Racine Tyler, a skinny widow, who received $4,000 from her late husband's life insurance policy and who drives a bakery truck with the original paint. Racine's phone number is 439-7123.

65. Opie carries his milk money in his shoes and gets out of school at 3:00 P.M.

66. Aunt Bee's china pattern is blue willow.

67. Nine hundred and forty-six jars of Miracle Salve were once delivered to Andy's house.

68. The town bus stop is in front of the drugstore.

69. Opie gave Aunt Bee a set of salt and pepper shakers for her birthday. He almost chose a new baseball hat.

70. Opie's most unforgettable character is Dr. Lou Bailey, Arnold's dad.

71. Two children were named after Andy Taylor: Andy Becker and Andelina Darling Wash.

72. Mayberry has had a drought, tornadoes (in the mid-1950s), a fire, and a flood.

73. Willow Avenue and Woods Way are quiet streets in Mayberry. The duck pond is on Willow Avenue.

74. Grover's Place is on Banner Street.

75. Jim Lindsey financed his car with the Mid-Mountain Finance Company.

76. The Miracle Sweep Vacuum is No. 1 in America.

77. Andy's courthouse desk faces east.

78. Celia didn't know that John married Beverly (on a radio soap opera that Aunt Bee listens to).

79. A bottle of Colonel Harvey's Elixir sells for $1.

80. Count Istvan Teleky lived in the eighteenth century.

81. The monster from Mars has four sets of teeth whereas the one from the moon has only three.

82. The new barber in town charges $6 for a hair style; that also includes a can of hair spray.

83. In the Regal Order of the Golden Door to Good Fellowship, the Keeper of the Door gets to wear a giant golden key around his neck. (Earlier lodge meetings were held on Fridays, but by the time Howard Sprague joins, lodge meetings are on Wednesdays.)

84. Speeder Elizabeth Crowley, rich kid Ronald Bailey, Esquirian Roger Courtney, and nurse Peggy McMillan all drive very similar Thunderbirds.

85. Barney sends money to this mother every month. (He's a good son.)

All keyed up—Goober guards the door to the Regal Order of the Golden Door to Good Fellowship

Miss Crump's Final Exams

I ain't got time to stand around here and discuss trivial trivialities.
  —Barney Fife

Fill in the Blank

1. _____Salve
2. The school crossing in Mayberry is at the corner of Haymore and_____.
3. Gomer joins the_____.
4. The capital of Colombia is_____.
5. Lost_____Cave
6. _____McBeevee
7. Checkout time at the Mayberry Hotel is at_____P.M.
8. Mayberry_____Bank
9. Old Man_____Woods
10. _____Minutemen
11. West Indian Licorice_____Delight ice cream
12. Dr. Harrison_____Breen of New York City
13. Boysinger's_____
14. Bernard P._____, M.D.
15. Mr. Higby_____the piano.
16. Peggy_____is a county nurse.
17. Emmett once conducted a special study of_____timers.
18. Helene_____Dubois
19. Barney says he has Thelma Lou in his_____pocket.
20. The_____sisters make moonshine in their greenhouse.

True–False Questions

1. Andy prefers angel food cake to applesauce cake.
2. Floyd has studied Latin.
3. Andy and Barney are cousins.
4. Leon is never heard to speak.
5. The secret ingredient in Clara's pickles is oregano.
6. Andy is allergic to poison ivy.
7. The Monday special at Morelli's is creamed chicken.
8. Opie is left-handed.
9. Ernest T. Bass is of English descent.
10. Goober's mother makes lemon pie the same way that Aunt Bee does.
11. Opie's three wishes, granted by the Count, all come true.
12. Six can't play bridge.
13. Mr. Weaver just mouths the words when singing "Leaning on the Everlasting Arms."
14. When it comes to potting petunias, Andy is a giant.
15. Mayberry is located in the southern part of North Carolina.
16. Floyd was in *The Mikado* when he was in the high school drama club.
17. Other than singing, none of the Darling boys is ever heard to speak.
18. Howard Sprague caught Old Sam in Myers Lake with potato salad for bait.
19. Barney remembers Al Becker.

20. Barney and Thelma Lou have had a standing date "every Wednesday night for years" to watch "that doctor show on TV" with a pan of cashew fudge between them.

Complete the Quote

1. "He's a_____."
2. "We defy the_____."
3. "Slow down. Take it easy. What's your_____."
4. "Judy, Judy,_____."
5. "All hail to thee, Miss_____."
6. "Hang it on the_____."
7. "Great_____, Aunt Bee!"
8. "It's not a whim anymore if you put on clean_____."
9. "That one makes me_____."
10. "Boy,_____are selfish."
11. "Goober says_____."
12. "_____, get me my house."
13. "_____ cucumbers."
14. "Another_____pointing the wrong way."
15. "How do you do, Mrs._____."
16. "Floyd Lawson, you're a miserable, deceitful_____."
17. "Water and air are_____."
18. "The dingo dog is indigenous to_____."
19. "The tears on my_____bespeak the pain that is in my heart."
20. "Lots of luck to you and_____."

Who Said It?

1. "Pipe down, Otis!"
2. "Spider bite!"
3. "The Shawnee. I lived among them. They're devils."
4. "I came to fill my vase."
5. "Fiddledeesticks."
6. "Goober, would you tell her to quit hanging her head out the window like a dog."
7. "Cockadoodle-doo!"
8. "How's about a Swiss cheese sandwich?"
9. "Those of us who chart the course of world events shall forever remain nameless."
10. "Them Coldcream Guards are fearless."
11. "I'm ept!"
12. "The bus bringeth and the bus taketh away."
13. "The dice are loaded against the evil–doer."
14. "Perfectly good hoot owl, just plum wasted."
15. "Aw, gee, Paw."
16. "I'm from Greensboro."
17. "I think I'll split over there and get some of those cool-looking potato chips."
18. "I do not choose to run."
19. "Call the man!"
20. "Yo!"

Easy Quiz

1. What is the name of the street in front of the Mayberry courthouse?
2. What city does Barney move to when he leaves Mayberry?
3. Does Floyd the barber wear glasses?
4. Who was the hero in the cave rescue?
5. How many wishes do two cards with flaming torches get from Count Istvan Teleky?
6. When was Jamestown founded?
7. Does "Slimy River Bottom" make Charlene Darling cry?
8. What is Opie's favorite nineteenth-century American short story?
9. What business is at the corner of Main Street and Garden Road?

10. What airline did the Taylors fly to Hollywood?

11. What is the last name of Emmett, the fix-it man?

12. Is Gomer Pyle the grandson of General Lucius Pyle?

13. What is television repairman Orville Monroe's other profession?

14. Who was the sixteenth president of the United States?

15. What is Andy Taylor's favorite magazine?

16. Who is "Opie Taylor, Sr."?

17. What street does Barney Fife live on in Mayberry?

18. What color is Sam Jones' barn said to be?

19. According to Goober, where can the best mashed potatoes in town be found?

20. Name one of Mayberry's mayors.

21. Where are the "fun girls" from?

22. What are the school colors for Mayberry Union High?

23. What is the name of Andy's prized fishing rod?

24. What is the name of Sam Jones' son?

25. Which door to the courthouse has the mail slot in it?

26. According to Andy, which piece of equipment is the most important one to a lawman?

27. What is the Mayberry squad car's license plate number?

28. What two portraits hang on the wall in Miss Crump's classroom?

29. What is Mayberry's "sister city"?

30. Who is Barney's favorite waitress at the diner?

31. How many jail cells are there in the courthouse?

32. What musical instrument does Andy play while sitting on the front porch?

33. What is Howard Sprague's occupation?

34. Where is Otis Campbell's "home away from home"?

35. What does Barney wear to dances and special occasions?

36. Who is Gomer Pyle's cousin?

37. Who is the best rock-thrower in all of Mayberry County?

38. What are the nicknames of Andy, Barney, Opie, and Goober?

39. Who has a dog named Sandy?

40. After Goober bought the filling station from Wally, who was his first customer?

Medium Quiz

1. Who is the guard at the Mayberry bank?

2. Mayberry's only Indian is a member of what tribe?

3. What is the "Pearl of the Caribbean"?

4. Who is the male lead in the movie *Picnic?*

5. How much are empty soda pop bottles worth in Mayberry?

6. Who pretends to be Andrew Paul Lawson?

7. Who drew faces on eggs for Opie?

8. Name two waitresses at Mayberry's diner.

9. What is the name of the "loaded goat"?

10. What town is said to have a poodle-trimmer?

11. Is Andy Taylor's middle name Samuel?

12. Who is the "Masked Singer"?

13. Who was nicknamed "Laughing Face" in Mayberry history?

14. Who was Frieburger?

15. What is Irene Phlogg's Hollywood name?

16. Did Opie take a bath this morning?
17. Where do the Hubacher brothers reside?
18. According to Floyd, what does *tempus edax rerum* mean in Latin?
19. What is the significance of these words: "Anybody know why these two people should not be wed, speak now or forever hold your peace"?
20. What does Andy keep in the crock cooler in the courthouse?
21. Where can Barney find an extra set of keys to the patrol car if he should lose his own?
22. What musical instrument does Briscoe Darling play?
23. Where does Barney stay when he vacations in Raleigh?
24. How many points are there on the stars of Andy's badge, the right shoulder patch of his uniform, and on the squad car door?
25. What day of the week is the *Mayberry Gazette* published?
26. What is the password needed to enter The Regal Order of the Golden Door to Good Fellowship?
27. What is Mayberry's largest department store?
28. Who is Opie's adult friend who jingles when he walks through the treetops?
29. What vehicle does Malcolm Merriweather use to see America?
30. What brand of gasoline does Wally's service station sell?
31. Who is Barney Fife's landlady in Mayberry?
32. For what offense does Gomer make a citizen's arrest on Barney?
33. Who is the sponsor of Mayberry's bowling team?
34. According to Barney, how do you fight fire and how do you handle a fox?
35. What is the identical first name of the wives of Emmett Clark and Rafe Hollister?
36. Where does Opie plan to attend college?
37. Where does Opie go for day camp one summer?
38. Where are the three telephones located in the Taylor house?
39. What is the name of Paul Revere's horse?
40. Who blackballed Howard Sprague from membership in The Regal Order of the Golden Door to Good Fellowship?

Hard Quiz

1. What is the most important crop in Mayberry County?
2. How many bathrooms are in the Taylor house?
3. What couple once abandoned its baby on the Mayberry courthouse stoop?
4. Who is Mrs. Parkins?
5. How many dogs does Clint Biggers claim at the courthouse?
6. How much does Doc Andrews charge for an office visit?
7. Whom did Opie once handcuff to the flagpole at the school?
8. Which direction do the Tomahawks face when taking their club oath?
9. Where are Mayor Purdy and Councilman Dobbs from?
10. When does Ichabod Crane pursue his travels homeward?
11. Why does Ernest T. Bass talk through his nose?
12. What is the first name of Otis Campbell's wife?
13. What do Mayberrians call the "Victory of Tuckahoosie Creek"?
14. What food of Aunt Bee's is Briscoe

Darling especially fond of?

15. According to Goober, where is the best fishing in the county?
16. What couple lives in Bannertown?
17. What has four wheels and flies?
18. Where is the company headquarters for the Emblem Oil Company?
19. What is the number that Henry Bennett selects from the hat during the church raffle?
20. Where can Andy find an extra key to Walker's Drugs?
21. What words does Andy chant over Opie's betrothal papers to make the Darlings think there are witches in the Taylor family?
22. How much does a jar of Miracle Salve cost?
23. What was the name of Aunt Bee's Chinese restaurant?
24. Where in his house does Andy keep a handgun?
25. What doctor delivered Opie Taylor at birth?
26. Where did Goober find the stuffed owl that Andy used to fool the Darlings about the Omen of the Owl?
27. Name the criminal whom Andy shot in the line of duty?
28. Wally had a contest at the filling station called Grab-Bag for Cash, but what did Goober want to call the contest?
29. How many hatfuls of water does it take for Mr. Darling to fill the radiator of his truck?
30. Name the two kids who have given Opie a black eye?
31. What is the magic word that a tramp tells Opie will make a gum machine give out free gumballs?
32. What three wishes did Opie request from the gypsy fortune-telling cards?

33. What was Keevy Hazelton's million-selling record?
34. Exactly how many quarts of "kerosene cucumbers" did Aunt Bee make?
35. Who removed Opie's tonsils?
36. Who wrote the book on fishing?
37. What tune does the town band practice in preparation for their evening band concert?
38. How many flying lessons does Aunt Bee take before she solos?
39. What is the number of the lane in which Howard bowls his perfect game?
40. Who is the "Merry Madcap of Mayberry"?

Real Hard Quiz

1. Mayberrians have been told to keep off the grass of what two Hollywood stars' lawns?
2. Where was Barney when the Darlings first came to Mayberry?
3. According to Andy, what are the names of the spirits of the fire, the water, and the air?
4. Where did Sarah's mother injure her hip?
5. Who makes ninety percent of the headstones in the Mayberry area?
6. What is special about Howard Sprague's suitcase?
7. What is Aunt Bee's cure for the hiccups?
8. How much does the lady shoplifter weigh with all of her stolen goods?
9. Who is Agent XYZ?
10. What contains root beer, orange juice, tomato juice, sherbert, and molasses?
11. How much does Barney the realtor think he can sell Andy's house for?
12. Who describes the "Kansas City Million-Dollar Heist" and the "Toledo

Payroll Caper"?

13. Whose tombstone had the inscription "A Fine Man and a Dear Husband 1908—1958?"

14. What is Andy's solution to the "Osgood vs. Welch Dispute"?

15. What is the alcohol content of Colonel Harvey's Indian Elixir?

16. When was the Greendale town hall erected?

17. Who threw the dipsy-doodle to Mickey Mantle?

18. From whom does Andy borrow a sewing machine one Sunday?

19. Who is described on the radio as being a gray-haired prowler and an ex-convict?

20. What Mayberry business prints the Marine Corps Hymn on its calendars?

21. Who is Martha Carruthers?

22. From whom does Ed Sawyer try to buy a filling station?

23. What is the total of Mrs. Mendelbright's life savings when she prepares to marry Mr. Fields?

24. From what city did Jim Lindsey order his guitar pick?

25. What math problem did Andy help Opie with once?

26. How long are Emmett's shoelaces?

27. Who is the first witness called in the Marvin Jenkins burglary trial?

28. What is the name of the bus driver of Southern Bus Lines?

29. Where does Opie keep his Scout hatchet?

30. Who is Mark Steele?

31. With what word did Helen Crump win the Kansas spelling bee state championship in the eighth grade?

32. What brand of mange cure does Dr. Pendyke claim he used before discovering the wonders of Miracle Salve?

33. What is Aunt Bee's winning answer when she appears on the "Win or Lose" game show?

34. Where are the three places that Barney keeps extra cash on himself?

35. How much is Goober's down payment when he purchases Wally's station?

36. What did Aunt Bee do with Andy's high school yearbook, *The Cutlass?*

37. What did Barney order when he and Andy ate at a fancy Raleigh restaurant?

38. What is selection No. 12 in the Mayberry Marching Band's brown book?

39. Who is Buzz Flewhart?

40. How much does the beer-can opener with the little umbrella on top cost at Weaver's Department Store?

Answers to Miss Crump's Final Exams

Fill in the Blank

1. Miracle
2. Rockford
3. Marines
4. Bogota
5. Lovers'
6. Mr.
7. 4
8. Security
9. Kelsey's
10. Mayberry
11. Mocha
12. Everett
13. Bakery
14. Fife
15. tunes
16. McMillan
17. toaster
18. Alexion
19. hip
20. Morrison

True–False

1. False
2. True
3. True
4. True
5. False
6. False
7. True
8. False
9. False
10. False
11. True
12. True
13. True
14. True
15. False
16. True
17. False
18. False
19. False
20. False

Complete the Quote

1. nut
2. Mafia
3. hurry
4. Judy
5. Mayberry
6. wall
7. beans
8. underwear
9. cry
10. giraffes
11. hey
12. Sarah
13. Kerosene
14. buffalo
15. Wiley
16. wretch
17. free
18. Australia
19. pillow
20. yours

Who Said It?

1. Barney
2. Gomer
3. Colonel Harvey
4. Otis
5. Aunt Bee
6. Andy
7. Barney
8. Howard
9. Barney
10. Goober
11. Newton Monroe
12. Floyd
13. The Reverend Tucker
14. Briscoe Darling
15. Opie
16. Lydia Crosswaith
17. Opie
18. Calvin Coolidge
19. Andy
20. Goober

Easy Quiz

1. Main
2. Raleigh
3. Yes
4. Deputy Fife
5. Three
6. 1607
7. Yes
8. "The Legend of Sleepy Hollow"
9. Wally's (later Goober's) Service Station
10. TWA
11. Clark
12. No
13. Mortician
14. Abraham Lincoln
15. *National Geographic*
16. Gomer Pyle
17. Elm
18. Red
19. The diner

20. Jenkins, Pike, or Roy Stoner
21. Mt. Pilot
22. Orange and blue
23. Eagle-Eye Annie
24. Mike
25. The one on the right as you enter the courthouse
26. Badge
27. JL–327
28. George Washington and Abraham Lincoln's
29. Mt. Pilot
30. Juanita
31. Two
32. Guitar
33. County clerk
34. His cell in the courthouse
35. His ol' salt-and-pepper suit
36. Goober
37. Ernest T. Bass
38. Ange, Barn, Ope, and Goob
39. Little Orphan Annie
40. Andy, who ordered a fill-up of super gas for the squad car

Medium Quiz

1. Asa Breeney (or Bascomb)
2. Cherokee
3. St. Benedict's Island
4. William Holden
5. Two cents
6. Andy Taylor
7. Malcolm Merriweather
8. Juanita, Flora, Olive, or Dorothy
9. Jimmy (Otis Campbell is also acceptable)
10. Mt. Pilot
11. No
12. Leonard Blush
13. James Merriweather
14. Mayberry sewer inspector
15. Teena Andrews
16. "No, why? Is one missing?"
17. The state prison
18. "Time heals everything"
19. They are the first words spoken on "The Andy Griffith Show" (spoken by Andy)
20. Spring water
21. In the top drawer of Andy's courthouse desk
22. The jug
23. A corner room at the "Y"
24. Six, five, and five
25. Wednesday
26. Geronimo
27. Weaver's
28. Mr. McBeevee
29. Bicycle
30. Acme
31. Mrs. Mendelbright
32. Making an illegal U-turn
33. Emmett's Fix-It Shop
34. You fight fire with fire and you outfox a fox
35. Martha
36. The University of North Carolina
37. Camp Winokee
38. In the living room, on the wall in the kitchen, and in Andy's bedroom
39. Nellie
40. Goober

Hard Quiz

1. Potatoes
2. One-and-a-half
3. The Garlands from Mt. Pilot
4. Imaginary cook (actually Andy)
5. Eleven
6. $5
7. Ralph Baker
8. Toward the rising sun (to the east)
9. Greendale
10. "The very witching time of night"
11. "So I can talk whilst I eat"

12. Rita
13. The Battle of Mayberry
14. Muffins
15. Hopkin's Lake
16. Mr. and Mrs. Parnell Rigsby
17. "A jet pilot on a skateboard" (garbage truck is not an acceptable answer)
18. El Paso, Texas
19. Six-and-seven-eighths
20. On the sill above the front door
21. "Ebum, shoobum, shoobum, shoobum"
22. Thirty-five cents
23. Aunt Bee's Canton Palace
24. On top of the hutch in the dining room
25. Dr. Bennett
26. At the Lodge
27. Luke Comstock
28. Goober's Gusher of Gold
29. Eleven
30. Sheldon and Cynthia (Helen Crump's niece)
31. Tuscarora
32. To get a new jackknife, to get a "B" in arithmetic, and to have Miss Crump as his teacher in the sixth grade
33. "Texarkana in the Morning"
34. Twenty-four
35. Dr. Thomas Peterson
36. Izaak Walton
37. "The Skater's Waltz"
38. Eleven
39. Ten
40. Howard Sprague

Real Hard Quiz

1. Gary Cooper and Cesar Romero
2. On a bus trip to Charlotte with his mother
3. Budjum Snark, Brillen Tramp, and Grovely Barch

4. At the bowling alley
5. Brian Jackson
6. It has a secret compartment for money
7. Hold your breath and take five sips of water
8. 163 pounds
9. Goober
10. Andy's punch supreme
11. $24,000
12. Gentleman Dan Caldwell
13. Tom Silby
14. Put up a chickenwire fence
15. Eighty-five percent
16. 1902
17. Whitey Ford
18. Louise Palmer
19. Saunders
20. Nelson's Funeral Parlor
21. Resident of Pleasantville, who became the Foster Furniture Polish Lady
22. George Sepley
23. $3,600.43
24. Winston-Salem
25. 169 divided by 14
26. Twenty-seven inches
27. Charles Keyes
28. Alf
29. In the same drawer as his underwear
30. Crab Monster
31. Hors d'oeuvres
32. Molly Harkins
33. Cinnamon with custard filling
34. In his holster, in his socks, and in his hat
35. $2,000
36. She gave it away to a disease drive
37. Snails and brains
38. "The Stars and Stripes Forever"
39. The man who studied the influence of atmospheric rays
40. A dollar and a quarter

Cast Credits

ANDY TAYLOR—Andy Griffith
BARNEY FIFE—Don Knotts
OPIE TAYLOR—Ronny Howard
AUNT BEE TAYLOR—Frances Bavier
FLOYD LAWSON—Howard McNear
OTIS CAMPBELL—Hal Smith
THELMA LOU—Betty Lynn
HELEN CRUMP—Aneta Corsaut
GOMER PYLE—Jim Nabors
GOOBER PYLE—George Lindsey
HOWARD SPRAGUE—Jack Dodson
EMMETT CLARK—Paul Hartman
WARREN FERGUSON—Jack Burns
CLARA EDWARDS JOHNSON—Hope Summers
BRISCOE DARLING—Denver Pyle
The DARLING Boys—(The Dillards) Doug Dillard, Rodney Dillard, Dean Webb, and Mitch Jayne
CHARLENE DARLING—Margaret Ann Peterson
ERNEST T. BASS—Howard Morris
ELLIE WALKER—Elinor Donahue
RAFE HOLLISTER—Jack Prince
MAYOR ROY STONER—Parley Baer
MAYOR PIKE—Dick Elliot
EMMA (BRAND) WATSON—Cheerio Meredith
BEN WEAVER—Will Wright, Tol Avery, Jason Johnson
JUDD and JUBAL FLETCHER, OLD MAN CROWLEY, and BURT—Burt Mustin
CHESTER JONES, CHONEY, and JASE—Joe Hamilton
ASA BREENEY, ASA BASCOMB, DOC ROBERTS—Charles P. Thompson
JOHN MASTERS—Olan Soule
LEON—Clint Howard

JOHNNY PAUL JASON—Richard Keith Thibodeaux
ARNOLD BAILEY—Sheldon (Golomb) Collins
SKIPPY—Joyce Jameson
DAPHNE—Jean Carson
CHARLIE FOLEY—Frank Ferguson
THE REVEREND HOBART M. TUCKER—William Keene
MR. MELDRIM and HARLAN FERGUS—Warren Parker
MRS. MENDELBRIGHT—Enid Markey
FRED GOSS—Fred Sherman
MRS. SPRAGUE—Mabel Albertson
MRS. EDITH PENDLETON—Ruth McDevitt
FLORA MALHERBE—Alberta Nelson
EDNA SUE LARCH—Maudie Prickett
LYDIA CROSSWAITH, JUANITA PIKE, and JOSEPHINE PIKE—Josie Lloyd
MARTHA CLARK and various townspeople—Mary Lansing
CYRUS TANKERSLEY—George Cisar
DUD WASH—Hoke Howell, Bob Denver
MALCOLM MERRIWEATHER—Bernard Fox
MARY SIMPSON—Julie Adams, Sue Ann Langdon
PEGGY McMILLAN—Joanna Moore
FRED WALKER—Harry Antrim
JIM LINDSEY—James Best
SAM JONES—Ken Berry
MIKE JONES—Buddy Foster
MILLIE HUTCHINS—Arlene Golonka
ORVILLE MONROE—Jonathan Hole
RITA CAMPBELL—Dorothy Neumann
WALLY—Norman Leavitt, Trevor Bardette, and Cliff Norton

HILDA MAY—Florence MacMichael

MYRTLE and various townspeople—Ruth Thom

JASON—Phil Chambers

ELMO—Vince Barnett

TREY BOWDEN—David A. Bailey

HOWIE PRUITT/WILLIAMS—Dennis Rush

KAREN BURGESS/FOLKER, SHARON PORTER/ McCALL—Ronda Jeter

CAPTAIN M. L. DEWHURST—Richard X. Slattery

VARIOUS STATE POLICEMEN—Ken Lynch and Roy Jenson

VARIOUS HEAVIES—Allan Melvin

VARIOUS TOWNSPEOPLE—Dabbs Greer, Roy Engel, Forrest Lewis, Jon Lormer, Owen Bush, Jim Begg, Amzie Strickland, Sam Edwards, Willis Bouchey, Mary Treen, Bob McQuain, Sara Seegar

VOICE OF LEONARD BLUSH—Howard Morris

"Lots of luck to you and yours."

Episode Summaries

There are 249 episodes (159 in black and white; 90 in color) of "The Andy Griffith Show." The following is a list, with brief plot summaries, of all the episodes. The order in which the episodes are listed is the order in which they were filmed and also the order in which they are most commonly aired in syndication. (The order in which the episodes were originally broadcast is slightly different.) Guest stars and prominent character actors are also listed, along with the writers of the episodes.

1. **The New Housekeeper:** Andy and Opie Taylor's housekeeper, Rose, leaves to be married, and young Opie finds it difficult to accept Andy's Aunt Bee as a replacement. Written by Jack Elinson and Charles Stewart.

2. **The Manhunt:** State policemen (led by Ken Lynch) comb the Mayberry area for an escaped convict and snub Andy and Barney's offer to help. (Watch for Barney's mother.) Written by Jack Elinson and Charles Stewart.

3. **The Guitar Player:** Andy tries to help Mayberry's best guitar player, Jim Lindsey (James Best), get a job with Bobby Fleet's (Henry Slate) Band with a Beat. Dub Taylor ap-

pears. Written by Jack Elinson and Charles Stewart.

4. **Runaway Kid:** Opie refuses to answer his father's questions because he doesn't want to break his promise to a runaway boy who is staying at their house. Written by Arthur Stander.

5. **Opie's Charity:** Andy gets upset with Opie because he donates too little money to a charity drive. Andy then discovers that Opie is saving his money to buy a gift for a girlfriend. Stuart Erwin appears. Written by Arthur Stander.

6. **Ellie Comes to Town:** Pharmacist Ellie Walker arrives in town and appears to be uncooperative because she won't give in to hypochondriac Emma Watson. This is the first appearance of Ellie. Written by Jack Elinson and Charles Stewart.

7. **Irresistible Andy:** Andy mistakenly believes that Ellie Walker is conniving to marry him. Written by David Adler.

8. **A Feud Is a Feud:** Andy must settle a feud between two farming patriarchs so that their children can marry in peace. Arthur Hunnicut and Chubby Johnson guest star. Written by David Adler.

9. **Andy the Matchmaker:** Andy arranges a fake hold-up to boost Barney's spirits, and also encourages him to court Miss Rosemary (Amzie Strickland). Written by Arthur Stander.

10. **Stranger in Town:** A stranger (William Lanteau) arrives in Mayberry and mysteriously seems to know everybody. This is the first episode in which Floyd appears. However, he is portrayed by Walter Baldwin, not Howard McNear. Written by Arthur Stander.

11. **The Christmas Story:** Scrooge-like Ben Weaver sees to it that Andy jails a man and his family, even though it is Christmas Eve. Written by David Adler.

12. **Ellie for Council:** Ellie runs for town council, the first time a woman has ever run for public office in Mayberry. Written by Jack Elinson and Charles Stewart.

13. **Mayberry Goes Hollywood:** A movie producer (Dan Frazer) is enchanted by Mayberry's small-town charm and decides to make a film there. Written by Benedict Freeman and John Fenton Murray.

14. **The Horse Trader:** Andy tries to get rid of the town's old cannon by stretching the truth about its history to an antique dealer. Written by Jack Elinson and Charles Stewart.

15. **Those Gossipin' Men:** A shoe salesman (Jack Finch) comes to town, and the menfolk mistake him for a talent scout and make fools of themselves. Written by Jack Elinson and Charles Stewart.

16. **Andy Saves Barney's Morale:** Barney arrests a number of the townspeople for minor offenses, and they refuse to take him seriously. Written by David Adler.

17. **Alcohol and Old Lace:** Andy and Barney have no idea that two sweet old ladies are brewing moonshine in their greenhouse. Written by Jack Elinson and Charles Stewart.

18. **Andy the Marriage Counselor:** Andy tries to make peace between an arguing husband (Jesse White) and his wife. Written by David Adler.

19. **Mayberry on Record:** When a record producer (Hugh Marlowe) tape records some of the local musicians, townsfolk convince him to publish an album. Written by Benedict Freeman and John Fenton Murray.

20. **The Beauty Contest:** Mayberry has a beauty contest, and it is up to Andy to judge the true beauty. Written by Jack Elinson and Charles Stewart.

21. **Andy and the Gentleman Crook:** A dapper criminal (Dan Tobin) butters up Barney, Opie, and Aunt Bee, while Andy remains wary of the conman's smooth-talking ways. Written by Ben Gershman and Leo Solomon.

Hugh Marlowe

Jesse White

22. **Cyrano Andy:** Andy pays a short visit to Thelma Lou to let her know how Barney feels about her. She then uses Andy to make Barney jealous. This is the first appearance of Thelma Lou. Written by Jack Elinson and Charles Stewart.

23. **Andy and Opie, Housekeepers:** Aunt Bee leaves Andy and Opie alone for a few days, and they make a mess of the house. After a neighbor cleans up, Andy realizes that Aunt Bee might feel as if she were not missed. Written by David Adler.

24. **The New Doctor:** A handsome new doctor (George Nader) sets up practice in Mayberry, and Andy thinks that Ellie and the physician have plans to marry. Written by Jack Elinson and Charles Stewart.

25. **A Plaque for Mayberry:** Someone in Mayberry is a direct descendant of a Revolutionary War hero, and Barney is confident that he's the one; instead, it turns out to be the town's most spirited citizen. Written by Ben Gershman and Leo Solomon.

26. **The Inspector:** A state official (Tod Andrews) observes Mayberry's lawmen in action and is astonished at Andy's old-fashioned methods. Written by Jack Elinson and Charles Stewart.

27. **Ellie Saves a Female:** Ellie turns a farm girl (Edris March) into a young beauty against her father's (R. G. Armstrong) wishes. Written by David Adler.

28. **Andy Forecloses:** Kind-hearted Andy must evict a struggling young family from one of Ben Weaver's houses. Written by Ben Gershman and Leo Solomon.

29. **Quiet Sam:** Barney suspects that a shy, secretive farmer (William Schallert) living just outside of Mayberry may be a criminal. Written by Jim Fritzell and Everett Greenbaum.

30. **Barney Gets His Man:** Barney accidentally captures a criminal who, vowing revenge, breaks loose and returns to Mayberry. Written by Ben Gershman and Leo Solomon.

George Nader

31. **The Guitar Player Returns:** Guitarist Jim Lindsey returns to his hometown bragging about his success, but Andy finds that Jim's career is not as prosperous as he makes it sound. This episode marks the last appearance of Ellie. Written by Jack Elinson and Charles Stewart.

32. **Bringing Up Opie:** Aunt Bee decides that the courthouse is not the proper environment for a young boy and forbids Opie from going to visit his father at work. Written by Jack Elinson and Charles Stewart.

33. **Barney's Replacement:** A lawyer (Mark Miller) interns as a deputy in Mayberry, and Barney gets the notion that Andy is going to replace him. Written by Jack Elinson and Charles Stewart.

34. **Opie and the Bully:** Opie faces up to a bully who is taking his milk money. Written by David Adler.

35. **Andy and the Woman Speeder:** Andy matches wits with a beautiful female speeder (Jean Hagen) as she tampers with the emotions of Floyd, Barney, and Opie, who are witnesses against her. Written by Jack Elinson and Charles Stewart.

36. **Barney on the Rebound:** Barney dates a beautiful new girl in town and becomes tangled in a breach-of-promise suit. Jackie Coogan guest stars. Written by Jack Elinson and Charles Stewart.

Edgar Buchanan

37. **The Perfect Female:** Andy dates Thelma Lou's cousin (Gail Davis) and tries to find out all he can about her before deciding to court. He discovers more than he expects at a shooting contest. Written by Jack Elinson and Charles Stewart.

38. **Aunt Bee's Brief Encounter:** A goldbricking handyman (Edgar Buchanan) sponges off the Taylors while courting Aunt Bee, but his intentions are not sincere. Doodles Weaver appears. Written by Ben Gershman and Leo Solomon.

Jackie Coogan

Andy Clyde

41. **Crime-free Mayberry:** An FBI agent comes to honor Andy and Barney because of the low crime rate in Mayberry. The agent is really a crook who has intentions of robbing the bank with his partner. Written by Paul Henning.

42. **The Clubmen:** Andy and Barney are invited to visit a posh men's club in Raleigh, but only Andy is asked to join. Written by Fred S. Fox and Iz Elinson.

39. **Mayberry Goes Bankrupt:** The town council begins to evict an old man (Andy Clyde) from his unkempt house until they discover he has a city bond and that the town owes him thousands of dollars. Written by Jack Elinson and Charles Stewart.

40. **Opie's Hobo Friend:** Opie befriends a drifter (Buddy Ebsen) whose shiftless ways begin to rub off on the boy. Written by Harvey Bullock.

Buddy Ebsen

43. **The Pickle Story:** Aunt Bee makes her horrible "kerosene cucumbers," much to the distaste of Andy, Barney, and Opie. Written by Harvey Bullock.

44. **Sheriff Barney:** After a nearby town offers Barney a job as sheriff, Andy lets Barney see what it's like to be sheriff for a day. Written by Ben Gershman and Leo Solomon.

45. **The Farmer Takes a Wife:** A farmer (Alan Hale, Jr.) comes to town looking for a wife and selects Barney's Thelma Lou. Written by Jack Elinson and Charles Stewart.

46. **The Keeper of the Flame:** Opie and his friends have a secret club that meets in a barn. When the barn

Doodles Weaver

Bill Bixby

burns down, Opie gets the blame. Everett Sloane, who wrote the lyrics to "The Fishin' Hole," guest stars. Written by Jack Elinson and Charles Stewart.

47. **Bailey's Bad Boy:** A spoiled, rich kid (Bill Bixby) is locked up by Andy for causing an accident. The teen-ager vows that his father will see that Andy loses his badge. Written by Ben Gershman and Leo Solomon.

48. **The Manicurist:** A beautiful manicurist (Barbara Eden) sets up in Floyd's Barbershop, and the women of Mayberry get jealous. Written by Jack Elinson and Charles Stewart.

49. **The Jinx:** The townspeople accuse a man (John Qualen) of being a jinx, and he eventually begins to believe it himself. Written by Jack Elinson and Charles Stewart.

50. **Jailbreak:** After Barney allows a criminal (Allan Melvin) to break out of the Mayberry jail, he and Andy must search the town for the man and his partner. Written by Harvey Bullock.

51. **A Medal for Opie:** Opie trains for the fifty-yard dash and learns a lesson about winning and losing. Written by David Adler.

52. **Barney and the Choir:** A vacancy pops open in the town choir, and sour-sounding Barney gleefully volunteers to fill it. Written by Jack Elinson and Charles Stewart.

53. **Guest of Honor:** Mayberry honors a man (Jay Novello) who is just passing through. After giving him the key to the city, Andy discovers the man is a pickpocket. Written by Jack Elinson and Charles Stewart.

54. **The Merchant of Mayberry:** Andy and Barney lend a helping hand to a door-to-door salesman (Sterling Holloway), thereby irritating department store owner Ben Weaver. Written by Ben Gershman and Leo Solomon.

55. **Aunt Bee the Warden:** Since the jail cells are full, Andy brings Otis home to serve his sentence, and Aunt Bee puts him to hard labor around the house. Written by Jack Elinson and Charles Stewart.

Barbara Eden

Michael Pollard

56. **The County Nurse:** Andy assists the county nurse as they try to persuade stubborn farmer Rafe Hollister to take his tetanus shot. Written by Jack Elinson and Charles Stewart.

57. **Andy and Barney in the Big City:** Andy and Barney visit Raleigh, where Barney gets tangled up with a jewel thief at a big hotel. Arte Johnson appears. Written by Harvey Bullock.

58. **Wedding Bells for Aunt Bee:** Because Aunt Bee believes she may be hurting Andy's chances of getting married, she allows the town laundryman to court her. Written by Harvey Bullock.

59. **Three's a Crowd:** Andy and the county nurse long to spend some time alone, but Barney keeps butting in. Written by Jack Elinson and Charles Stewart.

60. **The Bookie Barber:** Floyd realizes his dream of having a two-chair barbershop without realizing that his new barber (Herb Vigran) is really a bookie. Written by Ray Saffian Allen and Harvey Bullock.

61. **Andy on Trial:** A vengeful magazine publisher (Roy Roberts) sends a female reporter (Ruta Lee) to dig up some dirt on Andy. The result is a public hearing, with Andy's job on the line. Written by Jack Elinson and Charles Stewart.

62. **Cousin Virgil:** Barney's klutzy cousin (Michael Pollard) comes to visit. He fails at everything he tries, until Andy spies his real talent. Rance Howard appears. Written by Phillip Shuken and Johnny Greene.

63. **Deputy Otis:** Andy allows Otis to pose as a deputy in order that Otis can impress his visiting brother and sister-in-law. Written by Fred S. Fox and Iz Elinson.

64. **Opie's Rival:** Opie grows jealous of his father's courtship with a nurse and tries to break up the romance. Written by Sid Morse.

65. **Andy and Opie—Bachelors:** Andy's girlfriend, Peggy, cooks and tends for Andy and Opie while Aunt Bee is away. Andy then believes she has matrimony in mind and begins to avoid her. Written by Jim Fritzell and Everett Greenbaum.

66. **Mr. McBeevee:** Andy tries to get Opie to admit that a newfound friend (Karl Swenson) is imaginary. Written by Ray Saffian Allen and Harvey Bullock.

67. **Andy's Rich Girlfriend:** Andy quits courting Peggy when he fears that her wealthy background won't mesh with his simpler upbringing. Written by Jim Fritzell and Everett Greenbaum.

68. **Barney Mends a Broken Heart:** Andy and Peggy have a fight, and the well-meaning Barney sets up a blind

date with one of the "fun girls" from Mt. Pilot. This is the first appearance of the "fun girls." Written by Aaron Ruben.

69. **Andy and the New Mayor:** The new mayor doesn't approve of Andy's early release of a prisoner, so he keeps close tabs on Andy's work. Written by Harvey Bullock.

70. **The Cow Thief:** Cattle rustling strikes Mayberry, and the mayor sends for help from Raleigh because he doesn't believe Andy and Barney are capable of handling it. Malcolm Atterbury and Ralph Bell guest star. Writen by Ray Saffian Allen and Harvey Bullock.

71. **Floyd, the Gay Deceiver:** Floyd's pen pal (Doris Dowling) in a lonely hearts club comes to visit, and Andy helps deceive her by passing Floyd off as a wealthy widower. Written by Aaron Ruben.

72. **The Mayberry Band:** Since the mayor won't release funds for the sorry-sounding town band to make a visit to Raleigh, Andy smuggles jazz musicians into the group. Written by Jim Fritzell and Everett Greenbaum.

73. **Lawman Barney:** Barney has a tough time convincing two burly vegetable farmers that he represents the law and that they must move their vegetable stand. Written by Aaron Ruben.

74. **Convicts-at-Large:** Three female convicts hold Barney and Floyd hostage at a cabin near the lake. Reta Shaw, Jane Dulo, and Jean Carson guest star. Written by Jim Fritzell and Everett Greenbaum.

75. **The Bed Jacket:** Andy must trade his prized fishing pole to the mayor in order to obtain a bed jacket that Aunt Bee wants for her birthday. Written by Ray Saffian Allen and Harvey Bullock.

76. **Barney and the Governor:** After Barney tickets the governor's chauffeur (Rance Howard), the governor decides to pay him a visit. Written by Bill Freedman and Henry Sharp.

77. **Man in a Hurry:** Businessman Malcolm Tucker (Robert Emhardt) develops car trouble outside of town on a Sunday and can't get anyone to work on it. The slow pace of Mayberry frustrates him. Written by Jim Fritzell and Everett Greenbaum.

78. **The Bank Job:** Barney attempts to show the local banker how easily his bank could be robbed. Then real thieves decide to knock off the bank vault. Al Checco appears. Written by Jim Fritzell and Everett Greenbaum.

79. **One-Punch Opie:** When a new boy moves into town and stirs up trouble, Opie stands up to him, prepared to fight. Written by Harvey Bullock.

80. **High Noon in Mayberry:** An ex-convict (Leo Gordon) returns to Mayberry with "a little present" for Andy, who was responsible for putting him behind bars. Dub Taylor appears. Written by Jim Fritzell and Everett Greenbaum.

81. **The Loaded Goat:** Andy and Barney must figure out what to do with a goat that has eaten a bellyful of dynamite. Bing Russell appears. Written by Harvey Bullock.

82. **Class Reunion:** Andy and Barney organize a high school class reunion, and Andy wonders if his former sweetheart (Peggy McCay) will attend. Written by Jim Fritzell and Everett Greenbaum.

83. **Rafe Hollister Sings:** Earthy farmer Rafe Hollister enters the singing contest and winds up representing Mayberry. Written by Harvey Bullock.

84. **Opie and the Spoiled Kid:** A new kid in town, who is spoiled rotten, gives Opie some pointers on how to get a bigger allowance. Written by Jim Fritzell and Everett Greenbaum.

85. **The Great Filling Station Robbery:** A young man is accused of breaking into Wally's garage and stealing supplies. Andy must figure out who the culprit really is. Written by Harvey Bullock.

86. **Andy Discovers America:** Andy gets in hot water with Opie's schoolteacher when he criticizes her history curriculum in front of Opie and his pals. This is the first appearance of Helen Crump. Written by John Whedon.

87. **Aunt Bee's Medicine Man:** Aunt Bee plays hostess to a traveling medicine man (John Dehner) who sells an alcoholic Indian elixir. Written by John Whedon.

88. **The Darlings Are Coming:** When a mountain family comes down to Mayberry to meet a friend, the daughter develops a crush on Andy. This is the first appearance of the Darlings. Written by Jim Fritzell and Everett Greenbaum.

89. **Andy's English Valet:** An Englishman bicycling across America runs up a small fine in Mayberry and can't pay. Andy allows him to work it off by serving as a handyman at his house. Written by Harvey Bullock.

90. **Barney's First Car:** Barney buys a lemon from a crooked, little old lady (Ellen Corby). Written by Jim Fritzell and Everett Greenbaum.

91. **The Rivals:** Thelma Lou shows Opie a little special attention when he fails at romance, and Barney gets jealous. Written by Harvey Bullock.

92. **A Wife for Andy:** Barney worries because Andy doesn't have a wife and Opie doesn't have a mother. He then tries to set Andy up with every available female in town. Written by Aaron Ruben.

93. **Dogs, Dogs, Dogs:** Opie brings a dog into the courthouse, and ten more canines follow. Andy and Barney must find them homes. Written by Jim Fritzell and Everett Greenbaum.

94. **Mountain Wedding:** Mountain wild man, Ernest T. Bass, refuses to honor the marriage of Charlene Darling to Dud Wash. He gets one last chance to woo her. This is the first appearance of Ernest T. Bass. Dub Taylor appears. Written by Jim Fritzell and Everett Greenbaum.

John Dehner

95. **The Big House:** Two prisoners are temporarily housed in the Mayberry jail. As Barney teaches them about life at "the rock," they escape. George Kennedy appears. Written by Harvey Bullock.

96. **Briscoe Declares for Aunt Bee:** Mountain patriarch Briscoe Darling decides to court Aunt Bee, who wants nothing to do with him. Written by Jim Fritzell and Everett Greenbaum.

97. **Gomer the House Guest:** Gomer loses his job at the filling station and moves in with the Taylors while trying to find another job. Written by Jim Fritzell and Everett Greenbaum.

98. **The Haunted House:** After Opie loses his baseball in the town's haunted house, Andy, Barney, and Gomer go to explore its legends. Written by Harvey Bullock.

99. **Ernest T. Bass Joins the Army:** Ernest T. Bass tries to join the Army because he wants a uniform. Written by Jim Fritzell and Everett Greenbaum.

100. **Sermon for Today:** A visiting preacher (David Lewis) urges Mayberrians to slow down and take it easy. Andy, Barney, Aunt Bee, and friends then wear themselves out preparing for a relaxing band concert. Written by John Whedon.

101. **Opie the Birdman:** Opie accidentally kills a mother songbird and bears the responsibility of rearing her three young birds. Written by Harvey Bullock.

102. **A Black Day for Mayberry:** A gold shipment is scheduled to pass quietly through Mayberry, but after Barney spills the beans, the townspeople make the event a festive occasion. Rance Howard and Doodles Weaver appear. Written by John Whedon.

103. **Opie's Ill-Gotten Gain:** Because of his teacher's error, Opie gets all *A*s on his report card and Andy rewards him with a new bicycle. Written by John Whedon.

104. **Up in Barney's Room:** Barney is evicted from his apartment and tries to make up with his landlady, Mrs. Mendelbright. J. Pat O'Malley appears. Written by Jim Fritzell and Everett Greenbaum.

105. **A Date for Gomer:** Gomer takes his first fling at romance as he goes on a date with Thelma Lou's cousin (Mary Grace Canfield). Written by Jim Fritzell and Everett Greenbaum.

106. **Citizen's Arrest:** Barney jails himself after Gomer accuses him of making an illegal U-turn. Written by Jim Fritzell and Everett Greenbaum.

107. **Gomer Pyle, U.S.M.C.:** Gomer leaves Mayberry to enter the Marines, and Andy takes him to boot camp to see how he adjusts. Frank Sutton guest stars. Written by Aaron Ruben.

108. **Opie and His Merry Men:** Opie and his pals befriend a lazy hobo who tells them that lawmen cannot be trusted. Written by John Whedon.

109. **Barney and the Cave Rescue:** Andy and Helen are trapped in a cave. Barney heads up the rescue effort. Written by Harvey Bullock.

110. **Andy and Opie's Pal:** Opie gets jealous when Andy pays special attention to Opie's new friend. Written by Harvey Bullock.

111. **Aunt Bee the Crusader:** Aunt Bee is at odds with Andy as she drums up

support for a local farmer (Charles Lane) who is being evicted from his property. Written by John Whedon.

112. **Barney's Sidecar:** Barney adds a motorcycle and sidecar to the squad's rolling stock and endangers the lives and sanity of everyone in Mayberry. Written by Jim Fritzell and Everett Greenbaum.

113. **My Fair Ernest T. Bass:** Andy tries to pass Ernest T. Bass off as his suave, sophisticated cousin at a high society party. Doris Packer and Jackie Joseph appear. Written by Jim Fritzell and Everett Greenbaum.

114. **Prisoner of Love:** A female jewel thief (Susan Oliver) pulls at Andy and Barney's heartstrings while she is locked in the Mayberry jail. Written by Harvey Bullock.

115. **Hot Rod Otis:** Otis buys a car, and Andy and Barney fear the streets of Mayberry may become a disaster zone. (Andy, Barney, and Otis are the only characters who appear in this episode.) Written by Harvey Bullock.

116. **The Song Festers:** Barney prepares to sing solo in the town choir until it is discovered that Gomer has a beautiful voice. Barbara Griffith and Reta Shaw appear. Written by Jim Fritzell and Everett Greenbaum.

117. **The Shoplifters:** Because Weaver's Department Store is being robbed blind, Barney goes into action, not only investigating at night, but also posing as a manikin during the day. Lurene Tuttle appears. Written by Bill Idelson and Sam Bobrick.

118. **Andy's Vacation:** Andy takes a week off to relax, but Barney keeps butting in with trivial matters. Andy fi-

nally heads for the mountains, not knowing Barney has allowed a prisoner to escape. Written by Jim Fritzell and Everett Greenbaum.

119. **Andy Saves Gomer:** Believing that Andy has saved his life, Gomer tries to show his gratitude to Andy, but actually proves to be a nuisance. Written by Harvey Bullock.

120. **Bargain Day:** Aunt Bee buys a side of beef to save money, but her old freezer conks out, causing much consternation. Written by John Whedon.

121. **Divorce, Mountain Style:** Charlene Darling Wash leaves her husband (Bob Denver) in the mountains and comes to Mayberry hoping to snare Sheriff Taylor as her new hubby. Written by Jim Fritzell and Everett Greenbaum.

122. **A Deal Is a Deal:** Opie and his friends get stuck with selling worthless salve, but Barney and Gomer have a plan. Written by Bill Idelson and Sam Bobrick.

123. **Fun Girls:** Helen and Thelma Lou spot Andy and Barney with the "fun

Reta Shaw

girls" from Mt. Pilot and jump to conclusions. This is the only episode featuring both Gomer and Goober. Written by Aaron Ruben.

124. **The Return of Malcolm Merriweather:** The Englishman returns to Mayberry and works around the Taylor house, making Aunt Bee feel she is no longer needed. Written by Harvey Bullock.

125. **The Rumor:** Barney starts a rumor that Andy and Helen are going to be married. He, Thelma Lou, and Aunt Bee plan a huge surprise party for the couple. Rance Howard appears. Written by Jim Fritzell and Everett Greenbaum.

126. **Barney and Thelma Lou, Phfftt:** Thelma Lou finds out that Barney thinks he's got her in his hip pocket. She uses Gomer to make Barney jealous. Written by Bill Idelson and Sam Bobrick.

127. **Back to Nature:** Andy, Barney and Gomer take Opie and his friends camping, and Barney and Gomer promptly get lost. Written by Harvey Bullock.

(Courtesy Rance Howard)

Rance Howard

128. **Barney's Bloodhound:** Barney adds a bloodhound to the Mayberry police staff, but the dog is actually a harmless mutt. Arthur Batanides guest stars. Written by Bill Idelson and Sam Bobrick.

129. **Family Visit:** Relatives (James Westerfield and Maudie Prickett) of the Taylors' come to visit and more than wear out their welcome. Written by Jim Fritzell and Everett Greenbaum.

130. **Aunt Bee's Romance:** An old friend (Wallace Ford) of Bee's comes a-courting. He proves to be a bore, and Andy can't stand the idea that his aunt just might marry him. Written by Harvey Bullock.

131. **Barney's Physical:** In order to pass his physical, Barney must gain a few pounds and add an inch to his height. Aunt Bee feeds him some gargantuan meals, while Andy stretches him. Written by Bob Ross.

132. **Opie Loves Helen:** Opie develops a big crush on his schoolteacher, Miss Crump. Written by Bob Ross.

133. **The Education of Ernest T. Bass:** Ernest T. Bass wants a diploma to impress his girl back in the mountains, so Andy becomes his tutor. Written by Jim Fritzell and Everett Greenbaum.

134. **Man in the Middle:** When Barney and Thelma Lou have a lovers' quarrel, Andy tries to patch things up, but not before he and Helen are drawn into the maelstrom. Written by Gus Adrian and David Evans.

135. **Barney's Uniform:** A town bully (Allan Melvin) threatens to beat Barney to a pulp if he ever catches him out of uniform. Written by Bill Idelson and Sam Bobrick.

136. **Opie's Fortune:** Opie finds a wallet with $50 in it and must wait one week to see if the owner will return to claim it. Written by Ben Joelson and Art Baer.

137. **Goodbye, Sheriff Taylor:** Andy considers taking a job in Raleigh and leaves Barney in charge of the town for a day of chaotic events. Written by Fred Freeman and Lawrence J. Cohen.

138. **The Pageant:** Aunt Bee tries out for the lead role as Lady Mayberry in the town's Centennial Pageant. Written by Harvey Bullock.

139. **The Darling Baby:** The Darling clan comes to town searching for a young boy to betroth to Charlene's baby girl. Written by Jim Fritzell and Everett Greenbaum.

140. **Andy and Helen Have Their Day:** Andy and Helen plan to have a quiet day of picnicking at the lake, but Barney keeps popping up with insignificant problems. Howard Morris appears. Written by Bill Idelson and Sam Bobrick.

141. **Otis Sues the County:** Otis slips and falls in the courthouse, and an unscrupulous lawyer (Jay Novello) coaxes him into suing the county. Written by Bob Ross.

142. **Three Wishes for Opie:** Barney buys fortune-telling cards and a magic lamp, and Opie is granted three wishes. Written by Richard M. Powell.

143. **Barney Fife, Realtor:** Barney goes into the real estate business and persuades Andy to put his house on the market. Written by Bill Idelson and Sam Bobrick.

Larry Hovis

144. **Goober Takes a Car Apart:** Goober takes a car apart and puts it back together inside the courthouse, much to Andy's disbelief. Larry Hovis guest stars. Written by Bill Idelson and Sam Bobrick.

145. **The Rehabilitation of Otis:** Barney attempts to use psychology on Otis to help control his drinking problem and winds up driving him out of town and losing his friendship. Frank Cady appears. Written by Fred Freeman and Lawrence J. Cohen.

146. **The Lucky Letter:** Barney must qualify at the shooting range to keep his job, but he thinks fate is against him because he threw away a chain letter. Written by Richard M. Powell.

147. **Goober and the Art of Love:** Barney and Andy help Goober find a girl. Barney then teaches Goober how to court a girl. Written by Fred Freeman and Lawrence J. Cohen.

148. **Barney Runs for Sheriff:** Andy doesn't file in time for the election, so Barney heads up a write-in campaign for Andy, even though Barney is himself running for sheriff against Andy. Written by Richard M. Powell.

149. **If I Had a Quarter Million:** Barney finds $250,000 that a crook (Al Checco) tossed off a train and uses it as bait to trap the criminal. Written by Bob Ross.

150. **TV or Not TV:** Phony Hollywood filmmakers (Gavin MacLeod and Barbara Stuart) come to Mayberry to study the famous "Sheriff Without a Gun." In reality, they're staking out the bank for a robbery. Written by Ben Joelson and Art Baer.

151. **Guest in the House:** Helen becomes jealous when a pretty friend (Jan Shutan) of the Taylors' spends several nights at the Taylor house. Written by Fred Freeman and Lawrence J. Cohen.

152. **The Case of the Punch in the Nose:** Barney reopens an old wound between Floyd and Charlie Foley, and the whole town takes sides, with nose punches flying all around. Written by Bill Idelson and Sam Bobrick.

153. **Opie's Newspaper:** Opie and a chum put out a small paper, but it is full of gossip that the boys have overheard from Andy, Barney, and Aunt Bee. Written by Harvey Bullock.

154. **Aunt Bee's Invisible Beau:** Aunt Bee fabricates a romance with the Taylors' butter-and-egg man, but Andy finds out the man is married. Bobby Diamond appears. Written by Ben Joelson and Art Baer.

155. **The Arrest of the Fun Girls:** Andy and Barney arrest the "fun girls" for speeding. It turns out to be a big mistake because Helen and Thelma Lou become jealous. Written by Richard M. Powell.

156. **The Luck of Newton Monroe:** An inept peddler (Don Rickles) comes to

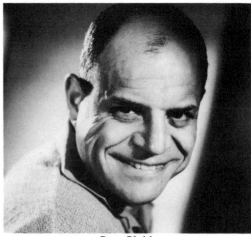

Don Rickles

town, and Barney gives him a few jobs around the jail. The man bungles them all. Written by Bill Idelson and Sam Bobrick.

157. **Opie Flunks Arithmetic:** Opie gets a low grade in math, and Andy forces him to study continuously, which only makes Opie do worse. Written by Richard Morgan.

158. **Opie and the Carnival:** Not knowing that the operators of the booth have rigged the guns, Opie tries to win a prize for his dad at a shooting gallery at the carnival. Billy Halop appears. Written by Fred Freeman and Lawrence J. Cohen.

159. **Banjo-Playing Deputy:** Andy tries to help an out-of-work banjo player (Jerry Van Dyke) by making him a temporary deputy. Lee Van Cleef and Herbie Faye appear. Written by Rob Ross.

160. **Aunt Bee, the Swinger:** Aunt Bee and a beau (Charles Ruggles) experience a whirlwind romance, but neither will admit to the other that the pace is much too quick. This is the first color episode. Written by Jack Elinson.

Charles Ruggles

161. **Opie's Job:** Opie and another boy compete for a job as delivery boy at a grocery store. Norris Goff appears. Written by Ben Joelson and Art Baer.

162. **The Bazaar:** Deputy Warren Ferguson arrests Aunt Bee and her friends for operating a bingo game at the charity bazaar. This is the first appearance of Warren. Written by Ben Joelson and Art Baer.

163. **Andy's Rival:** A handsome teacher (Charles Aidman) works with Helen

Jerry Van Dyke

on a school project, and Andy becomes jealous. Written by Laurence Marks.

164. **Malcolm at the Crossroads:** Ernest T. Bass and Malcolm Merriweather nearly come to blows over the job of manning the school crosswalk. Written by Harvey Bullock.

165. **Aunt Bee on TV:** Aunt Bee wins lots of prizes on a TV game show, but her friends tire of her talking about the gifts. Jack Smith and William Christopher appear. Written by Fred Freeman and Lawrence J. Cohen.

166. **Off to Hollywood:** When Andy receives $1,000 for the rights to make a movie about his career, the Taylors decide to take a trip to Hollywood. Written by Bill Idelson and Sam Bobrick.

167. **Taylors in Hollywood:** Andy, Opie, and Aunt Bee visit Hollywood and watch the production of *The Sheriff Without a Gun*. Gavin MacLeod and Hayden Rorke guest star. Written by Bill Idelson and Sam Bobrick.

168. **Hollywood Party:** Promotion pictures of Andy with a beautiful actress (Ruta Lee) reach Mayberry, and Helen grows jealous. Andy gets mad and dates the actress. Sid Melton and Herb Vigran appear. Written by Fred Freeman and Lawrence J. Cohen.

169. **A Warning from Warren:** Believing he has the power of ESP, Warren Ferguson makes things miserable for Andy and Helen. Written by Fred Freeman and Lawrence J. Cohen.

170. **A Man's Best Friend:** Opie and a friend put a walkie-talkie under a dog's collar and succeed in making Goober believe that the dog can talk. Written by Ben Joelson and Art Baer.

171. **Aunt Bee Takes a Job:** Not knowing that her employers are counterfeiters, Aunt Bee takes a job as a receptionist at a printing shop. James Millhollin, Milton Frome, and Herbie Faye appear. Written by Bill Idelson and Sam Bobrick.

172. **The Cannon:** The town cannon proves useful to Warren when thieves plan to rob the State Mobile Museum during its stop in Mayberry. Written by Jack Elinson.

173. **Girl-Shy:** Warren is shy with females except when he sleepwalks. As a somnambulist, he attempts to woo an astonished Helen Crump. Written by Bill Idelson and Sam Bobrick.

174. **The Church Organ:** The church organ goes kaput, and Andy locates one that would be just perfect. Unfortunately, the church can't afford it. Written by Paul Wayne.

175. **Otis the Artist:** Warren tries to divert Otis's attention from strong drinking by showing him how to work with mosaics. Written by Fred Freeman and Lawrence J. Cohen; story by Bob Ross.

176. **The Return of Barney Fife:** Andy and Barney attend their high school class reunion, and Barney has high hopes of rekindling his romance with Thelma Lou, who, like him, no longer lives in Mayberry. This is the final appearance of Thelma Lou. Written by Bill Idelson and Sam Bobrick.

177. **The Legend of Barney Fife:** Warren finally gets to meet his hero, Barney Fife. They team up to pursue an escaped criminal who is seeking revenge against Barney. Frank Cady appears. Written by Harvey Bullock.

178. **Lost and Found:** Aunt Bee loses a valuable piece of jewelry, receives the insurance money, and then discovers she still has the jewelry. Jack Dodson makes his first appearance as an insurance agent, not as Howard Sprague. Written by John L. Greene and Paul David.

179. **Wyatt Earp Rides Again:** A Wild West show comes to town featuring a man (Richard Jury) who claims to be the great-nephew of Wyatt Earp. The boastful Earp and his promoter (Pat Hingle) challenge Andy to a duel at high noon. Written by Jack Elinson.

180. **Aunt Bee Learns to Drive:** Goober teaches Aunt Bee how to drive. Andy worries. Written by Jack Elinson.

181. **Look Paw, I'm Dancing:** Andy helps Opie overcome his fear of making a clod of himself at the school dance. Written by Ben Starr.

182. **Eat Your Heart Out:** Goober falls for diner waitress Flora, but she has fallen for Andy. Written by Ben Joelson and Art Baer.

Pat Hingle

183. **The Gypsies:** A family of gypsies (Jamie Farr and Vito Scotti) camps near Mayberry and peddles cheap trinkets. When Andy tells them to move along, they put a curse on the town. Written by Roland MacLane.

184. **A Baby in the House:** Aunt Bee agrees to babysit for her niece, but the infant cries whenever Bee picks her up. Alvy Moore appears. Written by Bill Idelson and Sam Bobrick.

185. **The County Clerk:** Andy and Helen play matchmaker for Howard Sprague, but Howard's mother disapproves. This is the first appearance of Howard Sprague. Written by Bill Idelson and Sam Bobrick.

186. **Goober's Replacement:** Goober's girl, Flora, proves to be an able replacement for him at the station as Wally sells more gasoline than ever because of his attractive attendant. Written by Stan Dreben and Howard Merrill.

187. **The Foster Lady:** Aunt Bee becomes the Foster Furniture Polish lady and begins taping a series of commer-

Alvy Moore

cials. Ronnie Schell and Robert Emhardt guest star. Written by Jack Elinson and Iz Elinson.

188. **The Battle of Mayberry:** Mayberry's citizens have long been proud of the Battle of Mayberry; the true story is then revealed. Norm Alden appears. Written by John L. Greene and Paul David.

189. **A Singer in Town:** A pop singer (Jesse Pearson) vacations in Mayberry, and Aunt Bee and Clara pitch him a song that they have written. Written by Stan Dreben and Howard Merrill.

190. **Opie's Girlfriend:** Helen's niece visits with Opie and appears to be a better athlete. The result is a battle of the sexes. Written by Budd Grossman.

191. **The Barbershop Quartet:** Mayberry's barbershop quartet needs a substitute when Howard comes down with a sore throat. The best candidate is a chicken thief, but Andy doesn't know if he can trust him. Written by Fred S. Fox.

Ronnie Schell

192. **The Lodge:** Howard wants to join the men's lodge in town, but one of the members mysteriously blackballs him. Written by Jim Parker and Arnold Margolin.

193. **The Darling Fortune:** The Darlings come searching for wives, and the "Omen of the Owl" picks Helen to be a Darling bride. This is the last appearance of the Darlings. Written by Jim Parker and Arnold Margolin.

194. **Aunt Bee's Crowning Glory:** A visiting pastor (Ian Wolfe) enjoys the company of Aunt Bee; she doesn't know how to tell him she's been wearing a wig. Written by Ronald Axe.

195. **The Ball Game:** Opie and his team play Mt. Pilot for the district baseball championship, and Andy is selected to umpire the game. Teleplay by Sid Morse; story by Rance Howard.

196. **Goober Makes History:** Goober grows a beard and begins to believe that he's an intellectual; he actually bores everyone. Written by John L. Greene and Paul David.

197. **The Senior Play:** Helen and Mayberry High's senior class want to produce a controversial senior play, but the principal (Leon Ames) is firmly against it. Written by Sid Morse.

198. **Big Fish in a Small Town:** It's opening day of fishing season, and everybody hopes to catch Old Sam, the lake's legendary silver carp. Written by Bill Idelson and Sam Bobrick.

199. **Mind Over Matter:** Goober is in a minor auto accident, but his hypochondria makes him believe that he has been terribly injured. Written by Ron Friedman and Pat McCormick.

200. **Politics Begins at Home:** Aunt Bee decides to run for a seat on the town council, while Andy has already volunteered to back Howard Sprague. Written by Fred S. Fox.

201. **A New Doctor in Town:** A new young doctor (William Christopher) arrives in Mayberry, and nobody wants to be the first patient. Written by Ray Brenner and Barry Blitzer.

202. **Opie Finds a Baby:** Opie and Arnold find a baby on the doorsteps of the courthouse and try to keep it a secret from their fathers. Jack Nicholson appears. Written by Stan Dreben and Sid Mandel.

203. **Only a Rose:** Aunt Bee grows a beautiful rose for the Garden Club contest, and Opie accidentally destroys it. Written by Jim Parker and Arnold Margolin.

204. **Otis the Deputy:** Andy is captured by two bank robbers back in the hills, and Otis and Howard come to the rescue. Written by Jim Parker and Arnold Margolin.

205. **Don't Miss a Good Bet:** A stranger comes to town claiming to have a

Leon Ames

map to the lost Ross Raiders treasure, and a few of the townspeople offer financial backing. Written by Fred S. Fox.

206. **Dinner at Eight:** Goober mixes up some messages, and Andy winds up eating three spaghetti dinners on the same evening. Written by Budd Grossman.

207. **Andy's Old Girlfriend:** Andy's high school sweetheart (Joanna McNeil) moves back to town, and Helen becomes jealous during an overnight camping trip. Written by Sid Morse.

208. **The Statue:** The townspeople decide to build a statue to Seth Taylor, not realizing that he actually helped swindle their forefathers. Dal McKennon guest stars. Written by Fred S. Fox.

209. **Aunt Bee's Restaurant:** Aunt Bee opens a Chinese restaurant in Mayberry. Keye Luke appears. Written by Ronald Axe and Les Roberts.

210. **Floyd's Barbershop:** Howard purchases Floyd's Barbershop from the owners and raises Floyd's rent. Dave Ketchum appears. Written by Jim Parker and Arnold Margolin.

211. **A Visit to Barney Fife:** Andy visits Barney in Raleigh, and they attempt to solve a series of supermarket robberies. Written by Bill Idelson and Sam Bobrick.

212. **Barney Comes to Mayberry:** Barney comes home for a vacation and winds up as escort to an old girlfriend (Diahn Williams) who has become a famous movie starlet. Written by Sid Morse.

213. **Helen, the Authoress:** Helen writes a children's book, and a publisher accepts it. Andy becomes jealous. Written by Doug Tibbles.

Dal McKennon

214. **Goodbye Dolly:** Opie cares for a horse while its owner is on vacation, but for some reason the horse refuses to eat. Written by Michael Morris and Seaman Jacobs.

215. **Opie's Piano Lesson:** Opie eagerly begins taking piano lessons after school. An ex-pro quarterback then comes to coach the boys' football team, leaving Opie in a predicament. Written by Leo and Pauline Townsend.

216. **Howard, the Comedian:** Howard becomes an instant celebrity after he tells jokes on an amateur television show, but the homefolks believe he is making fun of them. Dick Haymes appears. Written by Michael Morris and Seaman Jacobs.

217. **Big Brother:** Howard becomes a Big Brother to a high school boy and promptly falls in love with the boy's older sister (Elizabeth MacRae). Peter Hobbs appears. Written by Fred S. Fox.

218. **Opie's Most Unforgettable Character:** Opie has a tough time writing a school paper on his most unforgettable character. Written by Michael Morris and Seaman Jacobs.

219. **Goober's Contest:** Goober holds a money-giveaway contest at Wally's station, and Floyd wins a $200 cash prize. This is Floyd's last appearance. Rob Reiner appears. Written by Ron Friedman and Pat McCormick.

Rob Reiner

220. **Opie's First Love:** Opie is excited about his first date with Mary Alice Carter (Morgan Brittany), but she drops him at the last second for the class heartthrob. Written by Douglas Tibbles.

221. **Goober the Executive:** Goober buys Wally's station and must learn to make decisions for himself. Bo Hopkins and Dave Ketchum appear. This is the first appearance of Emmett Clark. Written by Michael Morris and Seaman Jacobs.

222. **Howard's Main Event:** Howard begins dating Millie Hutchins, but her ex-boyfriend (Allan Melvin) shows up and threatens to beat up Howard. Written by Robert C. Dennis and Earl Barret.

223. **Aunt Bee the Juror:** Aunt Bee serves on a jury and is the only juror to believe that the man (Jack Nicholson) accused of burglary is innocent. Written by Kent Wilson.

224. **Howard the Bowler:** Howard subs on the Mayberry bowling team and has a perfect game going when the lights go out. Norm Alden appears. Written by Dick Bensfield and Perry Grant.

225. **Opie Steps Up in Class:** Opie goes to summer camp and makes friends with a rich boy. Andy and Aunt Bee then try to impress the boy's parents. Joyce Van Patten guest stars. Written by Joe Bonaduce.

226. **Andy's Trip to Raleigh:** Helen is jealous when Andy tries to hide the fact that he spent the weekend with a female lawyer (Whitney Blake) in Raleigh. Written by Joe Bonaduce.

227. **A Trip to Mexico:** Aunt Bee wins a trip to Mexico and takes friends Clara and Myrtle with her. Jose Gonzalez-Gonzalez appears. Written by Dick Bensfield and Perry Grant.

228. **The Tape Recorder:** After taping a private conversation between a bank

Whitney Blake

robber (Herbie Faye) and his lawyer, Opie and Arnold learn the location of the stolen money. Written by Michael Morris and Seaman Jacobs.

229. **Opie's Group:** Opie joins his friends' rock 'n' roll band, while Aunt Bee and Andy worry about how it may affect him. Written by Doug Tibbles.

230. **Aunt Bee and the Lecturer:** A lecturer (Edward Andrews) who is visiting Mayberry is attracted to Aunt Bee because she reminds him of his late wife. Written by Michael Morris and Seaman Jacobs.

Jack Albertson

Edward Andrews

231. **Andy's Investment:** Andy tries to earn money for Opie's college education by running a laundromat. Written by Michael Morris and Seaman Jacobs.

232. **Suppose Andy Gets Sick:** When Andy gets ill, Goober becomes deputy and chaos erupts. Written by Jack Raymond.

233. **Howard and Millie:** Howard Sprague and Millie Hutchins become engaged and then get into a series of

spats. Written by Joe Bonaduce.

234. **Aunt Bee's Cousin:** Bee's seemingly prosperous cousin (Jack Albertson) comes to visit, and Andy discovers that the man is not really so successful. Ann Morgan Guilbert appears. Written by Dick Bensfield and Perry Grant.

235. **Howard's New Life:** Howard leaves the world of Mayberry behind when he takes off for a new life in the Caribbean. Harry Dean Stanton appears. Written by Dick Bensfield and Perry Grant.

236. **Emmett's Brother-in-Law:** Emmett's successful brother-in-law (Dub Taylor) tries to get Emmett into the insurance business, but Emmett hates to leave the Fix-It Shop. Written by James L. Brooks.

237. **The Mayberry Chef:** Aunt Bee hosts a live cooking show for the TV station in Siler City, while Andy and Opie must make do for themselves at suppertime. Jack Bannon appears. Written by James L. Brooks.

238. **The Church Benefactors:** The church members must decide

whether to spend money on new church robes or on structural repairs for the church. Written by Robert C. Dennis and Earl Barret.

239. **Opie's Drugstore Job:** Opie takes a job at the drugstore and accidentally breaks an expensive bottle of perfume while the owner is away. Written by Kent Wilson.

240. **Barney Hosts a Summit Meeting:** Barney must find just the right house in Mayberry for a summit meeting between Russian and American diplomats. In a tight spot, Barney asks Andy if they can use the Taylor house. Paul Fix appears. Written by Aaron Ruben.

241. **Mayberry R.F.D.:** Farmer Sam Jones invites an Italian friend to come work for him, not knowing that the young man is bringing his family with him. Written by Bob Ross.

242. **Goober Goes to the Auto Show:** Goober meets an old friend (Noam Pitlik) at an auto show in Raleigh, and the friend makes Goober feel like he has not made a success of his life. Howard Hesseman appears. Written by Joe Bonaduce.

243. **Aunt Bee's Big Moment:** Believing that life has passed her by, Aunt Bee decides to take flying lessons, much to Andy's dismay. Written by Dick Bensfield and Perry Grant.

244. **Helen's Past:** Andy accidentally discovers that Helen was once arrested in Kansas City. Once the story gets out, her teaching position is endangered. Peter Hobbs appears. Written by Doug Tibbles.

245. **Emmett's Anniversary:** Emmett struggles with the decision of whether or not to buy his wife an expensive fur for their wedding anniversary. Ronnie Schell guest stars.

Teri Garr

Written by Dick Bensfield and Perry Grant.

246. **The Wedding:** After Howard Sprague's mother remarries, he remodels his house into a swinging bachelor pad and hosts a party. Teri Garr makes a cameo appearance. Written by Joe Bonaduce.

247. **Sam For Town Council:** Farmer Sam Jones runs against Emmett for a seat on the town council. Howard Hesseman appears. Written by Dick Bensfield and Perry Grant.

248. **Opie and Mike:** After helping a young boy deal with a bully, Opie must then cope with the problem of hero worship. Written by Doug Tibbles.

249. **A Girl for Goober:** Goober tries computer dating and winds up taking out a woman (Nancy Malone) who holds a Ph.D. Tod Andrews and Margaret Ann Peterson appear. Teleplay by Bruce Howard; story by Bob Ross.

Top Twenty Episodes

The following are two lists of what some Mayberry fans have voted to be the best episodes of "The Andy Griffith Show." The first list is based on a 1983 poll conducted among members of "The Andy Griffith Show" Rerun Watchers Club, and the second list shows the results of a 1994 poll of TAGSRWC members.

While these rankings are representative of the show's best episodes, there are, of course, many more episodes that could easily be considered among the twenty best. The difficulty in selecting "The Andy Griffith Show" top twenty demonstrates how consistently superb the show is:

1983 Poll

1. **Man in a Hurry** (episode 77)
2. **Barney's Sidecar** (episode 112)
3. **Sermon for Today** (episode 100)
4. **Goober and the Art of Love** (episode 147)
5. **Dogs, Dogs, Dogs** (episode 93)
6. **Opie the Birdman** (episode 101)
7. **My Fair Ernest T. Bass** (episode 113)
8. **The Pickle Story** (episode 43)
9. **The Christmas Story** (episode 11)
10. **Fun Girls** (episode 123)
11. **Citizen's Arrest** (episode 106)
12. **The Darlings Are Coming** (episode 88)
13. **Big Fish in a Small Town** (episode 198)
14. **Class Reunion** (episode 82)
15. **Mountain Wedding** (episode 94)
16. **Gomer the House Guest** (episode 97)
17. **The New Housekeeper** (episode 1)
18. **Convicts-at-Large** (episode 74)
19. **Mr. McBeevee** (episode 66)
20. **Stranger in Town** (episode 10)

1994 Poll

1. **Man in a Hurry** (episode 77)
2. **The Pickle Story** (episode 43)
3. **Convicts-at-Large** (episode 74)
4. **Mountain Wedding** (episode 94)
5. **Opie the Birdman** (episode 101)
6. **Barney's First Car** (episode 90)
7. **Barney and the Choir** (episode 52)
8. **Sermon for Today** (episode 100)
9. **Citizen's Arrest** (episode 106)
10. **The Christmas Story** (episode 11)
11. **Three Wishes for Opie** (episode 142)
12. **Barney's Sidecar** (episode 112)
13. **The Haunted House** (episode 98)
14. **Dogs, Dogs, Dogs** (episode 93)
15. **The New Housekeeper** (episode 1)
16. **Goober and the Art of Love** (episode 147)
17. **The Education of Ernest T. Bass** (episode 133)
18. **Mr. McBeevee** (episode 66)
19. **A Date for Gomer** (episode 105)
20. **Class Reunion** (episode 82)

Mayberry Memories

"Andy Griffith Show" fans agree—Mayberry is a most memorable town. We love watching it and we love talking about it. We wish we lived there. Many of us have grown up watching the show, and in a way, we are all naturalized citizens of Mayberry. But, if it were possible, if someone such as Count Istvan Teleky granted us a single wish, wouldn't it be wonderful to enter the television set and spend a day in Mayberry? How would we spend those precious hours on our visit?

Well, it'd be nice to start out at breakfast with a piping hot cup of coffee in Aunt Bee's kitchen—maybe served with a couple of fried eggs, sunny-side up, and bacon. Of course, we'd love to have a couple of homemade biscuits and blackberry jelly, too, but we'll pass on the marmalade.

Then, we'd cruise down to the courthouse in the squad car with Barney and Andy. Barney would already have more coffee simmering in the backroom, and we'd all share another cup apiece before starting the regular chores. We might meet Otis just as he

was letting himself out of his cell.

At about 10:00 A.M. or so, we'd walk next door to the barbershop and see what Floyd was up to. If business was slow, we'd come back outside and sit a spell on the bench, enjoying the warm sun. Howard Sprague might pop out of his office during his mid-morning break and say hello. Little Leon might walk by. Naturally, he'd offer us a bite from his peanut butter and jelly sandwich, but "No thanks, Leon."

A little while later, we'd drive down to Wally's Service Station and have Goober fill 'er up. Of course, Goober would check the air and oil also. Then he might ask if we wanted to catch a John Wayne movie later during the week at the picture show in Mt. Pilot.

We'd drive back into town and go on patrol with Andy while Barney held down the fort. By the time we got back to the courthouse, Barney would be locked in the cell and Andy would have to get the key and let him out, but not before a little good-natured ribbing took place. Barney would get riled up for a short while, but then he'd simmer down. Later, he'd call Juanita up and chitchat for a few minutes. Of course, we'd all know Sarah was listening in the whole time. Then at noon we'd all walk down the street and order the special at the Bluebird Diner and Barney would flirt harmlessly with Juanita.

After lunch we'd return to the courthouse and struggle to keep from falling asleep. Barney might clean his gun, and it'd probably go off, so Andy would take away his bullet. Opie might pop in for a short talk with his dad and pop back out again to go play baseball with Johnny Paul.

If we were real lucky, the Darlings might come down from the mountains and pick us a few bluegrass classics before getting on with their business in the big city. If by chance Ernest T. Bass followed them down, he'd probably chuck a few rocks in a couple of windows. But Andy would straighten things out and send him back up into the hills, where he belongs.

Not a whole lot would happen during the afternoon. We'd walk around the town and say hello to Mr. Foley, wave across the street to Ben Weaver, gossip with Clara Johnson, and say hey to Asa at the bank. Andy would drop by Helen's house for a few minutes. By this time, Barney would have nabbed a few unfortunate jaywalkers, and we'd return to the courthouse.

At about 6:00 P.M. we'd go back to the house with Andy and Barney, and Aunt Bee would be frying some chicken and making mashed potatoes and gravy. After a delicious supper, topped off by apple pie, we'd visit with the folks as we sat around peacefully on the front porch. We'd hear the crickets chirping nearby and see the fireflies flitting around the yard. Andy would get out his guitar and play us a few folk songs. Perhaps there'd be talk about getting a bottle of pop or maybe some ice cream for later.

Then, all too soon, our day in Mayberry would be over, and we'd have to return to the real world. But the sights, smells, and sounds of Mayberry would linger on in our memories—too real to be just a fantasy. We wouldn't forget the warm handshake and friendly smile of the good Sheriff Taylor, the nervousness of his thin deputy, the freckle-faced grin of his son, and the warm graciousness of his Aunt Bee. We'd treasure all our many wonderful experiences in Mayberry. We'd reflect upon the laugh of Ernest T. Bass, the chuckle of Howard Sprague, and the mannerisms of Goober.

There are just too many special moments to recall them all. But Mayberry lives in our memories and in our hearts. It's our hometown.

Mayberry Town Directory

Aiken, the Reverend

Akin, Red: sixteen; writes "Mayberry After Midnight" column for the *Mayberry Gazette*

Al: a World War I veteran

Albright, Beulah: she and son Harold play bridge with the Spragues

Albright, Nettie: now lives in Asheville; had a crush on Barney in high school

Alvin: Emmett wrecked the squad car into his car

Amanda

Ambrister, Mrs.: librarian; a little-bitty woman

Ambrose, Mrs.: her baby son, Jeremy, sleeps in the jail cell while she shops

Anderson, Dr.

Andrews, Doc

Ankrum, Ramona: niece of Mrs. Wiley's; charmed by Ernest T. Bass

Annabelle

Apple, Rhoda: engaged

April

Avis: Jeff Pruitt hoisted her up once

Bailey, Dr. Lou, and Mrs.: Arnold's parents

Baker, Kenny: sings, sometimes as a soloist

Barstow, George: the butter-and-egg man

Bartlett, Effie: watches wrestling on TV

Barton, Mrs.: her daughter Cindy throws a birthday party

Bascomb, Asa

Baskins, Ella: grows prize-winning pansies

Baxters, The: some dern trespasser stole their "No Trespassing" sign

Beamon, Claude, Sr., Claude, Jr., plain Claude, Claudette: four generations; all have the Beamon overbite

Beasley, Andrew: has a daughter

Beasley, Charlie: has strong arms

Beasley, Juanita: a waitress at the Junction Cafe (phone number 142R) and later at the Bluebird Diner (phone number 242)

Beasley, Lorraine

Beasley, Oscar: works at the butcher shop

Beasley, Virginia: engaged to Earlie Gilley

Beaslo, James Arthur: works at butcher shop; sweet on Lydia Crosswaith

Becker, Al: has a collie dog

Becker, Lilliane: member of Class of '45

Becker, Samuel W. and Lily: have a baby son, Andy; he farms the old Birch place, is a Korean War vet, and cuts his own hair

Becktel, Mary Lee: member of Class of '45

Bedlow, Tom

Bedlow, Miss

Bektoris, Ramona Wiley: a high school sweetheart of Barney Fife's; married to Harry; has a son and a daughter

Belfast, Harvey: the most popular kid in town when Andy was a boy

Bell, Mr. and Mrs.: Opie spent the night at their house once

Bellfield, Gordon: took a trip to Hollywood once

Ben: stationmaster

Bennett, Dr. and Mrs.: the town doctor for forty years; delivered half the people in Mayberry, including Opie

Bennett, Henry: the town jinx

Benson, Old Joe: his front tooth is missing

Benson, Dr. Robert (Bob): engaged to be married

Benson, Spooky: fills in for Goober at the gas station

Benson, Mr.: runs a vegetable stand

Bernice: works at the beauty parlor

Bertha: Jeff Pruitt's girlfriend

Beth: a hairdresser who lives in the back of the shop

Betty Ann: was once punched in the nose

Biggers, Clint: has a pack of dogs

Biggers, Tom: a realtor

Bill

Bishop, Erma: wins a Mayberry beauty pageant; produces, plays the piano, and makes costumes for the Founders' Day play

Blair, Wilton: died in 1960; Thelma Lou and Barney became acquainted at his funeral

Blair, Mrs.: tallies election votes

Blake, Harry: an Elks Club member

Blake, Rose: got new teeth in Raleigh, where her niece lives

Blanche

Bluett, Mr.: believes gypsies control weather

Boone, Fred and Jennie: a fighting couple

Bosworth, Harry: the head of the Mayberry Department of Water and Power

Boysinger, Mr.: owns the bakery

Bracey, Merlin: saw Ernest T. Bass break a street light

Bracey, Nate: Class of '45; moved away

Bradshaw, Charlie: on the church building and safety committee

Bradshaw, Herb: head of the town council; moved to become head teller at the Raleigh Security Bank

Branch, Purcell: father of Tyler; arrested in 1931 for driving down Main Street with the cut-out open on his Reo Flying Cloud

Branch, Tyler: Purcell's son

Branch, Mr.: lives across the street from the Taylors; never speaks, just nods his head

Brand, Emma (Watson): the town hypochondriac and jaywalker

Breeney, Asa

Bricker, Mr. and Mrs. George: a mailman and his wife

Briggs, Mrs.

Bristol, Mr.: the eggman; talks to his chickens as if they were people

Bronson, Mr.: works at the meat market

Bunker, Harvey: a former scoutmaster; debunked for dating Mavis Neff

Buntley, Robert and William: twin babies; William has a mole on his right ear

Burnett, Old Man and Old Lady

Burnette, Lucy: owns the dry goods store

Burnside, Dr.: a dentist–physician

Burton, Mr. and Mrs. Sam: he hits the sauce

Burton, Mr.: the engineer in charge of dynamite blasting on the highway

Bushy, Nate: a bachelor; always takes his mother to town dances

Butler, Mr.: newspaper publisher; can't spell "Fife"

Cal: was stopped at a roadblock by Barney

Caldwell, Bunny: was given a parking ticket by Gomer

Callahan, Fred: a deceased tenor

Calvin, Mr.: lives on Elm

Campbell, Otis and Rita: the town drunk and his wife

Campbell, Mr. and Mrs.

Canfield, Jim: an ex-congressman; retired; a Shriner

Carl: plays first clarinet in the town band

Carrington, Ida: broke her leg

Carson, Ella: a friend of Aunt Bee's; in the Garden Club

Carson, Elmer

Carter, Mr.: his family has feuded with the Wakefields for eighty-seven years; has a daughter, Hannah

Carter, Mr.: a businessman

Cartwright, Clara: works three days a week at the bakery; birthday is August 21

Celdridge, Charlie: member of Class of '45

Charlie: a councilman, town loafer, and lodge member; works at diner

Chase, Frank: in charge of the Founders' Day parade

Choate, Henry: the owner of Old Blue

Choney: a town loafer

Clairburn, Mrs.

Clark, Emmett and Martha: Mr. and Mrs. Fix-It

Clark, Mr. and Mrs.

Claude: works at the post office

Cleaver, Harriet

Clete: a lodge member

Clifford, Clark: Clara's beau who slits his shoes

Clint: works at the post office

Coleman, Edgar: glued covers on hymnals with Thelma Lou

Conroy, Flip: an ex-pro football player who played for the Giants for ten years; moved back to Mayberry to coach Opie's team

Conroy, Mr.: Flip's father; has his own business

Conway, Jonas: raises prize pigs

Corey, Mrs.

Cox, Mrs.: a second-grade schoolteacher

Crane, Mrs.: a snoop

Cranston, Doc

Crawford, Jess: had a chicken stolen

Crawford, Mr. and Mrs.: a pharmacist; owns Crawford's Drugs

Crenshaw, Wallace: backed his car into Benson's vegetable stand

Cripe, Glen: sings bass in the choir

Cripps, Miss

Crosswaith, Lydia: dated Goober for a while; house number is 598

Crowley, Herb (Art): owns a grocery store

Crowley, Old Man

Crump, Helen: a schoolteacher; phone number is 2389; her address is 895

Cruteck, Mrs.: has a cat named Queenie

Cundiff, Willis: Ninety-one years old; in traction in Mt. Pilot Hospital

Curtis, Ben: a substitute milkman

Dan

Davis, Mrs.: member of school board

Davis, Old Man: sold Otis a cow under false pretenses

Dean, Merle: his truck needs new shocks

Dennis, Mrs.: a hostess of the musicale

DeBois, Pearly May: Class of '45; moved away

DeSpain, Sharon: Andy's high school sweetheart; now living in Philadelphia; does design work

Devereaux, Mr. and Mrs. Charlie: she's as ugly as homemade soap and he's no prize

Devereaux, Cliff: has a big, fine-looking home

Devereaux, Mr. and Mrs. Wayne: he carries a picture of Myrna Loy in his wallet

Dick: Pansy is his daughter, and he has a son

Dilbeck, Fletch: a farmer

Doakes, Ed: owns a grocery

Dobbins, Old Man: daughter Sharon was Miss Potato Queen

Dobson, Mr.

Dockins, Elroy: nineteen; used to be a soda jerk at Crawford's Drugs but went to work in Mt. Pilot

Dooley, Pete

Doris: a Keevy Hazelton fan

Doris: a girlfriend of Sam Jones'

Dorothy: a waitress at the diner

Dorsett, Clarey: deceased

Downey, Morton: sings well

Drum, Mrs.

Drumhiller, Agnes: jilted at the altar by

Horace Frizee in 1949; they later married, and she gained weight and dyed her hair blond, but it turned orange; she has a brother

Duane: a playwright for the Centennial Pageant; penned "paleface speaks with forked tongue"

Earl: a bandleader at dances

Eaves, Charlie: rents a house on Grove Street

Ed

Eddenger, Mr.: has a carpentry shop

Edgar: a reporter for the *Mayberry Gazette*

Edwards, Barbara: moved away

Edwards, Dixie Belle: hunts black bears with Mary Pleasance

Edwards, the: have a son, Douglas; moved to Raleigh

Egbert, Jack: moved away; he's no prize

Eldridge, Jarvis

Eli

Ella: writes a society column for the *Mayberry Gazette*

Ellis, Mary T.: Goober's friend

Elmo and wife Margaret: he works at the drugstore

Emerson, Fletcher and Mrs.: used to own a hardware store

Emily: loved Aunt Bee's party for Bradford Taylor

Epley, Sam: rides a motorcycle

Ethel

Fairchild, Irene: a county health official

Farley, Mrs.: has a son, Devon (a Cub Scout), a fat cat, and a thin face

Farley: works at the post office

Farmer, Louise

Farrar, Richie: owns a hardware store

Felcher, Howard and Lorraine: getting a divorce

Felton, Miss: a good cook

Fenton, Miss: a former schoolteacher

Ferdie: Clara Edwards Johnson's nephew; plays the accordion

Fergus, Harlan: a banker and the town treasurer

Ferguson, Warren: deputy sheriff

Ferris, Mr.: a plumber

Fife, Barney: deputy sheriff, phone number is 431; first lived at 411 Elm; later moved into Mrs. Mendelbright's boarding house

Fife, Mrs.: Barney's mom

Finch, Augusta (Gussie): deceased; born the same year as Aunt Bee

Finney, Mr. and Mrs.

Flatt, Mr.

Fletcher, Judd (also goes by Jubal and Burt): a town loafer; "Old Geezer"; the lodge secretary

Fletcher, Tate (Fletch) and Cornelis: a farmer and his wife

Fletcher, Mrs.: cooked for Sam Jones for twelve years

Flint, Mr.: has a daughter Frankie (Frances); a farmer

Floss: organizes a class reunion

Flowers, Bruce: a former tenor in the town choir

Foley, Charlie: a groceryman

Folger, Craig and Millie

Forbes, Donna: has arthritis; moved to Raleigh

Fossett, Harold: parks with Juanita at Myers Lake

Foster, Earl

Foster, Jubal: a farmer and moonshiner

Foster, Miss: a history teacher

Foster, Mrs.: lives on Elm Street; makes terrible chicken a la king, which tastes like wallpaper paste

Frank: works at the diner; is in the bowling league and a lodge member

Franklin: a banker

Fred: works at the hotel

French, Carter: the father of Carter French, Jr.

Frieburger: a former sewer inspector who once ticket Barney's father for speeding

Frisby, Mr.: Taylors' butter-and-egg man; moonshiner; has a rooster, Beauregard

Frizee, Horace: left Agnes Drumhiller at the altar in 1949, they later married

Fudd, Horace: a fishing buddy of Goober's

Fuller, Mr.

George: works for Goober at the station

George: a TV and radio repairman

Gertrude: a Keevy Hazelton fan

Gil: plays cards with Fred Boone and Cliff

Gilbert, Linley: Phoebe's brother

Gilbert, Phoebe: works at the beauty parlor; gossips; Barney once took her out to the Blu-vue

Gilbert, Mr.: a prosecuting attorney

Gilley, Earlie: drives a convertible; owns a gas station in Mt. Pilot and sponsored the Line-up for Loot contest; Little League umpire, engaged to Virginia Beasley

Gilley, Henry: courted Tyla Lee Vernon for sixteen years before they married; lives in the little yellow house two up from the corner near the courthouse

Godsand, Mr.

Gordon Boys, The: Billy, Ike, Junior, and Sherman; moonshiners

Goss, Fred H.: runs the cleaners; tailor

Grace

Gratham, Mrs.

Graves, Wendall: school board member

Grayber, Denise: married Elmer Carson's first cousin

Gresham, Ned: friend of Floyd Lawson's

Gribble, Robert (Bobby): engaged to Emma Larch

Griffin, Skinny: a friend of Gomer's; likes to bird hunt

Grisby, Harold and Sue: live on Willow Ave.; own half interest in a sawmill; she's a blond right out of the bottle; he's terribly jealous

Gurney, Cecil: has two sets of false teeth but won't admit it

Hammond, Mr.: a printer

Hampton, Mr.: Mayberry High principal

Hannah

Hanson, Jed and Prothro: brothers caught stealing from Wally's Service Station

Hanson, Lars: celebrates Mohammed's birthday

Hanson, Old Man: used to own the print shop (out of business)

Harkins, Mr.: an old butcher

Harlan: married; has a daughter named Corlis

Harley: he dammed up Snakeskin Creek

Harmes, Vicky: schooldays girlfriend of Barney's; moved away

Harney, Katherine: moved away

Harper, Alice: an ex-girlfriend of Andy's who moves back to town after a ten-year absence; her parents have a cabin by the lake

Harper, Mr. and Mrs.: have a rose garden

Harriet: a bank teller

Harris, Vern: moved away; used to date Katherine Harney

Harris, Johnny: kicked in the head by a mule; deceased therefore

Harry: runs a fruit stand

Harry: ace who punches Howard Sprague

Harry: a tax man

Harry: fishes at Miller's Pond

Harry: operates Harry's Pond, a trout pool

Hartley, Fred: a neighbor of the Taylors'

Hartzel, Lillian: played "Flight of the Bumblebee" on the saxophone for Aunt Bee's political campaign; works at library

Harvey, Doc

Harvey: nabbed for illegal U-turn once

Harvey: subs for Goober at the station; delivers telegrams

Haskins, Mrs.

Hawkins, Mr. and Cathy: expecting a baby

Haynes, Ralph: high school jock; his wife went to Paul Revere High School in Chicago

Hazel: plays piano for the town choir

Hendricks, Mr.: owns the Spare Rib Tavern

Hendricks, Mr.: a Little League umpire

Hennessey, Wilbur: a drunk who fell out of the window of hotel room 209

Henry, Fred: rumored to be courting Widow Saunders; in the church choir

Hicks, Warden: runs the county work farm

Higgins, Sally

Hilda May: Barney's second sweetheart

Hobbs, Laura Lee: works at the dime store

Hollister, Rafe and Martha: a farmer and moonshiner; he's an extra fine singer

Hook, Miss: has a Boston bulldog

Hooper, Jared: deceased at ninety-three; left $500 to the Community Church in his will

Hopfleisch, Hugo: an old German soldier; confidante to Barney

Hopkins, Ilene: a Tony Curtis fan

Hosh, Virgil: pitches horseshoes

Hostel, Mrs.: a librarian; sax player in Carl Benson's Wildcats

Hudgins, Cy (Hudge): his goat ate some dynamite

Hudgins, Mrs.: overweight

Huey: a farmer

Huff, Weddy: had a cow stolen

Humboldt, Charles: friend of Aunt Bee's

Hutchins, Millie: works at Boisinger's Bakery; dates Howard Sprague

Irene: couldn't go out with Goober because she was having her appendix removed

Jack, Willie: his car needs new brakes

Jackson, Brian: a sculptor and headstone-maker; wife ran away with a traveling salesman

Jackson, Mr. and Mrs. Rick: he's a junior high schoolteacher

Jackson, Vic: had his tonsils and adenoids removed

Jackson, Mrs.: has a son Jimmy

Jason, Mr.: works at the post office

Jason, Mr.: has a repair shop; niece can play xylophone

Jason, Mr. and Mrs.: Johnny Paul's parents; they also have a daughter

Jason: hotel clerk; his daughter, Margaret, can do bird calls

Jason: a town crony; plays clarinet in the town band

Jeffries, Mrs.: with the Ladies' League

Jenkins, Buzz: a chicken thief

Jenkins, Ed: an insurance agent

Jenkins, Lou: a member of the bowling team

Jenkins, Mayor

Jenkins, Mr.: a farmer with four sons

Jennie: turned Goober down for a date

Jim

Joe: a printer

John: in charge of the Mayberry marching band

Johnson, Bonnie: got married; gained weight

Johnson, Charlie: runs the Laundercoin Laundromat

Johnson, Clara Edwards: a close friend of Aunt Bee's

Johnson, Earl: the key broke off in his car ignition

Johnson, Fluffy: works at the Gas Company; wears false fingernails and eyelashes; likes Orville Portnoy

Johnson, Pete: has nice eyelashes

Johnson, Mr.: has wild parties

Johnson, Miss: a schoolteacher

Johnson, Mrs.: has a son, Wendell

Jones, Chester: a town loafer

Jones, Sam: a farmer; head of the town council

Jones, Mrs.: a neighbor of the Taylors'; loves babies

Jordan, Lou: Goober's fishing buddy

Juanita: not the one who works at the diner

Judson, Mr.

Karen: a Keevy Hazelton fan

Kelsey, Mrs.: Barney takes in her laundry

Kester, Harvey: used to repair Gloria Swanson's radio

Kester: was once in the drum and bugle corps; played third bugle

Kincaid, Tillie: a backyard neighbor of the Taylors'; grows roses; Garden Club member

Kingsley, Jeff

Kitcherly, Alfred: drove an Essex

Kohler, Maggie: attended an adult history class

Koontz, Myra: works at the lingerie shop; there's a story going around about her

Lacey, Doris: a friend of Aunt Bee's

Larch, Mrs. Edna Sue: a friend of Aunt Bee's; has a second cousin who lives in Colorado

Larch, Emma: engaged to Bobby Gribble

Larson, Pete and Edie: their son, Joe, was an Army buddy of Ed Sawyer's

Lathan, Mr.: a town loafer

Lavinia

Lawson, Floyd and Melba: the town barber; they have a son, Norman

Layton, Joe: a good friend of Andy Taylor's

LeGrande, Mrs.

Lee, Charlie: a cook at Aunt Bee's Canton Palace; originally from Pittsburgh (Wong Soo's Canton Palace)

Lee, Jack: Charlie's nephew; working on his master's degree in psychology at the University of North Carolina; Phi Beta Kappa

Leonard, Buzzy

Leonards, The

Leroy: a hotel clerk

Lewis, Mrs.

Lillian: makes horrible meatballs

Lincoln, Barbara Sue: enters beauty contest

Lincoln, Sam: the father of Barbara Sue; sells peat moss

Lindsay, Bill: teaches an adult history class

Lindsey, Clara: the town gossip

Lindsey, Jim: a Mayberry guitarist who joins Bobby Fleet's band

Link, Mr.

Lockridge, Mr.: a school board member

Lou: owns the diner; lodge member

Lowell: a tree man

Lucus, Ben

Lukens, Mrs.: owns Lukens' Style Shop

Luther: plays saxophone in the town band; hard of hearing

MacAvery, Jed: talks to himself; lived alone for twenty-five years

MacConker, Viola: dips snuff by her barn

MacKnight, Old Man Joe: 103 years old; gave Andy his first job

MacKnight, Mrs.: lost a lot of weight

Madge: lives in a room at the Mayberry Hotel

Magruder, Mr. and Mrs.: she cleans the bank

McCabe, Old Man Lucian: has an apple orchard and a fine house; wealthy

McGrath, Sue Anne: works at the dime store

McGuinness, Mr.: has apple trees that are good for climbing

McIntyre, Jed: lived alone in cabin for twenty-five years; smiled and talked to himself

McMillan, Peggy: a county nurse; works at the hospital; father owns R&M Grain Elevators in Raleigh; drives a station wagon, then a convertible; house number is 323

Malherbe, Flora: Goober's girlfriend; works at the diner

Marcus, Jane: a friend of Helen Crump's

Marion: turned down Howard Sprague for a date

Martha

Martha, Miss: a neighbor who makes Opie eat grits and prunes when she baby-sits

Martin, the Reverend

Martinelli, Mr.: runs a meat market

Marsh, Sally: the "end of the line" for a date; turned Goober down

Mary, Miss

Mary: a friend of Bee and Clara's

Masefield, James: hates Lillian's meatballs

Mason, Fred: works nights

Mason, Mrs.: the drugstore proprietor; develops film

Masters, John: reservations clerk at the Mayberry Hotel; town choir director

Matt: a vegetable farmer

Matthews, Bill: brother of Lucy

Matthews, Lucy: valedictorian; Capricorn; blue is her favorite color; likes hot fudge sundaes and dancing

Maudie and Naylor: feud a lot

Max: a clerk in the sporting goods store

Meldrim, Mr. and Mrs.: he's a banker at the Mayberry Security Bank

Melvin: puts up fake disease signs in his yard to scare people away

Mendelbright, Maude: has a sister, Cora, in Mt. Pilot; they talk on the phone every Sunday while their feet fall asleep

Merle: a town councilman; chairman of the dance committee for the Apricot Blossom Festival

Mildred: Mrs. Wiley's maid

Milkin, Abigail

Miller, Bert: a door-to-door salesman who eventually gets a job at Weaver's Department Store; has "versitas" in his shoulder and hates "ringing doorbells"; usually feels "middlin' "

Millstones, The: have a farm

Milo Boys, The: World War I veterans

Mingus, Mrs.: Ernest T. Bass broke a street light in front of her house

Monroe, Orville: a TV repairman and funeral parlor operator

Moody, Harry: excels at painting plates

Morgan, Mr. and Mrs. Jess: a farmer/moonshiner and his wife

Morgan, Jimmy: teenager; good mechanic

Morrison, Jennifer and Clarabelle: moonshining sisters who grow flowers

Morton, Mr. and Mrs.

Muggins, Sam and Bess: have two children, Effie and Billy; spend Christmas Eve in jail for moonshining

Mundt, Mr.: fined $2 for parking in front of a fire hydrant

Muriel

Myers, Frank: possess a $100 Civil War bond issued by Mayberry in 1861 with 8½% interest; city owed him $349,119.27; makes berries for women's hats; has a letter from Jefferson Davis; his house is the first one as you drive into Mayberry from the north

Myrtle: a friend of Aunt Bee's

Nate

Nathan, Alice: a do-it-yourself mechanic; Quaker

Naylor and Maudie: fight with and about food

Neff, Mavis: works at the drugstore; dated Andy once

Neil: a vegetable farmer

Nellie

Nelson, Jeff: a chicken thief; sang in the barbershop quartet

Newman, Cissy: in the church choir

Neylands, The: had an anniversary party

Norbett, Mr.: a tire on his pickup truck meets the shoe on Barney's foot

Norman

Norris Boy, That: fills in for Goober at the filling station

Oakely, Nurse: works for Dr. Thomas Peterson

Olive: a waitress at the diner; widow with four children

Ollie

O'Malley, Charlie: his father-in-law owns the patent on Jenson's Orthopedic Loafers; has a cabin near the lake

Osgood, Ted: neighbor of Huey Welch

Palmer, Doug and Katherine: he has elderberry wine stains on his shirts

Palmer, Louise

Pamaley, Cliff: hard of hearing; tenor; he plays hearts

Parker, Gilly and Alice: Gilly skips choir practice to play poker

Parker, Tom and Betty: their parents work for a carnival; Howard Sprague is Tom's "Big Brother"

Parmaley, Old Man: used to own the Taylors' house

Parsons, Stell

Parsons, Millie: dyes her hair blond

Pat

Peabody, Sam: an alderman

Pearl

Pearson, Jesse: owns Pearson's Sweet Shop

Peggs, Mrs.: has a sister named Tillie with a gum condition and long teeth; Tillie was nicknamed "The Beaver" in school

Perkins, Doyle: runs a clothing store

Perkins, Mr.: a stag line regular

Perkins, Mrs.

Peters, Burley: in the town band

Peters, Jenny: a friend of Bee's

Peters, Maggie: a friend of Bee's

Peterson, Dr. Thomas (Tom): single; plays golf; drives a convertible

Peterson, Rafe: a lawyer who sells aluminum siding on the side

Peterson, Wes

Peterson, Mrs.: her cat, Fluffy, had kittens

Phelps, Charlie: did sign work on Barney's motorcycle; owns a hardware store

Phillips, Milford: moved away; donated the plaque for the town cannon

Phlogg, Irene: grew up to be actress Teena Andrews

Pike, Earl: gave his fifty-seven-year-old son a car for a birthday gift

Pike, Mayor and Mrs.: have three daughters (two are Juanita and Josephine) and a son, Nat

Plummer, Fred: worked at Foley's Market

Plummer, Perry: sings a little

Polk, Clarence: a lawyer and baseball umpire

Polk, Mrs.: a friend of Mrs. Wiley's

Pollock, Mabel: friend of Aunt Bee's

Pomeroy, Franklin: has a nice nose; works at the bank

Porter, Alpha

Porter, Mrs.

Portnoy, Orville: a nightman at the bakery

Poulice, Fred: works for Louise Farmer

Poultice, Eleanora: gives singing, dancing, and piano lessons

Powell, Mr.

Pleasance, Mary: a bank notary; hunts black bears with Dixie Belle Edwards

Plummer, Fred: worked at Foley's

Pendleton, Edith: a PTA member on the school board; snoop

Primrose, Miss: a saleslady at a clothing store

Pritchard, Jeff: a possible fill-in as a temporary deputy

Pritchard, Ralph: a first tenor who drops out of the town choir

Pritchard, Mrs.

Pruitt, Arnold: works at the record store

Pruitt, Jeff: one of the best farmers in the county

Pruitt, Mrs.: Howie's mother

Pudney, Hollis

Purdy, Mrs.: Opie throws a baseball through her back door window

Purvis, Mr. and Mrs.: he climbs trees when they fight

Purvis: hangs around the barbershop

Pyle, Gomer: a gas pump boy at Wally's; later joins the Marines

Pyle, Goober: runs Wally's Service Station, which he later buys himself; phone number is 371J

Pyle, Mrs.: Goober's mom

Quincy, the family: moved to Mayberry from Raleigh; son Steve was born in Richmond; the father is a salesman

Ralph: a town councilman who moved away

Rayburn: went to high school with Andy

Red

Regis: a hermit from the hills fighting against the gold standard

Reiner, Luke: moonshiner

Rigsby, Parnell and Mrs.: RFD 1, Bannertown; he lost $50

Rinnecker, Dick: wears a toupée

Ritter, Miss

Ritter, Mrs.

Roach, Mrs.

Robertson, Dorothy: a friend of Bee's

Roberts, Dr.: a medical doctor who also treats animals

Roberts, Fletch: drives a truck; works at the depot

Roberts, Mr.: the head attorney for the county's legal department

Rodenbach, Mrs.

Rodney: subs for Goober at the filling station

Rosemary, Miss: Barney's first sweetheart—he walks her to church

Rosemary

Ross, Charlie: a junk dealer

Roundtree, Mrs.

Rudy: a leading businessman

Rupert, Tracey: carved the initials "T.R." in the town cannon

Sally

Sam: owns a hardware store; leading businessman; fishes; smokes a pipe

Sarah: the switchboard operator

Saunders, Widow: survives her husband, Wilbur; collected $6,500 from his life insurance; has been stepping out with a dish towel salesman from Raleigh

Sawley, Sueler: has a son

Sawyer, Ed: moves in from New York; buys Sepley's gas station; likes Lucy Matthews; an Army buddy of Joe Larson's

Schroeder, Eleanor: a friend of Bee's

Schwamp, Mr.: stag line regular; bench setter; in art class; lodge member; omnipresent

Scobey, Lester and Helen: have a daughter, Mary; rent their house from Ben Weaver; owe $52.50 on rent, $780 on balance; later employed at Weaver's Department Store

Sepley, George: sold his gas station to Ed Sawyer

Sewell, Ben: a moonshiner and potato farmer

Sharon: in the town choir

Sherman, Orville

Shirley: turned down Howard Sprague for a date

Shorty: fills in at the school crossing when Barney's out of town

Shumacker, Miss Violet Rose: works at the coal company

Silby, Annabelle and Tom: a proud woman; she chaired the underprivileged children's charity drive; she was embarrassed by her husband's drinking; he left home, was supposedly hit by a taxi cab in Charlottesville, and had the finest funeral the town ever saw; sang second tenor in the lodge choir

Simkins, Ed and Grace: he beats his wife

Simmons, Stuart: lives in nearby Triplett

Simms, Harry and Lila: live on Elmwood Street

Simms, Mrs. Marie: a friend of Aunt Bee's; a blabbermouth

Simpson, Mary: a county nurse; drives a convertible

Simpson, Walt: a milkman for Dogwood Farms Dairy

Sinsabaugh, Billy: friend of Aunt Bee's

Skinner, Oscar: owns the feed store

Slater, Jim: one of the town's leading businessmen

Slatt, Viola: the biggest gossip in town

Sloan, Rube: moonshiner

Slummer, Ernie: a realtor

Smedley Sisters: one is named Sarah

Smith, Hannie Lou: has a greenhouse

Smith, Robert and Rachel: good friends of Andy's

Smith, Sarah: bakes cookies

Snyder, Mr. and Mrs.: next-door neighbors of the Taylors'; have a cat

Speers, Mrs.: works at Norman's Groceteria

Spooner, Louise: moved to South Bend, Indiana; son Willis is a college student in Connecticut; Willis suffers with his adenoids

Sprague, Howard: a county clerk; phone number is 397

Sprague, Mrs.: Howard's mother; remarried to George Watkins and moved to Mt. Pilot

Springs, Doc

Stapleton, Alice

Sterling, Fred: a jeweler

Stevens, Burt: a World War I veteran

Stevens, Mr.: a scoutmaster

Stoner, Mayor Roy and Mabel

Strongbow, Tom: Mayberry's only Indian; a Cherokee; Rural Route 3, Box 222

Strumm, Mrs.: Gomer charges her battery

Summers, Mr. and Mrs. Jim: he operates a meat market; always wins the sack race at the town picnic

Swanson, Henrietta: daughter Darlene, nineteen, attended Miss Wellington's School for Girls in Raleigh and was voted most likely to become charming; needless to say, Darlene entered a local beauty contest and lost

Sweet, Jack: moved away

Swindell, Herbert

Taft, Luke: a bachelor; hits the sauce

Talbot: the postmaster

Tankersley, Cyrus: a banker; head of the Chamber of Commerce; lodge president

Tarbucks, Mr. and Mrs. Arthur

Taylor, Andy: has a son, Opie; lives at 322 Maple Road; phone number is 426; Mayberry's sheriff

Taylor, Beatrice (Aunt Bee): homemaker for Andy and Opie Taylor

Terwilliger, Efrem and Martha: daughter Honey married Hollis Pudney's brother

Thelma Lou: Barney's regular girl; home phone number is 247; work phone number is 596; house number is 830

Thickett, Mrs.: a former schoolteacher of Andy and Barney's

Thoke, Edna: on debate team; moved away

Thompsons, The: their son delivers the Taylors' newspaper

Thurston, Farley: new butter-and-eggman for the Taylors; widower for fifteen years

Tillman, Mrs.: someone stole her apple pie

Tom

Tracy, John: Mayberry high school principal

Trotter, Mabel: in church choir

Tucker, the Reverend Hobart M.: lives on Maple Street; preaches at the All Souls Church

Tucker, Myra: a friend of Aunt Bee's

Tuttle, Lamar: Floyd Lawson's cousin

Upchurch, Farley: publisher, reporter, and photographer for the *Mayberry Gazette*

Varney, Charlie: holds rummy games on Friday and Saturday nights; bought Otis's car

Vernon, Tyla Lee: married Henry Gilley

Vickers, Mrs.: thinks dynamite blasting is Yankee cannons

Vincente, Mr.: has two children, Mario and Sophia; Italian immigrant who works for Sam Jones

Virginia Lee: Floyd's niece; enters local beauty contest

Vogel, Mrs.: home economics teacher; made costumes for the senior play

Von Roeder, Mrs.: a former schoolteacher of Andy and Barney's; "beast of the fourth floor"

Wainwright, Cissy

Wakefield, F.: owns a beauty salon

Wakefield, Josh and Hannah Carter: married, which helped end their families' feud

Wakefield, Mr.: has been feuding with the Carters for eighty-seven years

Walker, Early

Walker, Elinor (Ellie) May: a pharmacist at her Uncle Fred's drugstore

Walker, Fred: owns a drugstore

Walker, Gilly: a hot rodder

Walker, Harry: a realtor

Wallravens, The: need to paint their house on Elm Street

Wally: owns the filling station and town laundry; has a married daughter, Verdi

Wally: in the barbershop quartet

Warner, Mrs.: the schoolteacher replaced by Helen Crump

Warren, Tate: a store owner

Warren

Waters, Joe: a frequent parking violator; drives a truck

Watkins, Al

Watkins, Bill

Watson, Ray: a medal-maker

Watson, Shorty: the shortest of the Watsons; used to run a grocery store; fishing buddy of Goober's

Weaver, Ben: owns Weaver's Department Store; one of the richest men in town; fishes with Andy; can be ornery

Welch, Huey: raises laying hens

Wendall: has hunting dogs

Wessing, Edith

Wiley, Edna: attended adult history class

Wiley, Mrs.: a Mayberry socialite

Williams, Doris: played Mary Merriweather in the Centennial Pageant

Williams, Mr. and Mrs.: have a son, Howie, and a house the Taylors admire

Wilson, Mr.: has a noisy fan belt

Willick, Harvey: owns a shoe store; hypochondriac

Winkler, Mr. and Mrs. Simon: have a son, Arnold; just moved from Raleigh

Winslow, Halcyon Loretta: "Beasto Maristo"; father owns a third interest in a prune-pitting factory; she's still ugly, single, and pitting prunes

Winters, Ab and Emmie: Ab likes basketball and poker

Winters, Doc

Yelton, Don: friend of Andy's

Zachary, Doc (Zack)

Mt. Pilot Directory

Al: Daphne's boyfriend

Bentley, Neil: attorney-at-law and a notary public; represented Otis Campbell; office number is 205

Bernie: friend of Flora Malherbe's; runs a wholesale fur business

Blush, Leonard: has a morning radio show on YLRB; does vocals for Ethel Page's organ recitals on the third Tuesday of each month; known as "The Masked Singer" on WMPD

Brady, Bill and Mary: brother and sister; victims of "Goldbrick" Wheeler

Branson, Judge: a friend of Andy's

Carlin: manages the Mt. Pilot Comets

Coefield, Mr.: owns a barbershop chain

Cranston, Judge

Daphne: a "fun girl" who likes Andy

Dickerson, Mr.: a jury foreman

Edgar and Maude: Edgar is Aunt Bee's cousin; Maude has "the versitis"

Frank: bowls for Trucker's Cafe

Franklin, Mr.: an associate of Dr. Edith Gibson's; works on computer dating

Garland, Mr. and Mrs.: abandon their baby on the Mayberry courthouse stoop

George: on the Mt. Pilot bowling team

Gibson, Dr. Edith: has a Ph.D. in psychology from State University; works at Scientific Introductions; dated Goober, phone number is 4872

Grady, Mary and Bill (siblings)

Hagen, Jesse Earle: plays bass in Mayberry's marching band

Hank: on the Mt. Pilot bowling team

Hendricks, Orville and Martha: have a son, Eric; in the butter-and-egg business; they deliver eggs to the Taylors on Saturdays

Izamoto, Mr.: Barney's judo instructor

Jenkins, Marvin: tried for burglary of Brice's Department Store

Joe: works at the bowling alley
Johnston, Mr.: the registrar at the Mt. Pilot Sheriff's Barbershop Quartet Contest

Kelly: a hobo who lives in the woods
Keyes, Charles

Lenny: a partner in the Miracle Salve Company
Luke: a town drunk

MacDonald, Mr. (Mac): runs a flying school
Mendelbright, Cora: has a sister, Maude, in Mayberry
Mitchell, Sheriff
Monroe, Newton: works in the hardware store

Page Ethel: used to perform organ recitals at the Pot O'Honey Restaurant on Sunday afternoons, sang with a canary
Plaunt, Clyde: a sewer worker; used to date Millie Hutchins

Robinson, Harlan: a farmer who lives on Oakmont Road; sells an organ to the Mayberry church for $2,000

Skippy: a "fun girl" who likes "Bernie"; phone number is 327
Simmons, Mr.: in the nursery business; emcees Mayberry Flower Show; his great-grandfather was an industrialist/swindler
Smith, Mr.: court observer
Stevens, Jim: owns Stevens' Department Store

Watkins, George: marries Mrs. Sprague
Whitley, Cyrus: a graduate of the Bradbury Business College; doing five years for embezzlement
Williams, Sheriff
Wilson, Sheriff Blake

The Mayberry Yellow Pages

Al's Poultry Headquarters
All Souls Church
Ankrum Charcoal Company
Antique Store
Artistic Weavers

Barclay's Jewelry Store
Biggs' New and Used Furniture
Blu-vue Motel
Boysinger's Bakery: fresh daily—bread, rolls, cakes; cinnamon buns are seven cents each; cakes are $1.25
Burford's

Candy Shop
Carroll's of Mayberry: men's clothing
Coal Company
Cornwell's Gas Station
Crawford Drugs
Crowley's Market

Dave's Coffee Shop
Davis Store
Doakes' Grocery
Dog Pound
Dogwood Dairy Farms: milk, cream, cheese

Downey's: sells candies, among other items
Draperies
Duncan's Hot Dogs: fifteen cents each

Eddenger's Carpentry Shop
Emmett's Fix-It Shop

Feed and Grain: established 1890
Firehouse
Floyd's Barbershop
Foley's Groceries and Meats
Franklyn Pharmacy: 109 Main Street
Fraser's: sells candy
Freight Yard
Furniture Factory
Furniture Store

Gas Works
Gem Hotel
Gibson Hotel
Goober's Service Station

H. Goss: tailor and cleaners
Half-Moon Roadhouse
Half-Moon Trailer Park: on River Road

Hanson's Print Shop: 177 Main; now closed
Harry's Pond: trout pond
Harry Walker Real Estate Company
Harvey Willick's Shoe Store
Hospital

Jewelry Store
Johnson's Sporting Goods Store
Junction Cafe: truck stop

Kinkleheimer's: rents tuxedos

Lamps and Shades
Laundercoin
Library
Lucy Burnett's Dry Goods Store
Lukens' Style Shop

Madame Olga's
Martinelli's Meat Market: no parking between 9:30 A.M. and 11:00 A.M. on Tuesdays and Thursdays
Mayberry Community Center
Mayberry County Clerk
Mayberry County Legal Department
Mayberry County Unemployment Agency
Mayberry Courthouse
Mayberry Department of Water and Power
Mayberry Diner (the Bluebird): the diner
The Mayberry Grand: Saturday and Sunday matinees and late show on Saturday night; second show starts at 8:30; thirty-five cents admission to orchestra seats; twenty-five cents for balcony seats
Mayberry Hotel (built 1878): single room with bath, $2.50 (later raised to $3); single room without a bath, $1.75; no televisions
Mayberry Ice House

Mayberry Security Bank (later called Bank of Mayberry): closed Saturdays and Sundays; has about $50,000 in the vault on Fridays
Mayberry Tax Assessor
Mayberry Town Council
Mayberry Union High School
Mendelbright Park Apartments
Meyer's Real Estate
Mom's Diner: home cooking
Moravian Church
Morelli's
Mort's Clothing
Mrs. Mason's Drugstore: develops film
Murphy's House of the Nine Flavors

Nelson's Funeral Parlor
Nelson's Hardware
Nick's Cafe
Norma's Beauty Shop
Norman's Groceteria

Orville Monroe's: TV repair, mortician

Palmerton Cafe
Palmerton Drugs
Palmerton Theater
Patterson's: Barney bought a shirt here once
Pearson's Sweet Shop
Perkins' Realty
Perkins' Clothing Store
Pete's
Phelps' Hardware
Phoebe's Beauty Salon
Pickle Factory
Post Office
Prune-Pitting Factory

Records
Roadside Rest

Sawmill

Smith's Hardware

Snack Bar

Snappy Lunch: serves great pork chop sandwiches

Sneedling's

Spare Rib Tavern: sold beer; out of business

Spencer's Pipe and Tobacco

Sterling Jewelers

Tate Warren's Store

Ted's Pet Shop

Used Clothing

F. Wakefield Beauty Salon

Walker's Drugs

Wally's Service Station: phone number is 363

Weaver's Department Store: 501 Main Street

Weenie Burger

Ye Olde Book Shoppe

Three's company

Mt. Pilot Yellow Pages

Barbershop
Bradbury Business College
The Bombo Pilot
Bowling Alley
Brice's Department Store

Ching Lee's
Copper Kettle Restaurant
County Line Cafe: sells liquor

Dave Hong Kong: Chinese restaurant
Diamond Jim's Meat Market: has sawdust on the floor
Donut Bakery
Drive-In Theater

Earlie Gilley's Service Station
Embassy Dance Hall
Essex Bank

Fatty's Place
Furrier

Glifford's

Hendricks' Butter and Eggs

The Hoffbrau: serves German cuisine

Ideal Construction Company

Jolly Time Snack Bar

Kit Kat Club
Klein's Coffeehouse: American cheese and *garni.*

Lonas, Hill and Davison Attorneys: Room 108
Lumber Plant

Martin Phillip's Company: door-to-door household goods
Meat-Cutting Vocational School
Miracle Salve Company: Room 106
Monroe Nursery: had great azaleas, but nursery burned down
Mt. Pilot Cemetery
Mt. Pilot High School
Mt. Pilot Judo Society
Mt. Pilot Sheriff's Office

Peggy's Beauty Salon

Pickle-Bottling Plant
Pilot Pines Funeral Parlor
Poodle Trimmer
Pulp Mill

Scientific Introductions
State Police Building

Stevens' Department Store

Tip Top Cafe: favored by the "fun girls"
Trucker's Cafe

Williams' Interiors

Andy

Otis and Big Jack Anderson (Nestor Paiva) encounter spirits in the Old Remshaw House

"The Andy Griffith Show" Rerun Watchers Club

"**T**he Andy Griffith Show" Rerun Watchers Club (TAGSRWC) was founded in the fall of 1979 in Nashville, Tennessee. The club was started purely for fun by four devoted "Andy Griffith Show" watchers at Vanderbilt University. "The Andy Griffith Show" Rerun Watchers Club has since grown to a membership of approximately 20,000 Mayberry lovers. The club has more than 800 chapters throughout the United States and in several foreign countries.

The club's mission is simple: to promote the watching and airing of "Andy Griffith Show" reruns. TAGSRWC tries to operate in a way that captures the true spirit of Mayberry. There are no rules governing what members can or must do. Club members may "Taylor" their chapters to their own desires. The club publishes a quarterly newsletter, *The Bullet,* which, like its namesake in Barney's pocket, is a threat to fire at any time. Membership dues for TAGSRWC are $10 per year.

Most of all, though, TAGSRWC remains a lighthearted way for people to share their earnest devotion to watching "Andy Griffith Show" reruns. Below is a list of those TAGSRWC chapters that have selected names. The variety of names demonstrates a widespread appreciation for the special humor of "The Andy Griffith Show."

Andy—Nashville, Tennessee

Barney—Greensboro, North Carolina

Aunt Bee—Cookeville, Tennessee

Opie—Orlando, Florida

Otis Campbell—Jackson, Mississippi, and vicinity

Floyd—Camden, Tennessee

Gomer Pyle—Lexington, North Carolina

Goober—Gainesville/Pensacola, Florida

Ernest T. Bass—Durham, North Carolina, and vicinity

The Darlings—Louisville, Kentucky

Rafe Hollister—San Francisco, California, and elsewhere

Thelma Lou—Jackson, Mississippi, and vicinity

Leon—Athens, Alabama

Juanita—Pensacola, Florida

Sarah—Charlotte, North Carolina

Helen Crump—Gulfport, Mississippi

Howard Sprague—Framingham, Massachusetts

Malcolm Merriweather—Tallahassee, Florida

Asa Breeney—Montreat, North Carolina

Leonard Blush—Doraville, Georgia

Malcolm Tucker—Asheville, North Carolina

Mr. McBeevee—Memphis, Tennessee

Cousin Ollie—Lake Charles, Louisiana

Bert Miller—Nashville, Tennessee

Mayor Stoner—Louisville, Colorado

The Griffiths—Mt. Airy, North Carolina

Mayberry—Knoxville, Tennessee

Mt. Pilot—Pilot Mountain, North Carolina, and Madison, Wisconsin

Salty Dog—Atlanta, Georgia

The Loaded Goat—Los Angeles, California

Dingo Dog—Desmarais, Alberta, Canada

Barney's Bird Dogs—Hayden, Indiana, and vicinity

Lake Loons—Baton Rouge and Ruston, Louisiana

The Omen of the Owl—Jacksonville, Florida

Fearless Fife Fanatics, M.D.—Huntsville, Alabama

The Bud Nippers—Chattanooga, Tennessee

Mayberry Marketplace for Brides—Madisonville, Kentucky

Wally's Filling Station—Harding College, Searcy, Arkansas

Bluebird Diner—High Point, North Carolina

Floyd's Barbershop—Little Rock, North Little Rock, Arkansas

Mayberry Union High—Longview, Texas, and vicinity

The Corner Room at the Raleigh Y—Raleigh, North Carolina

The Rock—Tulsa, Oklahoma

The Front Porch—Boynton Beach, Florida

The Esquire Club—Cullman, Alabama

Bloody Mary's Rock—Wassau, Wisconsin

The Courthouse—Chapel Hill, North Carolina

Mayberry in Maine—Hallowell, Maine

Old Remshaw House—Greenville, North Carolina

Maximum Security Cell No. 1—Valdosta, Georgia

JL–327—Lumpkin, Georgia

Squad Car—Whittier, California, and vicinity

Miracle Salve—Richmond, Virginia

The Regal Order of the Golden Door to Good Fellowship—Montgomery, Alabama

Carl Benson's Wildcats—Ann Arbor, Michigan

Ernest T. Bass Brick and Rock Brigade—Salisbury, North Carolina

Two Fun Girls from Mt. Pilot—Charleston, West Virginia

Eagle-Eye Annie—Greensboro, North Carolina

Mayberry Minutemen—Graysville, Alabama, and vicinity

Mayberry Marching Band—Quantico, Virginia

The Moulage—Savannah, Georgia

Taylor Pack—Novato, California

Salt-and-Pepper Suit—Amory, Mississippi

One-Bullet Barney—Atlanta, Georgia, and vicinity

$1.75—Lawrenceville, Georgia

Mayberry After Midnight/"Judy, Judy, Judy"—Hickory, North Carolina

"How Do You Do, Mrs. Wiley?"—Madison/Decatur, Alabama

Floyd's Friends—Euless, Texas

"My Darling Romeena"—Neenah, Wisconsin, and vicinity

"Goober Says Hey!"—Dallas, Texas

Kerosene Cucumbers—Concord, North Carolina, and elsewhere

"Citizen's Arrest!"—Birmingham, Alabama

"Nip It in the Bud!"—Madison/Mayodan, North Carolina

Checkpoint Chickie—Savannah, Georgia

"Pipe Down, Otis!"—Atlanta, Georgia

"Shazam!"—Lincoln, Nebraska

"All God's Children Got a Uvula"—Simpsonville, South Carolina, and vicinity

"Hey, Paw"—Brooklyn, New York

"It's Me, It's Me, It's Ernest T."—Buies Creek, North Carolina

"He's a Nut!"—Tuscaloosa, Alabama

"Watch It, Al"—Saudi Arabia

"There's Andy, There's Me and Baby Makes Three"—Sylacauga, Alabama

"I Remember Poindexter"—Lenoir, North Carolina

"Sarah, Get Me My House"—Metairie, Louisiana

"There Went the Duck Pond"—Detroit, Michigan

"Shakedown!"—Wilmington, North Carolina

"Boy, Giraffes Are Selfish"—Chapel Hill, North Carolina

"He'd Kill You, Barney"—Bristol, Tennessee

"You Beat Everything, You Know That?"—Greer, South Carolina

"Hey to Goober"—Tallahassee, Florida

"Get a Bottle of Pop"—Gadsden, Alabama

"Poor Old Horatio"—Clemson, South Carolina

"Great Beans, Aunt Bee!"—?!

"Go Home Take a Shower . . . Yup, Go Home . . . Go Home"—Louisville, Kentucky

The Monster From Out of Town—Washington, D.C.

"Spider Bite!"—Thomasville, Georgia

"Aw, Now Barney"—Manteo, North Carolina

Don't Hit Your Granny With a Big Ol' Stick—Auburn, Alabama

Barney, Locked in the Cell Again—Opelika, Alabama

"Tick-a-Lock"—Fayetteville, Arkansas

"Check Your Oil, Andy?"—Boulder, Colorado

"You Get a Line and I'll Get a Pole, Babe"—Tuscaloosa, Alabama

"Now, Here at the Rock"—Aiken, South Carolina, and elsewhere

Mayberry in Martin—Martin, Tennessee

Hooty-Hoots—Jena, Louisiana

Wynken, Blynken, and Nod—Daytona Beach, Florida

"Blooey!"—Berlin Heights, Ohio

Fast-Gun Fife—Greenville, Kentucky

"I'm Sorry I Broke Your Heart, Mother"—Boonville, North Carolina

Keepers of the Candle—Cary, North Carolina

Hoot Owl Pie—Troy, Alabama

Barney's Mussed-Up Hair—Hamilton, Alabama

"Hey, Ange? Yeah, Barn"—Atlanta, Georgia

Barney Fife's Gonna Diversify—Montgomery, Alabama

"Fluffy and I Have Been Friends for Years"—Cornelia, Georgia

Gold Tooth for a Dollar—Lawrenceville, Georgia

The Lone Bullet—Conway, Arkansas

"The Boys Sure Are Talkative Today"—Joliet, Illinois

"Stick with Me, Ange"—Shelby, North Carolina

"Aw, Pa"—Dania, Florida

Bobby Fleet's Band with a Beat—Raleigh, North Carolina

The Fife Five—Amarillo, Texas

Jubal Foster—Metairie, Louisiana

Bernard P. Fife, M.D.—Augusta, Georgia

Mayberry Vice—Hinesville, Georgia

My Hip Pocket—Toccoa, Georgia

Tuscarora—Breckenridge, Colorado

"Rock and Roll Helps Me Study, Paw"—Richmond, Virginia

Escargots et Cerveaux du Boeuf—Alexander City, Alabama

Old Man Kelsey's Ocean—Myrtle Beach, South Carolina

The Mayberry Founders' Day Committee—Wyoming, Michigan

Johnny Paul Jason—Alexandria/Pineville, Louisiana

Sheriff's Office—East Point, Georgia

Bat Eggs—Albany, Georgia

Howard Sprague Goes to Paris—Paris, France

"Do You Like Me, Andy? I Like You"—Montgomery, Alabama

"Sick as a Dog But Having the Time of My Life"—Millen/Statesboro, Georgia

Shoes on the Cow—Greenville, Mississippi

Count Iz Vantelecky—Clarkston, Georgia

"Oh, Morrelli's!"—Waco, Texas

Bernard Milton Fife—St. Peters, Missouri

Barney Fife—Llano, Texas

"Will You Help Us?"—Columbus, Ohio

"We Will Not Sing!"—Athens, Ohio

"Mayberry—Gateway to Danger"—Charlotte, North Carolina

The Hey Makers—Austin, Texas

Vestavia Hills Knot-Tying Club—Vestavia Hills, Alabama

Howard McNear's Wonderful World—Lexington, Kentucky

The Volleyball Court Maintenance Crew—Jefferson, North Carolina

"Beasto Maristo"—Heflin, Alabama

The Sermon for Today—Dallas, Texas

The Robert E. Lee Natural Bridge—Maryville, Tennessee

"Just Had to Have an Apple"—Vidalia, Louisiana

Andrew Paul Lawson—Springfield, Oregon

Roscoe—North East, Pennsylvania

Lawson Enterprises—Shelbyville, Kentucky

"Subject's Imbibed"—Rainsville, Alabama

"Tell Me What It Is and I'll Give You Fifty Cents for It"—San Francisco, California

The Barney Fife Subconscious Prober-Primer—Lynn Haven, Florida

The Therapetics—Stamping Ground, Kentucky

Barney's Special Deputies—Boone, NC

Asa's Gun Club—Columbus, GA

Kleptomenerac—Sanford, NC

"Hello, Doll"—Hendrix, OK and vicinity

The Mighty Cloven Hooves—Greenwood, IN

The Haunted House—Lubbock, TX

"It's Therapetic"—Russellville, AR

"Dr. Pendyke and My Associate, Mr. Opie Taylor Sr."—Brownsville, TN

"They's All Keyed Up"—Erie, PA

The Compelsion Nuts—Kingsport, TN

"East to West! East to West!"—Greensboro, NC

The Dipsey Doodles—Roanoke Rapids, NC

Old Man Schwump—Peacan Island, LA

"You Wanna Get That, Barn; You're Closer"—Columbia, SC

"Well, Bless His Heart"—Sioux City, IA

"Pepperelli Pizza"—Fayetteville, NC

Andy's Porch—Sedalia, MO

"Barney, Get Me the Highway Folder"—Monore, LA

"If I Was a Spider, That's Where I'd Go"—Glencoe, AL

"But, Andy"—Mobile, AL

"I'll Do It"—Baton Rouge, LA

"She's Nice!"—Clarksville, TN

Thelma Lou is Betty Lynn—Johnson City, TN

"Nita . . . Juaaaaaaaanita"—Jacksonville, FL

"The Tears Upon My Pillow Bespeak the Pain in My Heart"—Goodland, KS

Myers Lake—Fort Worth, TX

"No Thank You, Leon"—Kankakee, IL

"Call the Man"—Austin, TX

Henrietta Perkins—McHenry, IL

"One of Them Traveling Religions"—Senatobia, MS

"Don't Wear My Hat, Ange"—Blacksburg, VA

The Bus to Raleigh—On the Road

"Rule Number One: Obey All Rules"—Athens, WV

"You Don't Believe I Can Get Guitar Sounds Out of This Jug?"—Eastanollee, GA

"It's a Jungle Out There"—Ashland, OR

Nactarine Crush—Rock Hill, SC

"Just Run Up an Alley and Holler Fish"—Franklin, TN

"Barney Parney Poo"—Carbon Hill, AL

Stokes County—Lake City, FL

". . . And a Mr. Potato Set"—Paducah, KY

Green River Ordinance—Salisbury, MD

"Aw, He's Gonna Study"—Chicago, IL

"There Once Was a Deputy Named Fife . . ."—Auburn, AL

"I Always Wished I Had a Name With A Y in It"—Banner Elk, NC

Mayberry Bears—Huntsville, AL

Mayberry, My Home Town—New Haven, CT

Ange—Birmingham, AL

"No Coffee, Tea, or Punch Thank You"—Timmonsville, SC

"Everybody Back on the Truck"—Statesville, NC

St. Clair Darlings—Marysville, MI

"She Called Me a Creatster"—Tullahoma, TN

"Al's Fine Too"—Des Moines, IA

"Heartaches!"—Gainesville, GA

The Pounded Steak—Hamilton, OH

Nelson's Funeral Parlor—Mayfield, KY

"Barney's Beach Bums"—Miami Beach, FL

Cashew Fudge—Dyersburg, TN

The Big Freeze—Canon, GA

"He's Ugly But He Ain't Stupid"—Tarrant, AL

"Only a Little Bit, On My Mother's Side"—La Crosse, WI

The Mayberry Gazette—Anderson, SC

Thumbs in Pockets—Tallahassee, FL

Ernest T. Bass Rock-Throwers—Augusta, GA

"Johnny Unitas of the Baltimore Colts"—Arnold, MD

Convicts-at-Large—Cortland, OH

"Why'd You Throw a Tomato at Me, Barney?"—Avon, CT

The Philomathian Literary Society—Mt. Juliet, TN

"Glue-Dipper Down at the Furniture Factory"—South Bend, IN

Santa Lucia—Jonesboro, AR

"Phantom Fife Strikes Again"—Gladeville, TN

Weaver's Department Store—Henderson, TN

"I'm Dead Sober, Andy, But I Expect I'll Get Over It"—Winterville, NC

"The Bus Bringeth and the Bus Taketh Away"—Columbia, SC

Barney's Judo Class—Fredericksburg, VA

"Jailsick, Kiss My Mouth"—Lockland, OH

"No More Peanut Butter and Jelly Sandwiches"—Montevallo, AL

Rudolph Rabbit—Spring Hill, FL

The Snappy Lunch—Morehead City, NC

"The Best Rock-Throwers in the Countee"—Morehead City, NC

"Big, Really Big, Big, Big"—Sacramento, CA

"I'm Gonna Get Me a Uniform"—Valley, AL

"Charlene, I Love You"—Peoria, IL

"I Think I'll Find a Cave and Hermitize Myself"—Grand Ledge, MI

"Aw . . . Big Ain't the Word for It"—Kannapolis, NC

"Me They, Me They"—Cincinnati, OH

The Light Classics—Toronto, Ontario, Canada

"Rule Number Two Is Don't Write on Walls"—While Sulphur Springs, WV

"The Quick and the Dead"—Austin, TX

"Don't Do That, Ollie; Don't Do That"—Wynne, AR

Fellow Followers of Fife—Bradenton, FL

The Legend of Barney Fife—Marietta, GA

"Heartaches! Nothing But Heartaches!"—Lexington, KY

"Good Old 14-A"—Mesa, AZ

Mr. Independent Wheels—El Cajon, CA

The Moody Gypsies—Roopville, GA

A Cappella—Midway City, CA

"All Us Fifes Are Sensitive"—Springfield, MO

Cousin Virgil—Tiptonville, TN

"Rabber Buby Guggy Bumpers"—Talledega, AL

"Sheriff, You Shore Can Render"—Aurora, CO

"Walk Like Chester"—Abbeville, AL

"Pow Pow Pow!"—Tallahassee, FL

"Good, Extry Good!"—Navasota, TX

Eleanora Poultice's Songbirds—Wichita, KS

"Trigger-Happy Fife"—San Francisco, CA

"You're Not No Account, Ernest T.; You're Just Ignorant" —Mauldin, SC

"Pickups and Splashes from Floor and Fool"—Nashville, TN

"5"—Spartansburg, SC

"Better Phone Him, Al"—Fargo, ND

The Young Swingers—The University of Tennessee-Knoxville

Rifle Fife—Nashville, TN

"Here Blackie, Here Boy!"—Richmond, MO

"Here's Wilbur, Barely Cold in the Ground"—Middleport, OH

The Barney Fife Marksmanship Society—Independence/Florence, KY

The Mayberry Mainstreeters—Horsham, PA

The Ankrum Charcoal Company—Dallas, TX

"Gluttons, Gluttons, Glut-tons"—Las Vegas, NV

"They're Doin' It!"—Russellville, KY

Mr. Schwump's Hairpiece—Houston, TX

"The Mayberry Theme Song" Whistler's Club—Broken Arrow, OK

The G. and C. Garage—Horicon, WI

Virginians Very Andy—Hampton, VA

Frank E. Myers—Sacramento, CA

"Where's My Bullet?"—Locust, NC

"Keep Your Money in Your Shoe and It Won't Get Wet"—Thomson, GA

"Sweet Juanite"—Billings, MT

"Jailsick Walk With Me, Jailsick Talk With Me, Jailsick Kiss My Mouth"—Pensacola, FL

Ernest T. & the M.G.'s—Lexington, KY

Karen—Manchester, ENGLAND

Otis' Snoot Full—Quantico, VA

"Surprise, Surprise! I Can See It in Your Eyes!"—McMinnville, TN

Otis Campbell's Horse—Crossville, TN

"Got Time to Breathe, Got Time for Music"—Blountville, TN

Eleanora Poultice's A+ Breathers—London, KY

Barney's Buddies—Flat Rock, NC

"Mayberry Says Thanks and Happy Motoring"—Scottsdale, AZ

Sigmund Frude—Florence, SC

"Dirty Me, Dirty Me, I'm Disgusted with Myself"—Decatur, AL

Warren—Milwaukee, WI

Emmett Clark—Kennesaw, GA

"Yeah, Boy!"—Washington, IA

Sheriff Without a Gun—Marion, VA

Bullet Maintenance—Traveling around

"The Barney Fife Peter Piper Nose-Pinching Test for Drunks"—Cockrum, MS

"Jubal, Jubal, Jubal"—Buckhead, GA

The Fishin' Hole—Frankfort, KY

Tiger Fife—Blacksburg, VA

"Barney's in Jail, Barney's Jail"—Antioch, TN

"Just Jump in and Hang on"—Birmingham, AL

Okay, You Guys; Come on, You Guys; All Right, You Guys; "Let's Go, You Guys"—Gainesville, GA

Mrs. Mendelbright's Boarding House—Marion, IN

Pistol-Packing Barney Fife—Oswego, IL

"Naw, That One Makes Me Cry"—Shaker Heights, OH

"Not so as You Could Notice"—Eldora, IA

"Ain't You Got a Jack?"—Matthews, NC

"Sing Along with Barn"—Donelson, TN

Barney's First Car—Roanoke, VA

"Clep-Clep, Clep-Clep"—Lakewood, OH

"Hellow Sarah, Get Me Juanita Down at the Diner"—Gilbertsville, KY

"More Power to Ya"—Denton, MD

"She's Blonde—Blonde Out of a Bottle"—Alameda, GA

"The McAllister Case"—London, Ontario, Canada

Pockets on the Slants—Ashland College, Ashland, OH

Dry as Dust—State Road, NC

Mr. Schwump's Stag Line—Towson, MD

"My Mother's the Same Way"—Westerville, OH

"Fuss and Foderol"—Parkin, AR

Al Becker—Greensboro, NC

"Gaw-aw-aw-lee!"—Chesapeake, VA

The Old Orange and Blue—Carlisle, PA

"Larnyx and Voicebox Calisthenics"—Vestavia Hills, AL

"Six Can't Play Bridge, Goober"—Kansas City, MO

Rock 'n' Roll Rosie from Raleigh—Hendersonville, TN

"That's Adventure Sleeping"—Griffin, GA

"Thirty Cents a Ding"—Sylacauga, AL

"Two Chairs, No Waiting"—Rockford, IL

"Barney Fife the Bulkhead"—Muscle Shoals, AL

Andyana Hoosiers—Ligonier, IN

"Thank You, Cousin Andy"—Erwin, TN

"No Hunt Beware Open and Closed No Credit"—Taylors, SC

"All Right, Three, Watch It"—Reidsville, NC

Andrew Jackson Taylor—Newport, RI

Gardenia Blossom—Honolulu, HI

"Local Barber Captures Escaped Convicts"—Roselle Park, NJ

"Dance Till Your Stockings Are Hot and Raveling"—Grand Junction, CO

"On a Case, Barn?"—Kearney, NE

Floyd's Barbershop Boys—Woodstock, VA

"Say It Again"—Urbandale, IA

"Floyd Ain't Much with People, But He's a Great Cat Barber"—Elizabethtown, KY

County Line Cafe—Jonesboro, AR

"Meat!"—Ames, IA

Mayberry Good Government League—Virginia Beach, VA

Greasy Trigger Finger—Jasper, TN

Emma Brand—Seattle, WA

"Two Young People Lost in a World of Pills"—Tempe, AZ

The Barney Fife Jrs.—Murfreesboro, TN

"I Requires Not to Soil My Vest"—Taylorsville, NC

"Crazy-Gun Barney"—Kansas City, KS

"You Saved Mah Life"—Westminster, MD

"I Don't Know How They Do It for Eighty Cents"—Phoenix, AZ

"I'm Gonna Whup Up on You!"—Thomson, GA

Gravy Sandwich—Tupelo, MS

"Us Fifes Is Wiry"—Baton Rouge, LA

"What's Your Hurry?"—Florence, AL

"He May Have Been on the Wrong Team Back in '18, but He Was a Heck of a Soldier"—Heide, West Germany

The 79¢ Blue Plate Special Over at the Diner—Columbus, GA

"I Passed It! I Didn't Heave It"—Nashville, TN

"Welcome Sweet Springtime" (14A)—Weakley County, TN

"No Account Mule"—Pine Bluff, AR

"Shoo Fly . . . He's Dead"—Martinsville, IN

"92"—Milton, FL

"Watch Out for Flying Lead"—Williamson, SC

"Juanita? . . . "Barn.""—Warsaw, IN

"Just Leave It to Big Barn"—Memphis, TN

Barney Fife Pistol-Packers—Gallatin, TN

"She's a Beast!"—Waldorf, MD

"Taters!"—Indianapolis, IN

"Odd Facts Known by Few"—Atlanta, GA

"The Little Brown Church"—Marietta, GA

Old Sam—Toronto, Ontario, CANADA

"Genuine Ceramic Pelican"—Toronto, Ontario, CANADA

"But Barney, I'm Your Mother!"—Memphis, TN

The Gem Hotel—Franklin, TN

"Hey Boys, Who's Malloy?"—Needmore, IN

"We Shall Meet, But We Shall Miss Him"—Clarksville, AR

"Mother Figure"—Auburn, AL

Thelma Lou's Arkansas Cousin—El Dorado, AR

The Mayberry Bucket Brigade—St. Petersburg, FL

WMPD, Mt. Pilot—The Spirit of Grovely Barch—Cookeville, TN

"Al Dances With Sally"—Louisville, KY

The Ebo Walkers—Harrodsburg, KY

"Hay-yup-pa-yah!"—Athens, GA

"Mindin' It for Regis"—Louisville, KY

"We the People"—Greensboro, KY

Doctor of Psychic Phenomenon—Nashville, TN

"She'll Take Eight"—Dover, TN

"Don't Look Back, Barn"—Ormond Beach, FL

The Mayberry Porch-Rocking Apple Peelers—Roanoke, VA

"He's Got a Snoot Full"—West Jordan, UT

"But that's Not Where I'm from . . . I'm from Greensboro"—Greensboro, NC

"Fracture of the Petula Oblongata"—Billings, MT

Stranger in Town—Falls City, NE

"There's Nobody Here"—Spartanburg, SC

"Don't Sound Like Much of a Club to Me"—Evansville, IN

Slimy River Bottom—Binghamton, NY

"Gomer, Get Down There with Them Spiders"—Winston-Salem, NC

The Mayberry Malfeasances—Lexington, KY

"Maybe You'll Talk if I Shine this Light in Your Eyes"—Arab, Al

Deputy Fife Hero in Daring Cave Rescue—Lexington, KY

"Well, What Would They Laugh at, Floyd?"—Hazelwood, MO

Frick and Frack—Sheridan, IN

The Mayberry Crock Cleaners—Charlotte, NC

The Torn Calciums—Nashville, TN

"Suck in that Gut!"—Tuscaloosa, AL

"Boy, Old Arnold Sure Knows How to Throw a Party"—Bainbridge, GA

Siler City—San Antonio, TX

"Putintame. Ask Me Again, I'll Tell You the Same"—Danville, VA

"The Boys at the Lab"—Little Rock, AR

"We Better Hit It"—Alma, KS

"Who Stepped on Maw?"—Cleveland, OH

All Souls Church—Catlettsburg, KY

"Pure Gala"—Newport News, VA

"All I Wants Me a Uniform"—USS Simon Lake

The John Masters Choral Society—Lebanon, OH

Mayberry Junior High—Ringgold, GA

The Barney Fife Foundation for the Sensitive and Nave—Huntsville, AL

Finiculee-Finiculaa—Iowa City, IA

"Comicalness Don't Win No Medals"—Albertsville, AL

"I've Got the Magazines to Swing It"—New York, NY

Edgar Coleman—Loveland, CO

The Seventy-Six Documented Cases of Malfeasance"—Springfield, MO

"Me, Myself, and I"—Chicago, IL

"It Will Be a Pleasure, Dear Lady, to Be Incarcerated in Your Domicile"—Knoxville, TN

"I Got a Rude"—Mobile, AL

"Lot's of Luck to You and Yours"—Macon, GA

"Eatin' Speaks Louder than Words"—Sewanee, TN

Banjo in the Holler—Nashville, TN

May 16th—Varnville, SC

"If It's Charity, We Want No Part of It, 'Cause We Aim to Hang on to Our Position in the Community"—Jeffersontown, KY

"Let the Midnight Special Shine Its Ever-Lovin' Light on You"—Beckley, WV

Old Man Kelsey's Woods—Roanoke Rapids, NC

"Can't . . . Can't Go Out in the Sun; It Gives Me the Herpes"—Winterville, GA

322 Maple Road—Charlotte, NC

Taut Ship—Minneapolis, MN

"Ebum, Shoobum, Shoobum, Shoobum"—Atlanta, GA

"The Monster that Ate Minnesota"—Bemidji, MN

Mayberry Texans—Houston, TX

Nate Bracey Bunch—Asheboro, NC

"Studying to Be a Doctor"—St. George's, GRENADA

"Just Arch Your Back and Purr"—Wilmington, OH

"Gun, Blue"—Hattiesburg, MS

"I Fell Awake"—Montezuma, GA

"What in the World Brings You Down Outta the Mountains?"—Pompano Beach, FL

Opie's Choice—Methuen, MA

Barney's Fire Brigade—New Haven, CT

"I Want Gomer Near a Window"—Fergus Falls, MN

"You Ain't Heard the Last of Ernest T. Bass"—Sylvester, WV

"Tough Talk's Just Talk"—Omaha, NE

"When You Learn Something, You Learn It"—Williamsburg, KY

"Swept Into the Dustbin of History . . . Exit Barney Fife"—Jacksonville, FL

"Go Home! Take a Nap! Go to Thelma Lou's and Watch TV! Just Do It"—Greenfield, IN

"Barney, A Nick for Bernard"—Banks, AL

"Exactilioso!"—Springfield, IL

Septic Tank Pumpers—Norfolk, VA

U. T. Pendyke, D.V.M.—Boise, ID

"I Wonder What Causes That"—Little Valley, NY

"Disorderly Corpses"—Fort Dodge, IA

"Let's Get that Vehicle Our of Here"—Washington, DC

"You Really Are a Pioneer"—Harrisonburg, VA

"The High Sheriff of Greendale"—Elwood, IN

"Hog Winslow's Daughter, Hogette"—Ft. Smith, AR

"You Can Tell the Governor to Put that in His Smipe and Poke It"—Boaz, AL

"She's Nice . . . REAL Nice!"—Vera Beach, FL

"I'll Get You for This, Deputy"—Whiteville, TN

"Boy, Oh Boy, Oh Boy"—Sumter, SC

"Flibbertigibbet!"—Albuquerque, NM

"Oh . . . Shoes!"—Prescott/Tucson, AZ

"One False Move and Blooey!"—Isle of Palms, SC

"I Can't Hear His Ameninies"—Cordova, TN

"It's Just Like a Tale Outta Two Cities"—Weber City, VA

"Thank You, Johnny Shaftos"—Edmond, OK

Mayberry Tigers—Auburn, AL

"Sure, Mike, Sure"—Corbin, KY

Man in a Hurry—Natchez, MS

Miracle Salve Dealers—Fayetteville, NC

Breckenridge Against Rerun Nipping—Breckenridge, CO

"I Let this Baby Do My Talking"—Brookhaven, MS

"Blue Steel Baby"—Spartanburg, SC

"A Wink's as Good as a Nod to a Blind Mule"—Abington, VA

"Mayberry Unit #1"—Gastonia, NC

"Fire by Constriction"—Vinton, VA

"Hey Barney, When Are You Going to Get Johnny Paul's Head Out of the Sewer?"—San Diego, CA

"We Know What Century It Is!"—Burlingame, CA

"Hit Her with a Leg of Lamb!"—Simpsonville, SC

"If You Flew a Quail Through this Room,

Every Woman in It Would Point"—Toney, AL

Mayberry Volunteer Fire Brigade—Prescott, AZ

"I Picked a Pocket and Paid"—Lakewood, CO

"Nate Bracey, Nate Bracey, Nate Bracey, Nate Bracey!"—Arrington, TN

"Just a Bed and a Bible"—Rockvale, TN

"Look Down that Lonesome Road"—Falls City, NE

Andy Griffith Theological Society—Mooresville, IN

Old Man Kelsey's Crick—Janesville, WI

"Let Andy Make the Scene"—Kansas City, MO

"Don't Toy with Me, Otis!"—Columbus, OH

"Blockhouse Lookout"—Birmingham, AL

"Colonel Tim's Talent Time"—Hopkinsville, KY

"The Count Sure Is Lively Tonight, Ain't He?"—Paris, TX

"The Lowdown Pesky Buzzards"—Edmonton, KY

"All Right, Let's Cool It. Let's Let Andy Make the Scene, O.K., Gas It Up Chickie."—Elyria, OH

"Act Like Somebody"—Huntsville, AL

Mayberry Hotel—Mt. Airy, NC

"Compelsion Complex"—Paw Paw, MI

"I'll Get You, Sheriff Taylor, I'll Get You with My Possum Stick."—Grand Rapids, MI

"That's the Couch I Was Telling You About."—Hawkinsville, GA

"Music to Snip By"—Toronto, Ontario, CAN

Clara Edwards Johnson—Valencia, CA

"Well, I Want You to Know You're the Only One I Ever Gave a Hoot For."—Hartsville, SC

"Let Me Guide You into the Land of Rhythm and Pleasure"—Atlanta, GA

"What's Wrestling to Some Is Dancing to Others"—Lawrence, KS

"Where There's Smoke, There's Firewater"—Mansfield, TX

A Cherry for Thelma Lou—Decatur, IL

"Chickie Baby"—Selmer, TN

"Boy Needs a Haircut"—Huntsville, AL

"Just Jump in Where You Can and Hang On"—Boulder, CO

Bannertown Branch—Mt. Airy, NC

Electronal Marvels—Huntington, IN

"Use Your Head, Man!"—Bloomington, IN

"Old Sig Had This Thing Pegged Years Ago"—Grosse Pointe, MI

"Hi Bernie." "Hi Doll."—Scottsdale, AZ

Daphne and Skippy, the Fun Girls—Nashville, TN

"Gravy Is No Joke, No Siree"—Rochester, MN

"Thank You for the Dance"—Biscoe, NC

"Home Away from Home"—Talladega, AL

"Regional Sales, Northeast North Carolina, Emblem Oil Co., El Paso, Texas"—Evansville, IN

"Barney Fife for Sheriff: Honest, Fearless, Incorruptible"—Chardon, OH

"Doggone Firefly Hit Me . . . Knocked Me Right Down"—Vincennes, IN

"I Have a Fortune of Meat in There"—Denver, CO

Mary Grace—Burlington, NC

"Oh, Bernie, You're a Scream"—Chattanooga, TN

Hodie Snitch—Huntsville, AL

"Where Did You *Get* the Liquor?"—Columbus, OH

"Mayberry—We're Declarin' for You"—Hartselle, AL

"Miss Bee, I'm Declarin' for You"—Venice, FL

"You're Not Talking to a Jerk, You Know"—Jefferson City, TN

Sidecar Express—Birmingham, AL

"Clock in the Stomach"—Columbus, IN

"I'se Right Out There in It"—Savannah, GA

F.B.I. Handshake—Fernandina Beach, FL

Rafe Hollister Sings—London, KY

"Blew the Scram-A-Voo"—Herzliya, ISRAEL

Floyd Lawson's Lonely Hearts Correspondence Club—South Salem, NY

"Maude, Al! If Those Hamburgers Are Ruined, I Won't Be Responsible."—Ft. Wayne, IN

"During Our Lifetime, We Travel Many Roads"—Durham, NC

The Mayberry Union High Orange and Blue Alumni Association—McAllen, TX

"Andy, If You Give 'Em 25, They'll Take 30"—Swannanoa, NC

"What Would You Say That Your Average Rainfall Would Be Up Here in Wheeling?"—Natchez, MS

"Horatio Who?"—Fayetteville, AR

"The Boys in Khaki"—Crawfordsville, IN

Nathan Tibbs—Operation Desert Storm

"That's the Mark of Us Fifes"—Jefferson City, MO

"That's One Subject You Just Can't Talk Enough About—Sin"—Marion, NC

"I'm Tensed"—Bentonville, AR

Mt. Pilot Supper Club—Cincinnati, OH

"Such Goin's on, Such Goin's on"—Winston-Salem, NC

"The Case of the Pig-headed Deputy who was Killed by a Berserk Sheriff"—Parma, OH

"Don't Give Him My Mr. Cookie Bar, Andy"—Lewiston, ME

"Toot-Toot-Tootsies"—Chillicothe, OH

"Hail to Thee, Miss Mayberry"—Webb City, MO

"Where's the Footprints of the Cow?"—Brasilia, BRAZIL

"E's for Empty, F's for Full"—Lorton/Springfield, VA

"If You Want a Good Suit, You Gotta Go to Mt. Pilot"—Normal, IL

The Tomahawks—Waco, TX

"Greater Mayberry Historical Society and Tourist Bureau, Limited"—St. Cloud, MN

Barney Fife, Our Hero—Clarksdale, MS

The Governor's Parking Ticket—Washington, DC

Mayberry Sheriff's Department—Niagara, WI

"Ain't We Pickin' Our Peaches Before They're Fuzzed Up Good?"—Harrison, OH

The Mayberry Civic League—Bakersfield, CA

"I'm in It for Keeps"—Albertville, AL

Barney Fife's Bongo Fury—Schaumburg, IL

Opie's Motley Crew—ISLE OF CRETE

The Barney-Fest Fanatics—Bridgman, MI

"Water and Air's Free—Gasoline's Thirty Cents a Ding"—Milton, FL

"One of Those Rabbit Girl Clubs"—Pacific Grove, CA

"Ebo Walker Was A Mighty Fine Fiddle Player"—Berks, ENGLAND

"Don't Tell My Daughter-in-Law"—Leawood, KS

"Anxiety Magnifies Fearsome Objects"—Redstone Arsenal, AL

Noogatuck's Neighbors—Ukiah, CA

"It's Been a Gas"—Piedmont, SC

"Keep a Good Thought"—Ashland, KY

"I Keep Gettin' My Britches Caught on My Own Pitchfork"—Golden, CO

"You Smell Gas? I Smell Gas"—Opelika, AL

"Grinnin' Like a Mule Eatin' Briars"—Alexandria, VA

Fife Realty—Woodbury, TN

Girl Campers of America—Nashville, TN

"We Don't Smoke Marijuana in Mayberry"—Muskogee, OK, USA

"Please Leon! I'm on a Case—Turlock, CA

Ralph Henderson—Ellenwood, GA

"What It Does Is Give You a Buzz"—Sunrise, FL

"The Lord Bless You and Keep You"—Grapevine, TX

Chief Strongbow and the Tuckahoosie Creek Tribe—Durango, CO

Compelsive Kleptomeneracs—Richmond Hill, GA

"Oh, They Twang My Buds"—Niwot, CO

"From Somewheres Else"—Carlinville, IL

Left Pocket, One Bullet—Greeley, CO

"There's My Darling Person"—Albuquerque, NM

"Chickey-Chee"—Rock Island, IL

"Nip It, Nip It, Nip It!"—Grove Hill, AL

Adventure Sleeper—Nashville, TN

The Old Scramez-Vous—Wilmington, NC

"I'd Rather Be in Mayberry"—Guthrie Center, IA

"When My Turn Comes"—Tallahassee, FL

"I Don't Chew My Cabbage Twice"—Cincinnati, OH

"Just Kidding, Andy"—Decatur, AL

Mr. Schwump Appreciation Society—Greenwood, MS

The Schwumpsters—Stephens City, VA

The Mayberry Town Dump

"It's Definitely No Fun When That Iron Door Clangs Shut"—Ft. Thomas, KY

Mayberry Town Council—Belding, MI

Emmett's Fix-It Shop—Clayton, GA

Sheldon Leonard—Baltimore, MD

Andy of Mayberry—Bluffton, IN

"Don't Pick Your Peaches Til They're All Fuzzed Up"—Madison, IN

Hootie-Hoo Houndogs—Kingsport, TN

"I Crawled Right Over to the Phone"—Ft. Loramie, OH

"Mulberry Squeezin's"—Greer, SC

Jack Nicholson—Dallas, TX

"You're Beginning to Get to Me"—Vienna, AUSTRIA

"Shape It Up Maybe, Comb It, but Shave It—Never!"—Cedar Rapids, IA

"How About Dooley?"—West Chester, OH

"Proud, Proud, Proud, Proud, Proud"—Syracuse, NY

"Oh, What a Tangled Web We Weave When First We Practice to Deceive"—Terre Haute, IN

"Reliable Barney Fife"—Cincinnati, OH

Tokyo, R.F.D.—Tokyo, JAPAN

"Give It to 'Em Firm"—Homewood, AL

Pocket Bullets—Danville, IL

"It's Old Sam"—Clinton, MA

"Who's Been Messin' Up the Bulletin Board?"—Prodigy Network/Internet

"Trivial Trivialities"—Georgetown, SC

"Andy's Got Hot Knees"—Alamance County, NC

Mayberry, USA—Morton, IL

"This Is a Jailhouse! Let's Show Some Respect!"—W. Monroe, LA

The Baby Blue Persuaders—Edmonds, WA

Mayberry Enterprises—Rochester, NY

"You Smell Good Enough to Take to the Picture Show"—Rolling Meadows, IL

"Let Me Up, Ange"—West Grove, PA

"Spy in the Sky"—Baton Rouge, LA

"Cockadoodle-doo!"—Salem/Smith's Station, AL

Mayberry Nabors—Pawnee, IL

"Naughty Deputy"—Pinson, AL

"Well, If It Ain't Daddy Longlegs!"—Anderson, SC

The Dusty Gun and Rusty Knife Fife Club—Glen Alpine, NC

Burlen Arms—Mesa, AZ

Barney and Blue—"Barn, That Dog Don't Like That Whistle!"—Ft. Walton Beach, FL

The Fun Girls and Friends—Pittsford, NY

Big Maude Tyler—Caldwell, WV

Up at State Prison—Craigsville, VA

"Miss Crump, I Love You"—Avondale Estates, GA

"I Am Nice to My Besters, But You Are One of My Worsters"—Winston-Salem, NC

"Quit Rubbin' Opie's Head"—Midlothian, VA

" '60 With a '61 Grill"—Roanoke, VA

"Number Two Amber Alert: A Man Awake at All Times"—Oxford, AL

"Can't Sing a Lick"—Scotts, MI

"Za Zu Zaz"—Broadway, VA

"Oh-h-h-h . . . A Little Sugar on the Jaw!"—Benton, AR

"This Is Where We Keep the Keys . . . On the Peg Outside the Cell Door"—Burgaw, NC

"Fire Too Hot, Jump in the Pot"—Lompoc, CA

The Society Faithfully Dedicated to Preserving the Dignity of Mister Schwamp—Munson Township, OH

Sazerac—Newport Beach, CA

"Bloodhound of the Law, Sniffing Out Crime"—Crossville, TN

"Hi, Bernie"—London, KY

"Watch-Out, Big Ears! There's a Crazy Owl Flying Around"—Maiden, NC

"I Ain't No Rockefeller"—Big Stone Gap, VA

"Name Ain't Clem. It's Andy, Andy Taylor"—Lebanon, IN

Murphy's House of the Nine Flavors—Keyser, WV

"Hearty Eatin' Men and Beautiful, Delicate Women"—Northport, AL

"I Think I've Heard Just About Enough About That Tomato"—Tuscola, IL

Mayberry Cider Sippers—Bridgeport, CA

"I Was a Pawn in the Hands of a Wily Woman"—Plainview, NE

Mayberry Sightings—Landover Hills, MD

The Big Ones Take Care of the Little Ones—Collinsville, IL

"I've Heard About Your Bullet"—Plano, TX

Mrs. Mendelbright's Bulb-Snatchers—Cedar Falls, IA

"That's the Most Disgusting Sound I Have Ever Heard"—Rockledge, FL

150 Pounds of Beef—Topeka, KS

Ignorant Laypersons—Grenada, MS

Barney Backers—Clarksdale, MS

"Clean Your Gun, Jump in the Truck"—Memphis, TN/ W. Memphis, AR

"Lookin' Like a Dang Fool"—Wabash, IN

Meehawken State Prison—Windy Hill Bch, SC

Peggy McMillan—Vinton, VA

"Will You Love Me When I'm Old and Ugly?"—Rushville, IL

"There Goes a Happy Man." "There Goes a Happy Nut!"—Carthage, TN

"Of Course You Smell Gas. What You Think It Runs on—Kerosene?!"—Spring, TX

"Stop That Wedding!"—Camden, AR

Aunt Bee Haven—Anniston, AL

Emma's Pain Gang—Ottawa, IL

Mayberry's Finest . . . No Interlopers—Brownsburg, IN

Licorice Seeds—Cincinnati, OH

"I'll Be Righct Chere, Barn"—Denver, CO

Mayor Pike—Stoughton, WI

"It's Just Not Right to Falsify"—Madisonville, KY

Wally's Service—Bradford, OH

"If I Didn't Think You Were Kiddin', I'd Hit You With a 912"—Kings Mtn., KY

Jerry's Kids—Ellwood City, PA

Cell Keys Hangin' on the Wall—Belleville, IL

Opie Taylor Sr.—Lucedale, MS

"Oh Barney, You're a Scream!"—Charlotte, NC

"How Much Do I Owe You?"—Solvang, CA

Andy's Front Porch Pickin' Parlor—Alvin, TX

"Otis Campbell, Where Is the Still?"—Lexington, IN

"Us Town Drunks Have a Code We Live by"—Mattoon, IL

"The Bigger They Are, the Nicer They Are—Hey Chuck!"—Princeton, WV

"I Guess That Makes You Sheriff Now"—Bowling Green, KY

"I Wouldn't Marry You if You Were the Last Man on Earth!"—Angola, IN

"That Ain't Right!"—Ottawa, OH

"You Wanna Buy a Ship in a Bottle?"—Belvidere, IL

"Ain't It a Dinger, Paw!"—Edgewood, KY

Eagle-Eye Annie Goes to Alaska—Anchorage, AK

Bee and Clara—Latrobe/Greensburg, PA

Mayberry Courthouse—Naples, ITALY

Colonel Harvey's Elixir—Jacksonville, FL

"We're the Esquire Types"—New Castle, IN

"Snoop! Snoop! Bulb-Snatcher!"—Muncie, IN

Philosphical Meanderings—Guadalajara, MEXICO

Fish Muddle—Yukon, OK

Deputy Barney Fife's Bud Nip-o-teers—Moody, TX

Thatcher's Woods—Rochester, NY

Desperate Female Hunters and Pals—Daniels, WV

"Hogwash—Eh?"—Kingston, Ontario, CANADA

"We Defy the Mafia!"—Florence, AL

"Damp Under There. Could Be Spiders"—Omaha, NE

"Trouble Check"—Fergus Falls, MN

"Somebody Just Called to Say I'm Dead"—Curtice, OH

The Mayberry Barber—Reed City, MI

"Yes, Yes, Go Boy Go!"—Leland, MS

Hagen's Heroes—Shreveport, LA

"I Can Take a Bossy Mouth, But I Ain't About to Be Beat to Death with No Spoon"—Oxnard, CA

Mayberry on My Mind—Clearwater, FL

Mayberry, NC 27599—Morgantown, NC

"Hey to Barn, Hey to Goob"—Pella, IA

Mayberry, Michigan—Pottersville, MI

"No, But I've Been Pointing It a Lot Lately"—Atlanta, GA

" 'Specially When I'm Dancin'!"—Ashland, AL

"What's Your Hurry, Take It Easy"—West Palm Beach, FL

A Silk Purse and a Sow's Ear—Sacramento, CA

The Mayberry Knot-tying Class—Tulsa, OK

"My, You Look Good Enough to Be Buried"—Lenexa, KS

Mayberry Mind-Erasers—Arlington, VA

"Next Time We Go Tiger Hunting, We're Going to Take Our Tweezers"—Rochester, NY

"Come Over and Sit a Spell Righct Chere"—Evening Shade, AR

Fife the Fierce—Metairie, LA

Ange and Barn—Staunton, IN

"Hear That, Boys? No Yellin' at the Table"—Joplin, MO

"Hug Me, Bernie. I Just Love to Be Crowded!"—Whitakers, NC

"Didn't You Ever Do Anything for the Joy of Giving?"—Mount Gilead, NC

"Biggest Crock of Nothin' "—Cleveland, OH

Mrs. Lesch's Quality Used Cars—Caldwell, NJ

The Dickies—Burbank, CA

Old Aunt Maria—Adamsville, AL

"Hey, Ope"—Mentor, OH

Mayberry Utility Dept.—Buford, GA

The Mayberry Mounted Patrol—Seneca, SC

"Now, I'll Drive, So I'll Sit in the Front Seat"—Meridianville, AL

TAGS in Thailand—Bangkok, THAILAND

DC-269—Vilas, NC

"He Called Me a Boob!"—Dayton, OH

The Gigolo Club—Ft. Myers, FL

"Women, Women, Women—Fickle, Cruel Heartless"—Takoma Park, MD

Jim Lindsey—East Peoria, IL

"Something About a Girl in Cleveland, Ohio"—Pounding Mill, VA

Mayberry Mudcats—Zebulon, NC

"Now, There's Bullet Maintenance"—Andersonville, TN

"And the Cow Comes Right with It"—Vanceburg, KY

Mayberry Memories—Eau Claire, WI

"We . . . the . . . People . . . In Order to Form a More Perfect You!"—New Port Richey, FL

Barney's Badgers—Dodgeville, WI

"I'm a Little Mean, But I Make Up for It by Being Real Healthy"—Anniston, AL

"The Kitchen's Right Through that Door if That's What You're Gropin' for"—Brunswick, ME

"Hazel"—Kahoka, MO

The Lone Occupant of the Corner Room at the Y—Pasadena, TX

The Aunt Bees and the Bullets—Marion, NC

"Barney, Sing A Cappella"—Leavenworth, KS

Goob's Whiplash Club—Eureka Springs, AR

"Paw, Just What Can You Do with a Grown Woman?"—Birmingham, AL

"One Loaded Goat at a Time"—Radford, VA

"Web-footed, Red-crested Lake Loons"—McKinney, TX

The Town Drunks—Nashville, TN

The Riflemen—Sevierville, TN

"Your Hair's Drippin' "—Music Row

Jud and Choney—Johnson City, TN

"I Didn't Sell It for Money"—Madison, NC

"That's Right. I Am a Killer. I Just Killed a Whole Pint!"—South Haven, MN

The Traffic Jam—Mt. Holly, NC

"Help Someone Along Life's Way, Spread a Little Sunshine Every Day"—Hamer, SC

"You Wear Your Uniform, I'll Wear My Uniform"—Sandusky, OH

"Yep, That's the Plan; We're Gonna Pick a Name for Our Chapter"—New Freedom, PA

God Bless Mayberry—Decatur, IL

Up a Tree with Fluffy—Portland, IN

"I Stay in the House Too Much"—Walla Walla, WA

"Is that a Gun in Your Pants?"—Schaumburg, IL

Mayberry Preservation Society—Mt. Airy, NC

"All Right, Shakedown!"—Preetz, GERMANY

"Beep-Beep!! Outta the Way, Sunday Driver!!"—Ft. Lauderdale, FL

Barney and Thelma Lou—Rockholds, Ky.

The Mayberry Historical Society—N. Myrtle Beach, SC

Barney's Sidecar—Greenwood, SC

"But Don't the Trees Seem Nice and Full"—Forest Grove, OR

"It's Not a Whim if You Put on Clean Underwear"—Winston-Salem, NC

"For Mature Human Bein's, We're a Sight"—Minneapolis, MN

Corned Beef and Cabbage at the Diner on Tuesday—West Columbia, SC

"Little Sweet Tea and Spicy Talk"—Spokane, WA

"Didn't You Hear the Man? He Says He Can't Think Straight When He's Sober!"—Morris, IL

Dooley's Holler—Arlington, TX

David Mendelbright Memorial Horse Trough—Centre, AL

"Do You Want Me to Say 'Bait'?"—Colbert, GA

"We're the Cat's!"—Fort Erie, Ontario, CANADA

New Mayberry, New Hampshire—Portsmouth, NH

The Secret Ingredient: Oregano—Huntington, WV

Jensen Orthopedic Shoes—Puschendorf, GERMANY

Badge #3—Hartsville, SC

" 'Course, I Don't Fix 'em; I Just Put in the Gas"—Enniskillen Township, Ontario, CANADA

"When She's in the 'On' Position, She's Gonna Run on Ya"—Chapel Hill, NC

"Leaning on the Everlasting Arms"—Stockton, CA

"Also Starring Don Knotts"—Walnut Creek, CA

The Single Bullet Society—Canton, OH

"That Was My Daddy's Rock"—San Bernadino, CA

The Valdez Baked Alaska Mayberry Club—Valdez, AK

The Single Pocket Bullet Theory—Fairlwan, OH

The Cold Cream Guards (Lee Greenway Memorial chapter)—Rutherfordton, NC

Rev. Tucker's Congregation—Malvern, AR

Ellie Walker—Whiteville, NC

The Yo Club—Union, WV

Barney's Package—Morton Grove, IL

" 'I' Before 'E' Except After 'C' and 'E' Before 'N' in 'Chicken' "—Spartanburg, SC

Return to Mayberry Association—Tipp City, OH

"A Sandwich Sure Tastes Better With Milk"—Ft. Smith, AR

Good Right Hand of Barney Fife—Gauley Bridge, WV

Town of Mayberry, Building Department—Flagstaff, AZ

"You're a Treasure!"—Jackson, TN

"That's the Clunker I Sold to that Boob in Mayberry"—Washington C.H., OH

"2 and 2 Makes 4"—Springfield, OH

Sheriff Andy Taylor—Kissimmee, FL

"Ain't That Something"—Syracuse, IN

"Ernest T. Bass, You're a Low-down, Pesky Buzzard; Doggone Ya!"—Elkhart, IN

"Now, Don't Get Purposely Obtuse, Andy"—Williford, AR

"Wild Pheasant, Perhaps the Most Difficult Species of All to Ensnare"—Greencastle, IN

Anyone interested in joining "The Andy Griffith Show" Rerun Watchers Club (TAGSRWC) may write to the Andy chapter, the club's administrative chapter, 9 Music Square South, Suite 146, Nashville, Tennessee 37203-3203; enclose a long, self-addressed stamped envelope with your inquiry.